BANNOCK AND BEANS

BANNOCK AND BEANS

A COWBOY'S ACCOUNT OF THE BEDAUX EXPEDITION

BOB WHITE

Edited
with Foreword and Afterword
by Jay Sherwood

ROYAL **BC** MUSEUM
Victoria, Canada

Published by the Royal BC Museum, 675 Belleville Street, Victoria,
British Columbia, V8W 9W2, Canada.

Library and Archives Canada Cataloguing in Publication

White, Bob, 1902-1985
   Bannock and beans : a cowboy's account of the Bedaux Expedition / Bob
White; edited, with foreword and afterword by Jay Sherwood.

"The original Bannock and beans was produced in 1983 by the Piapot History
Group ..."--Foreword

ISBN 978-0-7726-6060-2

   1. Bedaux, Charles, 1886-1944--Travel--Northwest, Canadian. 2. Adventure
and adventurers -- Northwest, Canada. 3. Northwest, Canadian -- Discovery and
exploration. 4. White, Bob, 1902-1985. I. Sherwood, Jay, 1947- II. Royal BC
Museum III. Title: Cowboy's account of the Bedaux Expedition.

FC3826.B4W54 2009   917.11'85   C2009-902708-9

Contents

To the memory of Bob White
and the cowboys of the Bedaux Expedition.

Foreword

Jay Sherwood

Introducing *Bannock and Beans*

In 1934 a wealthy French entrepreneur living in the United States spent over $250,000 in an attempt to take five motorized vehicles across the northern wilderness of British Columbia. It was the middle of the Depression and the well-publicized Bedaux Expedition stirred the imaginations of many people of the time.

In the early 1980s Bob White, a cowboy on the Bedaux Expedition, wrote his memoirs of this unique adventure in British Columbia's history and his later involvement with Bedaux's planned Empire Ranch. He began by saying, "I'm not much at this letter writing business, not having spent much of my time in a school room, when I was growing up in the log house on the Ranch in the Cypress Hills of Saskatchewan." Then he produced a 371-page handwritten manuscript showing that he had a clear and detailed memory of events that had occurred almost 50 years earlier. White titled his account *Bannock and Beans*, after two of the basic foods that the cowboys ate while out on the trail.

Everyone who knew Bob White says that he was an accomplished storyteller, and the storyteller's voice is clear in his writing. *Bannock and Beans* is the most detailed record of the life of the cowboys on the Bedaux Expedition. Several of the professional personnel on the trip kept diaries, and accounts of the expedition generally focus on their viewpoint and on the main group of travellers.

The five Citroën vehicles that Bedaux's party attempted to drive through the northern BC wilderness constituted the unique element of this adventure. However, the Citroëns could only carry a limited amount of equipment. In fact, overloading the Citroens was one of the contributing factors to the failure of these vehicles and the extra gasoline they consumed.

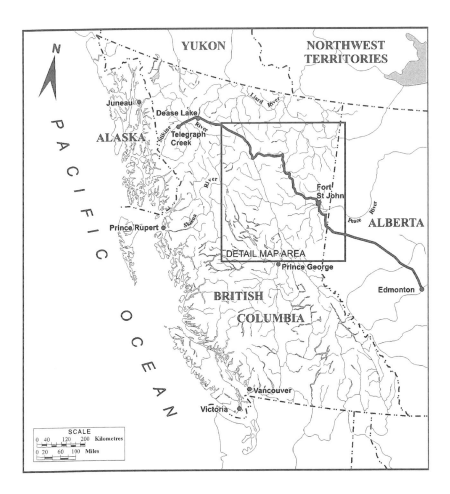

Ironically, the cowboys were the backbone of the expedition, for these men, along with more than 100 packhorses, transported the fuel, food, supplies and personal gear that were necessary for this adventure.

Bob White was part of the freight party that carried extra gasoline and supplies ahead of the main group for the first part of the expedition. Six men, along with 57 horses, travelled through the wilderness of northern British Columbia during a rainy summer under difficult and sometimes dangerous circumstances. Reading *Bannock and Beans* is like listening to a storyteller around an evening campfire. White's stories provide us with many of the details of daily life on the Bedaux Expedition. *Bannock and Beans* describes the hard work of the cowboys, and the camaraderie of men who thrived in this rugged environment. And despite difficult circumstances, White was able to appreciate the beauty of the landscape through which he travelled.

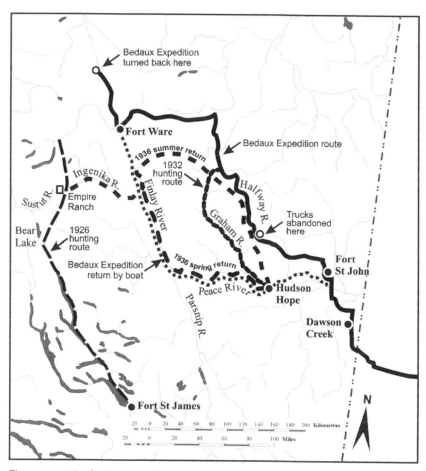

The map on the facing page shows the planned route of the Bedaux Expedition, from Edmonton to Telegraph Creek on the Stikine River.

The routes of Charles Bedaux and Bob White in northeastern British Columbia. The solid line is the actual route of the Bedaux Expedition, showing the places where Bedaux and company abandoned the Citroëns and where they turned back after attempting to complete the journey on horseback; the small-dotted line is the expedition's return route, by boat, along the Finlay and Peace rivers to Fort St John. The location of Bedaux's Empire Ranch is marked with an open square on the Sustut River; from there, Bob White's two return trips to Hudson Hope in the spring and summer of 1936 are marked with dashed lines. The routes of Bedaux's earlier hunting trips are also show, from Fort St James in 1926 and Hudson Hope along the Graham River in 1932. RBCM.

Some of the cowboys at Sifton Pass in September 1934 (left to right): Ernie Peterson, Bob Beattie, Henry Philpott, Einar Westergaard, Bill Pickell, Jack MacDougall, Bob White (on grey horse), Willard Freer, Art MacLean.
Frank Swannell photograph; BC Archives G-03841.

When the freight party joined the main group later in the summer, White was able to see that Charles Bedaux had many aspects to his personality: he showed generosity as well as selfishness; he was an egomaniac who could also be considerate of others; he thrived on efficiency in the business world, but was often inefficient on the expedition; he was frequently aloof, yet tried to relate to the cowboys; though he built his career on practicality, he sometimes had fanciful notions of life in the outdoors.

Bedaux hired a publicist to send reports about the expedition to major newspapers across North America, and he took along a Hollywood movie-maker to film events on the trip. The film segments that have survived contain many scenes involving the cowboys and show their importance to the expedition. The cowboys also participated in staged events and they liked acting for the movies. White is prominent in several scenes and his talent as a cowboy is obvious. It is also apparent that he relished being on the expedition. *Bannock and Beans* reflects White's enjoyment of the adventure despite its hardships, and his account includes lively descriptions of the theatrical aspects of the Bedaux Expedition.

White took a camera on the expedition. His photographs show the packhorses and cowboys at work as well as the landscape of northern BC, and they are the major record of the groups who were not part of the main entourage. White's pictures comprise one of the main sources of photographs of the Bedaux Expedition and copies are located at Library and Archives Canada, the BC Provincial Archives, and the Glenbow Museum, as well as regional museums in the Peace River area.

The Bedaux Expedition did not succeed in its goal of taking motorized vehicles across the wilderness of northern BC. By the end of the trip Bedaux had a plan to develop a ranch in northern BC. In 1936 White became involved with Bedaux's Empire Ranch. The second part of *Bannock and Beans* is his account of two trips to the ranch site during that year. The first adventure entailed a winter trip through the northern BC wilderness. Again, White took his camera, which gives us a photographic as well as a written record of his involvement with Bedaux's second major enterprise in BC. Bedaux had a genuine affection for BC's northern wilderness and he maintained a connection with this part of the province for 13 years. *Bannock and Beans* provides the basis for Charles Bedaux's story in northern BC.

The original *Bannock and Beans* was produced in 1983 by the Piapot History Group, a local history society in Maple Creek, Saskatchewan, where White lived after he left the ranch in the Cypress Hills. The society reproduced White's handwritten manuscript in a coil binding along with a selection of pictures; it printed about 200 copies of *Bannock and Beans*, and then returned the original material to White. Most of Piapot's copies went to White's family members and friends. A few made their way to BC, particularly the Peace River area where White maintained contact with several friends. Since his death in 1985 the family has kept White's manuscript and most of his photograph collection.

In this edition of *Bannock and Beans* I have kept the manuscript in its original state as much as possible. I have done a minimal amount of editing, mostly to correct spelling and grammatical mistakes; White often wrote long sentences with many commas, so I added periods and transitional words to produce shorter sentences and make the narrative flow more easily. The original manuscript had no breaks, so I have inserted chapter divisions with titles to highlight the stages of the expedition and create a distinct section for White's adventures around the Empire Ranch. Imperial measurements remain in this edition, because they were standard at the time. In the 1930s Hudson's Hope was usually called "Hudson Hope" and this spelling remains throughout the book.

This edition includes many of the photographs in the Piapot edition, along with some unpublished White photographs and pictures taken by other Bedaux Expedition members. I have added some extra research material relating to Charles Bedaux to recount his involvement in northern BC from 1926 to 1939.

The 75th anniversary of the Bedaux Expedition is an opportune time to produce *Bannock and Beans* for a wider audience and to commemorate a unique event in our province's history. Bob White's memoirs and photographs provide a new perspective on the expedition. All of his descendants have said that Bob White would be pleased to have his story told.

Charles Bedaux

Born in France in 1886, Charles Eugene Bedaux immigrated to the United States in 1906, arriving with only a small amount of money. Initially Bedaux lived in New York, but he soon travelled to the Midwest, working in a variety of jobs. In St Louis he met Blanche Allen whom he married in 1908. The following year Bedaux's only child, a son, Charles Emile Bedaux, was born. The marriage ended in a divorce, and in 1917 Charles Bedaux married Fern Lombard, the daughter of an attorney in Grand Rapids, Michigan.

Bedaux started his own scientific management company in 1917 and became one of the leaders in this field within a few years. The Bedaux System of management was based on B (Bedaux) units. The B unit was the combination of work and rest that would give the highest output over the day with the least strain to the worker. Each B unit represented one minute. The B unit measured human effort based on the work produced by a normal worker at a normal rate under normal conditions. Workers were guaranteed a basic rate of pay based on the B unit, but additional wages were given to employees who completed additional units of work. Bedeaux used time and motion studies to improve the efficiency of performing a specific task. He also filmed employees at work, looking for the most ef-ficient method to complete a task, and sought employee input into ways that they could do their job more efficiently and successfully.

In 1920 Bedaux moved from Cleveland to New York, where his company expanded rapidly in the flourishing economy of the 1920s. Within a few years he established branch offices in several countries throughout the world, including Canada. The pulp mill at Ocean Falls was one of his cus-tomers. Bedaux's clients included major corporations like General Electric, Campbell's Soup and Eastman Kodak. Eventually Bedaux established his main office in the prestigious Chrysler Building in New York and became one of the wealthiest people in the United States.

Like some other wealthy Americans in the 1920s, Bedeaux went on expensive hunting trips, often to places outside the United States. He also became interested in investing in gold mines, and so met Bob McCorkell, an American who had moved to British Columbia and was developing gold mines in the remote Cassiar region of the northern part of the province. McCorkell owned the Cassiar Ranch near Fort St James. He and his brother, Bert, had horses at the ranch that they used to transport supplies to their mines and bring back the gold. They also used the horses to take people on hunting trips. In the 1920s Cassiar was a well-known destina-tion for wealthy American hunters of moose, bears, mountain goats and sheep.

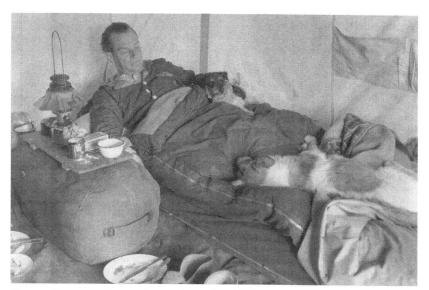

Charles Bedaux resting in his tent during the 1934 expedition. LAC e008300544.

In 1926 Charles Bedaux came with a hunting group to the Cassiar Ranch. He brought with him his wife, Fern, who liked the outdoors, and his son. Bob and Bert McCorkell accompanied this hunting expedition. The hunting party travelled by boat and scow up to Bulkley House at the head of Takla Lake. From there they took pack and saddle horses to the Thutade Lake area on a six-week trip. Initially, the hunting party planned to go to Telegraph Creek on the Stikine River and then travel to Vancouver by boat. But the horses had difficulty finding sufficient food, forcing the hunters to return to the Cassiar Ranch.

Bob McCorkell's memoirs of the trip note some of the features that were destined to be part of Bedaux's two future trips to British Columbia. "On return, Bedaux was more than liberal in gratuities to the crew. What was indeed exceptional was the request, by him and his wife, that each of the saddle horses that had been allotted to them and they now had grown attached to, were to be shipped to New York, there to be transhipped to their estate in Europe." The 1934 Bedaux Expedition has been nicknamed the Champagne Safari, because of the champagne and exotic foods that Bedaux brought on the trip. McCorkell wrote: "In addition to the conventional food, the Bedauxs had provided the choicest of special foods for themselves and their guests. The special food would include 'delices de Strasbourg', the duck and moose liver glazed with Madeira in aspic. Bedaux spared no expense to bring enjoyment to himself and guests."

McCorkell also noted Bedaux's attempts to relate to the cowboys:

He would insist that the men prepare a big campfire and he enjoyed soliciting conversation with the men. One of the campfire stories which later was related to me would be typical. This kind of trail story was told by one of the packers called Harvey. Bedaux had assumed that Harvey was the one fellow on the crew who knew the most about everything that pertained to trail life. This time they were watching a pair of loons in a small lake beside where his big party was camped. Bedaux then asked Harvey if anyone had ever eaten a loon. The answer from Harvey was, "Yes, certainly, Mr Bedaux. It is just knowing how to cook them that is necessary." Bedaux then expressed surprise that loons were used for food and then asked Harvey just how you did cook a loon. Harvey then spoke in his low casual tone: "First, you just pluck and prepare them, as you would a duck. Then you place them in the pot, fill it with water. Then you add a small solid round stone, placing the stone inside the pot. You then let them boil. You keep testing that stone with your fork and when the stone is soft you will know that the loon is ready to eat." This type of trail story would give Bedaux a good laugh.

An article in the *Prince George Citizen* on October 28, 1926, mentioned an unusual aspect of the hunting trip: "With two moving picture machines the members of the party secured a number of unique pictures of big game in their natural habitat."

In 1930 Bedaux made the first automobile trip across Africa, from Mombassa to Casablanca, in nine weeks. Unlike the 1926 hunting trip, where he did not want publicity, Bedaux sought to have his African adventures made known to the world. These *New York Times* headlines show Bedeaux's desire for the sensational:

BACK AFTER DRIVING CARS ACROSS AFRICA
Bedaux Says His Expedition Motored From Sea to Sea
in 3 Months and a Week.

ATTACKED BY WILD BEES
Tells of Exciting Experiences as He Returns Aboard the Bremen.

Fern once again accompanied Bedaux, along with his mistress, Marian Booth. Count Ledebur, a future Hollywood actor, was also part of the expedition.

Bedaux returned to British Columbia for another hunting trip in 1932, again with his wife, his mistress and Count Ledebur. The group travelled to Edmonton where Bedaux met and hired Jack Bocock, a geologist, to manage their trip. Bocock had spent the summer of 1929 and 1930 in the BC Peace River region as a geologist on the provincial government's PGE (Pacific Great Eastern) Resources Survey, and had worked earlier that summer on a mining venture in the upper Peace River. The party travelled to

The Bedaux party crossing the Caribou Range after a snowstorm in September 1932 (left to right): Charles Bedaux, unknown, Josephine Daly (the Bedaux's maid), Fern Bedaux, Marian Booth, Count Ledebur. LAC e008300547.

Hudson Hope where they hired Bob Beattie, a local packer. Beattie, several cowboys and more than 50 pack horses went on a six-week hunting trip into the Rocky Mountains north of Hudson Hope.

In her diary, Fern Bedaux worried about Bedaux's health. On September 2 she wrote:

> Camp is at 4400 feet. We climbed to 6400. It was a beautiful climb. Sunshine all of the time. What glorious views are seen from above. I loved every minute but didn't realize that Charles was overdoing it a bit. I thought he was only going slowly to get used to climbing again. We were back at six. Had dinner and shortly after Charles got a chill. He went to bed but it took lots of covers, a roaring fire and a rum toddy to get him over it. By 9 o'clock he was all right again but very weary and tired.

The following day she observed: "Charles and I were busy about camp all day. He is feeling better today but is really too weary to be doing this kind of a trip just now." In Fern's entry for September 12 she recorded: "Windy camp. 4000 feet. Terrible day. Moved camp to a better shelter. Charles went after a sheep with Beattie and Bocock. Too much for him. He came back exhausted. I won't write it!" The party remained at Windy Camp the next day. "Last night was the worst I have ever spent in the open. The wind was terrific. I thought our tent would fall any minute. Charles worried me. I waited minute by minute for morning." Fern's September 21 diary noted that, "Charles and I stayed around camp. He needs a good rest & is getting it."

Despite the often inclement weather and Charles' health, Fern revelled in the beauty of the country. On September 8 she wrote: "Charles & I took horses and with Mr Beattie went up on the mountain to have a look for

Showing off some bighorn sheep trophies in 1932. Charles Bedaux wears a fur cap, second from the left in the front row; Jack Bocock kneels beside him in the centre; and Count Ledebur crouches on the far right holding a rifle. LAC e008300548.

sheep. No game but a lovely day. Nice lunch – pretty ride – good walk and glorious view. We saw Redfern Lake – a fairy lake – and counted nine others from the top of the mountains. Wild fiendish and gorgeous." Two days later the hunting party crossed the Caribou Range. "The loveliest trail of the trip. Left camp and climbed up 2000 feet right away. Altogether we climbed 3000 feet, 3500 to 6490. What a view! We want so much to come back and camp here. Quick lunch up on top. Saw caribou. Parts look very much like Scotland."

Fern also wrote with delight about an unusual event that occurred on the trip.

> Last year Mr Clark left one of his horses on the trail. She was swayed & couldn't travel. That was back at about our September 2 camp. This morning she was sighted on the skyline – about 50 miles straight across mountain tops from where she was left. Bill Pickell, Fabe and Lucas went after her. She kept running from them then back again for a long time, and finally followed them happily back to camp. Think of it – a whole year alone out on the range, and ill to start with. It is the nicest story on the trip. She was in camp all afternoon looking so happy and contented. Her hoofs are worn right down to the quick.

At the end of the trip the *Peace River Block News* reported: "It is rumoured that Mr Bedaux intends within the next two years to ship three especially large and specially constructed caterpillar tractors that will blaze a road to Redfern Lake. A slash is to be made six feet in width, if plans mature, to the lake so that the trip can be made in two to three days."

After the adventure Charles Bedaux purchased Chummy and Mary Lou, two of the horses used on this hunting trip, and had them shipped to Candé, the chateau in France that he purchased in 1927. Earlier in the

Fern Bedaux with First Nations women who met the hunting party on the Sikanni River. LAC e008300550

summer these two horses had been out on one of Mary Henry and Knox McCusker's well-known botany expeditions to northern BC.

In 1933 Bedaux invested some money in a small mining company near Hudson Hope in which Jack Bocock was a partner. He also expressed an interest in investing in a gold mine in the Two Brothers area where he had hunted in 1926. Meanwhile, he continued developing plans for a motorized expedition across northern BC, and in September purchased five half track vehicles from the French vehicle manufacturer, Andre Citroën. These vehicles had wheels on the front and a caterpillar track on the back. Citroën had constructed similar vehicles for trips across Africa and Europe. In the fall of 1933 Bedaux hired Jack Bocock to organize his expedition.

Initially Bedaux planned to travel from the Fort St John area up the Halfway River valley to Redfern Lake, the route that he had followed on the return part of his 1932 trip. From Redfern Lake he wanted to travel by the old First Nations and Northwest Mounted Police Trail to Fort Grahame, and then proceed up the Finlay River to the area where he had hunted with Bob and Bert McCorkell in 1926.

In October 1933 Bedaux wrote to Bert McCorkell describing his planned expedition and asking McCorkell to work for him:

> What have you been doing this summer? More gold mines, more packing, more life free from cares and more of that wonderful laughter of yours, which can scare game for 20 miles around?
>
> What are your plans for next summer? Are you going to be tied up or will you sign up with me? It is no monkey business this time, no outfitting of a tenderfoot who wants to see the North. It is real hard work, dangerous at times and to you with what you know at the moment, a thing absolutely impossible. Nevertheless, I am planning it and what is more, I am going to do it. In 1926, with you leaving from Fort St

James, we tried to reach Telegraph Creek and we failed. Last year we went up into New Cassiar like a bunch of dudes and we didn't like it.

Next year, I am planning to take a train of five Citroën Caterpillar Motors from Pouce Coupe to Redfern Lake, across the divide, then still going west over the headwaters of the Finlay, reach the Indian trail to Telegraph Creek. It sounds crazy but I have some secret tricks of mine that will give me a good chance of success....

We would meet you some time during the summer, somewhere near Two Brothers Lake. We might even find a way to signal you at night from one of the high peaks of the Rockies just east of the Finlay.

The route that Bedaux planned to follow on the expedition was more than 300 kilometres from the Cassiar Ranch, and he and McCorkell were unable to come to an agreement on clearing a trail for the Citroëns.

In the fall of 1933 Bedaux returned to western Canada. This time he and Fern came to Edmonton, intending to go duck hunting in central Alberta. Instead Charles got sick, so they remained in Edmonton. In a letter to Bryan Williams, the BC game commissioner, Bedaux wrote:

It will be two weeks ago tomorrow that we arrived in Edmonton. My wife and her guest, Madame Chiesa, had travelled eleven days from Paris to reach Alberta and a camp I had ordered set up northeast of Vermillion. The day after we had arrived, I had to go to bed and I have been in bed ever since. In the meantime, all the ducks have flown over the Macdonald Hotel on their way to California and Mexico.

Bedaux also told Williams:

The love my wife and myself have for northern British Columbia is real. It dates back to our first attempt to enter Cassiar in 1926. At that time, if you will recall, we had tried to reach Telegraph Creek from Fort St James by way of Thutade Lake, and failed because our horses gave out. This, however, gave us a pretty good idea of the country west of Finlay River. Last year, from Hudson Hope, going beyond the Prophet River both by the high trail and by the low trail, we got a fair idea of the possibilities of the country which lies east of the Rocky Mountains. The combination of the information gathered on those two trips has led me to believe that it is not impossible, leaving Edmonton, to reach Telegraph Creek by means of specially designed caterpillar tractors, the said tractors supported by ordinary pack train.

From Edmonton Bedaux wrote to Bob Beattie, the head packer for his hunting trip the previous year:

I am sorry I will not see you this time – in fact I am sorry for many things indeed! All because ever since I got here, instead of shooting ducks as I wanted, I have been lying in bed sick. When I sent you my last wire, I still had hope of getting up quickly and getting on the way, and now my one idea is to get on my feet again so that we can run back east and on to France.

Frank Swannell.
Floyd Crosby photograph; LAC PA171461.

Ernest Lamarque.
Floyd Crosby photograph; LAC PA173879.

While Bedaux was in Edmonton he spent time with Jack Bocock planning the 1934 expedition. Bedaux returned to New York after a few weeks, leaving Bocock with a large amount of food and equipment to gather and men to hire in six months. The correspondence between Bocock and Bedaux shows the myriad details Bocock handled preparing for the expedition.

Bedaux realized that his original route followed known trails for a large portion of the route. Instead of going to Redfern Lake and travelling through Laurier Pass, Bedaux decided to continue up the east side of the Rockies and cross the more remote headwaters of the Muskwa River. Bedaux also altered his route by not following the more well-known Finlay River valley. After reaching Fort Ware on the Finlay River, Bedaux intended to follow up the Fox River, cross Fox or Sifton Pass, and then travel through remote country to Dease Lake.

Bedaux employed some scientists to make his expedition more credible and gain the support of the provincial and federal governments. On the recommendation of the surveyor-general of British Columbia, Jack Bocock hired Frank Swannell as geographer for the expedition. In 1929 Swannell and Bocock had both worked in the Peace River on the PGE Resources Survey. Swannell, a registered BC land surveyor who had spent a few years surveying in the Peace River area, was one of the province's best cartographers. Al Phipps, a member of Swannell's surveying crew for several years, was hired to be Swannell's assistant. Another BC land surveyor, Ernest Lamarque, was selected to locate the route the expedition would follow. Lamarque had spent several years in northern Canada working for

Charles and Fern Bedaux in conversation with Jack Bocock (left). LAC PA173770.

the Hudson's Bay Company, in part as a factor at the Hudson Hope post. He had done much of his surveying in remote areas of BC. Art Paul, from the Soils Department of the University of Alberta, and Earl Cuishing, who had worked with Jack Bocock's mining company, were hired as part of Lamarque's crew. Bocock was the expedition's geologist, while his brother, Cecil, was employed as mineralogist and supplies handler during the expedition.

Bedaux wanted his expedition to receive large amounts of publicity in the major newspapers in the United States, Canada and France. He hired a publicist to promote his expedition to the press, and a radio operator who would maintain contact between Bedaux and the outside world. Bedaux also employed Floyd Crosby, a young Hollywood filmmaker, to take movie footage of the expedition. Bedaux hoped that a film would be made of his adventure and that he would have a prominent role in this movie.

A press release from New York announced the expedition:

Preceded by trail-blazers who will plunge into the wilderness at Fort St John, BC, on April 1, the Bedaux-Canadian 1934 Exploration of Sub-Arctic Regions will make an elaborate attempt this summer to force passage through one of the few large unexplored areas in North America.

The expedition will use Edmonton, Alberta as its base and will hit the trail at Fort St John. Circling northwestward through unpenetrated regions in the Canadian Rockies and the Cassiar and Stickine Ranges, an effort will be made to reach Telegraph Creek on the Pacific slope before winter sets in.

Engaged in the undertaking will be 30 persons, 60 horses, several river boats, an amphibian plane, a radio broadcasting outfit and five caterpillar tractor trucks. The expedition is being financed by its leader, Charles E. Bedaux, inventor and head of the 12 industrial engineering corporations which bear his name in America and abroad.

Mr Bedaux led two previous explorations in British Columbia in 1926 and 1932. In 1929–30 he accomplished a feat which has not been duplicated, when he led an expedition in automobiles across 9,500 miles of the Libyan and Sahara Deserts, from Mombassa on the Indian Ocean to Casablanca on the Atlantic.

The press release also reported:

Floyd Crosby. LAC PA184672.

Tractors for the expedition are being specially made at the Citroën works in France and will be similar to those used by an expedition which crossed the Sahara in 1927 and another expedition which in 1932–33 was prevented by the Chinese Government from completing a two-way journey from the Near East into the Gobi Desert.

When reporters asked Bedaux why he wanted to undertake this expedition he replied: "It's fun to do things others call impossible. Everyone says to take a fleet of automobiles through the unmapped Rockies can't be done. I say it can! The Government hasn't much faith in me, but I've done the impossible before."

On April 5, 1934, Bedaux wrote to the lieutenant-governor of British Columbia on letterhead that read, "BEDAUX SUB-ARTIC EXPEDITION". He said:

Allow me to inform you that beginning April 15th, work will start at Fort St John on an expedition that I am organizing and wherein I will attempt to pass five caterpillar tractors from Edmonton to Telegraph Creek by way of Redfern Lake, Sifton Pass and Dease Lake. My object in planning this expedition is to prove that the country known as Cassiar is not impenetrable and my immediate object is to map, with the help of some of your geographers, the new country lying between Sifton Pass and Dease Lake.

As your chief geographer has been advised, all the scientific information we may gather will be placed at the disposal of your government.

He added, "I will have an expert cameraman and we expect to bring back a film of real interest."

Acting Provincial Secretary Arthur Wells Gray wrote to Bedaux on May 2:

With hesitancy, but at the same time feeling certain you would wish the publicity incidental to your expedition to be beyond dispute in detail, it is suggested that the title "Sub-Artic" is a misnomer. The "Arctic Circle" begins at Sixty Six degrees, Thirty minutes north latitude, approximately *four hundred and fifty* miles north of the northern boundary of the province of British Columbia. Your journey as outlined from Fort St John to Telegraph Creek will be wholly within British Columbia, the most northerly point of your route, according to your map being latitude 58°27 – about 107 miles south of the northern boundary of this Province, making a total from the Arctic of five hundred and fifty seven miles. A necessary reason for review of the title may be the printer's error in the spelling of Arctic.

Bedaux responded to Wells Gray:

The observation you make is absolutely correct. The name I had selected was "The Bedaux Cassiar Expedition", but my publicity agent, acting at the time of my departure from the United States late in February, selected the words "Sub Arctic" without any definite knowledge of where the Arctic Circle is. I hope you will not gather from this error in name, the impression that the expedition is not organized with all the seriousness that it deserves. I feel that, on the contrary, we have done everything conservatively and prudently.

The Bedaux Expedition was divided into four groups. On April 15 Tommy Wilde, one of the cowboys on the 1932 hunting trip, would take a group of men to begin clearing a route for the Citroëns at Bear Flat, west of Fort St John. There was a pack trail from there up the Halfway River valley. Wilde's instructions were to clear the route to six feet in width, leave no stumps more than six inches off the ground, and avoid side hills wherever possible.

The second group, led by Ernest Lamarque, would depart on May 1. Lamarque's work began at the end of the well-established trail up the Halfway River. From there Lamarque was to locate a trail through the Rocky Mountains and over to Sifton Pass.

On July 1 Nick Geake, a former British military officer, would leave from Fort St John with a small group of men and more than 50 packhorses. This freight group was to carry gasoline, food and supplies that the expedition would need later in the trip.

The main party of the expedition, which would include Bedaux and his five Citroëns, was scheduled to depart from Edmonton in early July.

During the spring Jack Bocock had to hire the personnel for the expedition. He had more than 2000 applications for the positions, partly because of the exotic nature of the expedition and the prospect for adventure, and also because Bedaux was paying good wages – $4 a day for the cowboys instead of the average wage of $2 – as well as promising about four months of work. Almost all the cowboys Bocock hired were from the Hudson Hope and Fort St John area, and many were men that he personally knew. Bob Beattie, head packer for the 1932 hunting trip, was chosen as head packer for the main Bedaux group. Jack MacDougall, Bill Pickell and Tommy Wilde also cowboys on the 1932 trip, were hired. Two of the cowboys that Bocock hired for the freight group were Bob White and Bob Godberson. Bocock knew White, who had packed for him on the PGE Resources Survey in 1930.

In June Charles and Fern Bedaux and their friend, Madame Chiesa (also reported to be Bedaux's mistress), came to western Canada where they spent a couple of weeks training in the mountains around Jasper with Joe Weiss, a Swiss guide who joined the main expedition. Then the group travelled to Edmonton, the starting point for the Citroëns and their planned trip of more than 1100 miles to Telegraph Creek on the Stikine River. By early July, after nine months of preparation and spending more than $250,000, Charles Bedaux was ready to start his expedition.

Bob White

Bob White was born in 1902 in the Saskatchewan region of the Northwest Territories, one of six children of Francis and Sybil White. Francis immigrated to Canada from England when he was a young man. Bob grew up on the family ranch in the remote Cypress Hills of southwestern Saskatchewan and lived there between 1902 and 1925, except from 1914 to 1916 when his mother took the children to New Brunswick.

Bob worked on the family ranch with his older brother John, but he wanted to travel and have some adventure. From the fall of 1925 through the spring of 1926 Bob lived in Banff where he worked on the construction of some outbuildings at the Banff Springs Hotel. In a letter to his sister, Agnes, in January 1926 he wrote: "Just a few lines to thank you for the cake and jelly, which sure were good." He also commented that, "I went up to the Cave and Basin and had a swim in the hot water, while I was swimming

Bob White.
Floyd Crosby photograph; LAC e008300198.

Bob White (left) and Paul Graham in the Cypress Hills at the beginning of their trip.
Glenbow NA 1095-9.

around in the pool, icicles froze on my head, Conny left me the camera, so I took a few snaps, I am sending you one that was taken in front of our shack."

Bob White returned to the family ranch. He was in his mid 20s. Though he liked working on the ranch his parents were not paying him much in wages and they did not offer him a share in the ranch. White began to plan a trip to the wilderness of northern BC. His brother John also wanted to go, but as the oldest son who would inherit the ranch, he remained behind.

On August 1, 1928, White and his friend, Paul Graham, left the Cypress Hills with saddle and packhorses planning to travel more than 1200 miles to the Peace River country in British Columbia. Their journey took the two men through Maple Creek in southwestern Saskatchewan, across the South Saskatchewan River, and into eastern Alberta. Riding north through the eastern part of that province, they visited the buffalo park at Wainwright before travelling on to Edmonton.

By early September, after a month of riding, the two men reached High Prairie in northern Alberta where they found work on a harvesting crew. White and Graham became friends with George Godberson, the steam engineer on the threshing outfit, and George's younger brother, Bob. Graham left in December, while White remained in High Prairie for the winter.

In early April White wrote to Agnes:

> Just a few lines to let you know that I am still alive, and to thank you
> very much for the cakes you sent me which I appreciated very much.
> I received the parcel, the day I drove out to Aggie (next station west
> of High Prairie) to haul tamarack posts, it was a pretty cold day, I was

A Beaver (Dunne-za) First Nations camp on Stoddart Creek, a traditional fishing area. White visited this camp on the 1930 PGE Resources Survey.
Bob White family collection.

eating cake most of the way, and it sure went good.

As for those buckskin or moose hide coats, you can't get them for less than $12.00 or $15.00 dollars, and as high a $50.00 for the more elaborate ones. Well I have got a pretty good place to work, I and an English man (Reg Lucas), started working for C. Spendiff, the first of April, and will work till the first of June and then we are going to head up-country; there may be another fellow come with us, we can't start much sooner as the grass is not very good here, till the first of June.

I had a mishap the other day, while playing catch with a ball one night, I knocked that false tooth out. I may have to go out to Edmonton, and get it fixed unless a dentist comes through here, as he does sometimes.

Reg and I have got a great job these days, clearing land, mostly young willow, and old stumps: by golly you won't catch me taking up a bush homestead, the frost is going out of the ground fast, had a little rain tonight, but I think we will be on the land next week, a fellow a few miles west has 10 acres of wheat in, there are a lot of people coming in to this country every day.

Lots of love to all, will write again,

Bob

During the winter, Godberson and Lucas became interested in White's adventure and decided to join him. They left High Prairie in early June 1929. At Peace River, Alberta, they took part in a rodeo where they met Frank and Charlie Hudson, ranchers on the remote upper Halfway River in the foothills of the Rocky Mountains northwest of Fort St John. The Hudson brothers invited the three men to accompany them on the return trip to

Godberson (left) and White with their fur catch, spring 1934. Bob White family collection.

their ranch and they accepted. When they arrived in the BC Peace River country Lucas set out on his own, while White and Godberson stayed to work for the Hudson brothers and other ranchers.

The two men spent the winter there, and in late January decided to snowshoe to Hudson Hope for mail and supplies. One night, at one of the trap-line cabins where they stopped along the trail, they encountered a man named Tom Cassidy, whom White had met previously. Over the winter, Cassidy stole goods from several houses and cabins, including some clothing that belonged to White and Godberson. Eventually he was arrested, and the clothing was part of the evidence used to convict him. Cassidy was sentenced to a year in jail, but he quickly escaped. When he was recaptured, the police discovered that he had been an accomplice to a murder in Calgary, and before that had been a gangster in Chicago. Cassidy was convicted of the Calgary murder and hanged.

In the spring of 1930 White broke horses for Billy Hill, one of the ranchers in the upper Halfway River area. Word spread through the area about his ability to handle horses. Jack MacDougall, who had packed for Jack Bocock on the PGE Resources Survey in 1929, needed an assistant packer for the 1930 season and he hired Bob White. In his government report Bocock wrote: "The party consisted, beside Bocock, of John Mac-Dougall, packer, and Robert White, assistant packer, cook, etc., both of Hudson Hope. The competence and willingness of these men, combined with the first class outfit provided by MacDougall, were important factors in covering the allotted area in the time available."

White spent the summer of 1930 travelling throughout the Peace River region. On a couple of occasions the party spent a few days at Fort St John while Bocock wrote reports and handled administrative work. White told the local game warden that he and Bob Godberson wanted to purchase

White working on a
deer hide.
Bob White family collection.

traplines in the upper Halfway River region. The game warden established adjacent trap lines for the two men on the headwaters of the Cameron River, one of the tributaries of the Halfway.

From 1930 to 1935 White and Godberson trapped in this area during the winter and worked as cowboys for ranchers during the rest of the year. When they came into Hudson Hope from the trap line in the spring of 1934 they heard that Jack Bocock was hiring cowboys for the Bedaux Expedition. In addition to the good wages and about four months of work, the expedition would give them an opportunity to travel through wilderness further north and to have new adventures.

On April 5 White sent a telegram to Bocock: "Dear Jack, is there chance of job preferably with horses?" Two days later Bocock replied, "I have received your wire asking for a position for you and Bob Godberson on the Bedaux Expedition. It is possible that I shall be able to offer you something later. I will wire you if that happens."

In early June Bocock offered both men work on the freight party that would gather at Fort St John in the beginning of July.

White (left) and Godberson on their saddle horses. Bob White family collection.

BANNOCK AND BEANS

Preface

I have written out this scrawl mostly for my own benefit – to keep in mind the life we led and who we worked with.

Many have said, "Why don't you make a story out of it?"

Well, to begin with I'm not much at this letter writing business, not having spent much of my time in a school room, when I was growing up in the log house on the ranch in the Cypress Hills in Saskatchewan. There were no schools out there in those early days – a few private teachers, then two years at school in St Stevens in New Brunswick from 1914 to 1916. About all I accomplished there was to acquire the name of Herring Choker.

Then in 1928 my life-long ambition came true for a long ride across the country. With a chum and two pack horses I rode 1400 miles to Hudson Hope in northern British Columbia, then onto traplines in winter and pack trails in summer.

I packed the summer of 1930 on a geological survey all over the Peace River Block – Jack Bocock boss, Jack MacDougall, horse wrangler and packer. It was more like a paid holiday, with wet days and mosquitoes thrown in. The only trouble I got into was burning a few bannocks for the crew of three. It was through my good friend Jack Bocock that I got on the Bedaux Expedition.

There have been a number of wild articles written about the Bedaux Expedition, some not very complimentary. One writer referred to our faithful pack horses as a bunch of slat-ribbed cayuses, another called his yarn the "Champagne Safari of the North" and said the cowboys never had it so good in their lives, living on caviar and champagne. All I can say to them is they should have been with us.

A few years ago I started to write about the Bedaux Expedition but didn't make much headway until Mrs Shirley Meiers of Medicine Hat took a hand. With her help and encouragement I completed the first section, so many thanks to you, Shirley. Then my good friends Morley and Ruth Wagner of Maple Creek encouraged me with the next section and pictures. Ruth is secretary of our Piapot History Club and has given expert help and advice. She even recruited some willing workers from the Club, Greba, Shelley and Mary Drever. So a big thank you to you all. Without your help I'm sure this scrawl would still be on the draw.

And readers, pleasant reading, but don't expect too much.

Sincerely,
Bob White, 1983

Bob White on his horse, Smoky, during the Bedaux Expedition. Floyd Crosby photograph; LAC e008300199.

Part One:
The Bedaux Expedition

Joining the Freight Party

It was a nice sunshiny day early in June of 1934. I had just walked over to our little log post office in Hudson Hope to pick up my mail and visit with our postmaster, Fred Monteith, a kindly man and a friend to everyone. In my mail was the long awaited telegram from my good friend Jack Bocock in Edmonton, informing us to go down to Fort St John to start work on the Bedaux Expedition. There were three of us from here who had been offered work as packers: myself, my trapping partner, Bob Godberson, and Willard Freer. We had our application in for a job with the outfit since the middle of the winter. I thought I had a pretty good chance of getting on since I had been out all summer in 1930 on a geological survey with Jack Bocock, who was to be second in command of the expedition. Those of us who did get on considered ourselves lucky for they had over 3500 applications for a job with the expedition.

After coming in off the trapline that spring Bob Godberson and I had busied ourselves at odd jobs, more or less putting in time to see if this Bedaux job was going to materialize. Bob went working in the Hope, while I broke a few horses to ride and also branded and dehorned cattle at several places along the river.

When anyone left our fair city of Hudson Hope it was always an excuse for a dance. The party hung on pretty late, so our departure the next morning was delayed. First we had to build a raft. We cut down a couple of dry jack pines just below town, then hauled a couple more small logs from Joe Turner's place with the team and wagon, along with our bedrolls and riding gear. We rolled the logs over the steep gravel bank and lashed our raft together with our saddle ropes, then piled on our bed rolls, chaps and spurs. The three of us, Bob Godberson, Willard Freer and I, stepped on and we were on our way.

Willard Freer (left) and Bob Godberson paddling a raft to Fort St John.
Bob White family collection.

We had 60 miles to drift with the current to the old Fort St John landing and were lucky to have a warm day. The old Peace was at a fair stage of water, so we made pretty good time. The rock reef above the Gates, about 10 miles downstream, was passed without difficulty for the swift water was in the main channel. We landed above the Gates, looked it over, picked our place and sailed right through. We called in at our friends, the Les Bazelys, on the Ralph Osborne place above the mouth of the Red River [Farrell Creek], where we enjoyed a visit and tea, then on down to the Ardills, where we enjoyed their hospitality and dinner. After that we went back down their hill, on to the raft and out into the current. We had a tarp rigged up as a sail to help speed us along, but only had the odd puff of wind, so it didn't help much.

We took turns taking naps to make up for the sleep we missed last night, for we intended travelling late to make the Fort if we could. We passed the mouth of the Halfway River, Bear Flat, and then past where Cache Creek enters from the north. It was quite late when we got to the slide area. By 11 o'clock we reached the mouth of the Moberly River coming in from the south. It was getting pretty chilly on the raft, so we decided to camp for the night. There was an old cabin on the bank. On going up to it we found it was occupied by Herb Taylor, an old-timer who was washing for gold along the river bank. He had been asleep, but made us welcome. He said he was glad for the company, so after we had tea and a bite to eat, we rolled out our beds on the floor, which was old Mother Earth. In the morning we had about 10 miles to go. There was a breeze from the west, so we rigged up our sail, which helped push us along, and we made the landing at the old Fort at 10 o'clock.

After unloading the raft we made up our backpacks and started up the steep hill to the north and the three or four miles to the new site of Fort St John. With fair packs we had to rest a time or two climbing the hill. On getting into the post we hunted up Edward Geake, or Nick as we called him. He was to be in charge of the advance freight outfit that we were to join. We went into camp a mile north of town on Bert Ambrose's place on Fish Creek.

Our first job was to pick out between 50 and 60 head of horses for our outfit. We had all kinds of fun trying out new horses. Bill Pickell had the job of buying the horses for the outfit and was to pay an average of $35 a head for pack horses and a little more for the saddle horses if he had to.

There were a lot of horses in the area, and many people were anxious to sell. Horses were brought in from all directions. I was with Bill when he looked several of them over. It was hard to tell what kind of a horse you were getting, for no doubt people wouldn't be selling their best ones. Bill did a pretty good job of picking them out, and got some cracking good horses. We got stuck with a few duds in our outfit, but also left a few for the outfit that was to follow us.

Some of the boys were put to work in the warehouse filling pack panniers, while Ernie Peterson and I started picking out the pack horses for our outfit and fitting them with pack saddles. We got about 40 head of pretty good horses, then had to start on the young unbroke ones. We put packs on them and turned them loose in the corral, and not too many would buck with their packs. Ernie picked a nice-looking bay gelding that we both thought would make a real good pack horse. He had nice legs and a good saddle back, but after getting the pack saddle on him, getting struck at and kicked, we sure didn't want him in our outfit. We

Bob Godberson.
Floyd Crosby photograph; LAC PA171488.

A Cowboy on the Peace River – 1934

I started the spring of 1934 at Jack Ardill's who lived seven miles up the Peace from the mouth of the Halfway River. Jack and Mrs Ardill and their four children were always very hospitable, and I looked forward to a stay overnight with them in my travels up and down the river. Quite often I would have a few pack horses along, but it would be all the same to them. Jack would just say peel off the rigging and turn your horses loose. That sort of treatment was sure appreciated by a waddy travelling through the country, and I was always glad of a chance to do something for them in return.

Jack was busy putting in some crops, so the boys and I started to round up the cattle. We usually had quite a bit of fun at our branding episodes, but this spring a little more so, as Jack had got hold of a few cows from Freeman Forsythe in trade for feed. These cows were some of the original Bert Erb bunch on Red River [Farrell Creek] and pretty wild. We got them all in the corral except for one wild cow, so after we had finished branding those in the corral Jack suggested we try and get a rope on her. We rode out and got between her and the bush. We traded horses as Jack figured I'd have the better chance. Mine was a young horse who had wintered out, so it wasn't in the best running shape. Jack's horse, a bald-faced bay called Bob, was in good condition. We took after the cow and got her headed toward the corral. I managed to get a rope on her and we finally got her down and tied up at the corner of the corral. She had a wicked set of horns, so we felt better when we got her all tied up. We built up the fire and got the irons hot and got the Â brand on her.

When we were through I held her with a rope from the saddle horn and her hind feet, while Albert Kem, a young chap not long out from Poland, pulled the ropes from her head. I said, "You better head for the corral or a pine tree nearby." He said, "Oh, she no bother." So I threw the rope off the horn. She scrambled up in a hurry with fire in her eye and darn near had Albert, who was just standing there. He barely made the lower limb of a pine tree. The bossy went under him with a snort and out for the open range.

My next job was at Lynx Creek, four miles below Hudson Hope, where we gelded some colts and branded a few cattle for the MacDougall brothers, Jack and Don. I had packed with these boys on different survey parties. We then went on up to brand and dehorn Joe Turner's cattle. Joe lived a mile and a half north of Hudson Hope, and his cattle ranged in the breaks to the north. We didn't quite get all of them in the roundup, but got the brand on 144 head. About half of them had horns and there were three- and four-year-old steers in the bunch. Joe's plan was to swim 90 or 100 head across the Peace River and work them south toward the railroad at Dawson Creek during the summer. Joe wanted me to take on the job, and I might have done so had the Bedaux work not materialized. But I agreed to try and swim them across the river if I had time before we went. The two days we put in working that bunch were sure grim, so hot the sweat just poured off us.

They were of the Aberdeen Angus breed with a Shorthorn cross that put horns on about half of them, a pretty snuffy bunch. Several of those old bossies put us all over the fence more than once. My help, George Brandon and Oscar Volding, weren't too keen on that wild stuff, but old Vic Peck, who was riding my horse, was right at home. He had spent his younger life punching cows in the States. One old bossy wouldn't go in the chute, so Vic just popped a rope on her and we stretched her out. After getting the S bar T brand on her left shoulder we let her up and all got out of the way except George Brandon, who headed for the fence with the cow right behind. George had to go over the fence head first and just made it. When old bossy hit the fence, George thought she was coming right through the rails, so he started crawling away to beat everything.

Some of the big steers had a great set of horns and bled quite freely after we sawed them off, so we gave them a week's time to heal. Then we decided to try and swim them across the river for our time was getting short. We rounded them out of the bush and into the corral for an early start the following morning. Before sunrise we started them for the Hope, about a mile and a half distant, for we wanted to get them in Shorty Pennington's corral in the centre of Hudson Hope before there were too many people around. We just got started into the settlement and all the doors opened up. The women and kids poked their heads out to watch this nice bunch of black cattle go by, and believe me they sure went. We tried to hold them together, but they split up just past the hotel, and about 20 head got away on us. It took about three hours riding through the bush until we finally got all but one or two.

Our plan was to put them down the bank from Shorty's corral and into the river, just above a rock bank, where they would be in swimming water right off. The water there was fairly swift and quite choppy. We had all the boats we could get lined up on the lower side to head the dogies out into the river. [The Peace River is about half a mile wide at Hudson Hope.] When the time came to start, a few of the boys let the cattle out of the gate, down the steep bank and into the river. Don MacDougall and I had the government canoe and were to try and get a few head to line out so that the rest would follow, but we had no such luck. Since the water was choppy all those critters did was mill around, and after that 90-odd head got into the water I never saw such a melee. It wasn't long until Don and I were in a hell of a fix with cattle swimming all around us, some trying to get into the canoe. To make matters worse we had a deluge of rain at that time. When we found we couldn't get them to line, all the boats drifted down with the current. We didn't want to take a chance of drowning any, although it looked for a time we might lose about half of them.

The dogies were determined not to head out into the river, and by the time we had drifted down the river 200 to 300 yards, most of the cattle were back on the same side they had started from. A few head had trapped themselves under a rock bank, and we had to go in with the boat and push them into the river to come ashore lower down.

This ended my attempt to get the cattle across the Peace, for we had got our call to start work for Bedaux at Fort St John. Bob Godberson and I were to help Joe trail the bunch out to the railroad at Dawson Creek in the cold January of 1936, but that is another story.

left him for the outfit that was to follow and heard later that they didn't want him either.

We put in a good husky snubbing post outside the corral where we tied the unbroke horses and the ones we found to be halter pullers. We left them there for a while to get used to their packs. They put on quite a show when they all pulled back at the same time, sometimes getting the snubbing post out of the ground altogether. But they never got away for they could never decide to go in the same direction. The worst was Old Red, a dark chestnut gelding, around 1200 pounds, a well-built horse but plumb ornery. He was supposed to have been broke but never did know anything. He'd buck, kick and throw himself any time he felt like it. He gave us trouble most of the time he was with us before finally drowning in the Muskwa River 250 miles up the trail. Geake said Old Red was too ornery to swim.

We had a lot of Riley & McCormick pack saddles shipped in from Calgary, but they had too small a tree for some of our horses. Frank Wagner, a trapper up the Halfway River, made a lot of pack saddles and we were lucky enough to get some of his for our bigger horses. There were a number of army pack saddles that were horse killers. We got stuck with a few of them. There weren't nearly enough saddle blankets so we opened up several bales of fair cotton and wool blankets. With a big string of pack

Having a bite to eat (left to right): Bob Beattie, Bert Ambrose, Art MacLean, Willard Freer, Bill Pickell, Flora Pickell and Jack MacDougall. BC Archives B-07376.

horses you don't unpack at noon, so it was necessary to have the saddles well padded.

We tried out about 30 head of horses before we picked the 6 saddle horses for our outfit. Some of them gave us quite a ride. It's funny how a horse will carry a pack sometimes and buck like the dickens when you go to ride him. All of us got pretty good horses. I settled for a flea-bitten gray horse from southern Alberta. He turned out to be a whale of a good horse – would stand with his lines down, a good swimmer, and good in fast water. When our boss asked who wanted to carry the company rifle on their saddle I volunteered and got to be the hunter for our outfit. Then I found that my Smoky was game shy. I had some trouble getting the meat back to camp for a while, but he soon got used to it.

The Bedaux Expedition was like Santa Claus to a lot of Fort St John people since money was scarce. The Bowes and Herron garage did well for they did most of the hauling from the railhead at Dawson Creek. They did good service and helped out in many other ways. The stores did a lot of extra business, as did the local blacksmith, Pete, and his helper, John Peck. We had all our pack horses shod in front and the saddle horses shod all around. We had to lead the horses the mile into town from camp. It took about three days to complete the job.

We held the horses in Bert Ambrose's pasture but the fence wasn't too good in the brush and 16 head got out one night. These horses had come from south of the river, so we assumed they would head for the river near

The Late Commander Geake, R.N.

Ernest Lamarque was a British Columbia land surveyor hired by Charles Bedaux to locate the route from Fort St John to Telegraph Creek. Lamarque wrote an unpublished article in 1938 after Nick Geake was murdered on a mining trip to Mexico. This is a portion of that article.

Spring had come in the valley of the Peace, but it was a laggard in that of the Halfway [River valley] where, a few miles north of the confluence of the Cameron, we had halted over Sunday – a bleak day with a bitter wind from the snow-clad mountains to the west – to allow our horses the full benefit of the scanty pasture. It was early in May, 1934, and the leafless aspens and cottonwoods shivered and bent before that icy blast, the straggling sunbeams, between the rain squalls, barely camouflaging the sheer inhospitality of that cheerless day.

Floyd Crosby photograph; LAC PA171472.

Camped close to the pack trail leading from the Peace to the Liard River country, a solitary horseman passed us that afternoon on his southward journey. A bare headed, alert, middle aged man with a well trimmed, pointed beard, lightly clad in sweater and shorts, his knees bare, there was something about him quite different to the ordinary settler-pioneer of that region. He led a string of three or four unloaded pack animals and was accompanied by two fine, big dogs. After a few words of greeting, he passed on his way. Geake was his name, and I learned that he had a homestead a few miles to the north where the Graham or West Branch enters the Halfway River and that he was an ex destroyer commander of the British Navy. He lived quite alone, it appeared, his "place" adjoining that of one Wagner, who came by, also southbound, an hour or so afterwards.

Later in the season, I met Geake again, far to the north on the divide between the Muskwa and Kwadacha rivers in the main range of the Rocky Mountains...Visiting him in his camp to arrange about supplies – his horses carried provisions and gasoline for the expedition – I found him standing around in the cold sleet and rain, re-organizing the loads for his pack animals. He had a rain cape over his shoulders, no hat, his legs quite bare below his shorts, his sockless feet merely encased in low rubbers.

Two days later, ere turning back to meet Bedaux's main party, with his horses he visited me in my camp just before we started on our journey down the Kwadacha on the westerly slope of the mountains. For once he was warmly clad in mackinaw clothes and gaiters, but still hatless.

On the whole, while he had his "place" on the Halfway, where he resided often for weeks or months at a time, he travelled about a great deal, sometimes visiting the coast, and also, it was said, going much further afield....

He wandered, too, a great deal in the northern wilderness. His journey to the Finlay in '34 was not his first one to that river or region for, a year or so before, he had ascended the Peace and Finlay at the vicinity of Sifton Pass. Then, rafting down the Fox River, which enters the Finlay near Whitewater, he and his companion are reported to have been marooned when their rough craft drifted away from its moorings.

No doubt there would have been more adventures, accidents, or incidents in his wilderness travels than with the average man, partly on account of his lack of experience and partly, also, because he probably not only courted adventure but also hardship, toughing it at times quite unnecessarily and in a manner no really experienced "old-timer" would think of doing, realizing, as the "old-timer" must, that there is enough hardship in any case in a life in the wilderness without deliberately seeking it.

However that may be, brought up in the rough, hard school of the Royal Navy, Geake was essentially a manly man who, at home though he may have been in society, preferred the more rugged life of the wilds.

the ferry about 14 miles distant. Bill Pickell got his gas wagon and loaded Edgar [Dopp] and me in with our saddles. Although we covered a lot of country by dark, we failed to locate them. There was a lot more bush in that country. We left word around. A fellow down by the river located them and drove them up to our camp for the reward.

Finally we got the horses and rigging sorted out and got busy making up the packs in Clark Finch's warehouse in town. We had 10 gas packs. There was a total of 20 containers with 10 gallons in each one. These containers were specially made in Edmonton but came without a baffle in them. We realized that the gas splashing back and forth with every step would murder a horse's back, so the tops were all taken off, the baffle welded in, and the tops welded back on. Those tanks were awkward things to get a pack rope to stay on, so we fitted them with rings wired on, and a rope to hang them from the pack saddle, which made for quicker packing.

Our flour was packed in canvas panniers. We'd put 50 pounds in the bottom, then make the pack up to 80 or 85 pounds with more perishable stuff, such as oatmeal, cornmeal, sugar and salt. Matches were put in tins and were distributed, as were a lot of other things, into as many packs as possible, so in case we lost a pack in a river or any place, we didn't lose all of everything. The very compact packs such as flour were up to 200 pounds per horse, but the weight was cut down for the more bulky packs. Our wooden pack boxes were packed the same way, with the canned goods in the bottom and the more perishables on top. This was done for many of the river crossings might wet the bottom of the packs. Each pack was numbered and the contents listed and marked on the pack. The lists were also entered in a book. Eventually we got all our packs finished and hauled down to our camp at Fish Creek.

The big day finally arrived when we began packing up for the start. We wrangled the horses at 5 am. After picking out our horses we put saddles on them, then started hanging the packs. It took us several hours. Eventually we put all our stuff on 51 pack horses, which, with the six saddle horses, made 57 horses all together in the outfit. There were six to go out with this outfit. Edward (Nick) Geake, who had been a major in the British Army, was to be in charge. Besides owning land near Pouce Coupe, Nick had located on a small place just below the forks of the Halfway. Nick knew that I had broke a lot of horses since I had come up to the Peace River country. In fact, I had worked on some horses in his own corral.

Willard Freer, who was to be our cook, grew up in the Peace River country. Ernie Peterson, an experienced trail hand who had a place on the North Pine was going out for the adventure. His packing partner, Art MacLean, was a young fellow raised in the Fort St John country. My packing partner was my trapping partner, Bob Godberson, raised around High Prairie, Alberta.

On the Trail
(July 4–15)

We turned the horses loose and had a little excitement when a few tried to buck their packs off, but finally they started to line out and down the narrow grade across Fish Creek. We headed north, then a little to the west to the Montney country: didn't make too long a drive for the first day, 10 to 12 miles, camping across Montney Creek by Alf Clark's place. Our horses camped well that night, considering they were from all over the country, but we were to experience considerable trouble later when we got into more bush.

Geake was a fine person and could sure handle men, but he had very little experience with horses. We wanted more bells to put on the horses to start out, but he said no. He was told the more bells you have the more bunches you have to find, which is true, but it takes time for horses to get used to and follow a bell. We said it's better to hunt for horses with a bell on than without, as we were to find out later. But we had our horses all on hobbles and wrangled them the next morning without too much trouble. The grass had been good and there was not too much bush.

We stocked up with a few eggs, butter and vegetables from the settlers, for this would be our last chance to pick up anything of that sort. There were only a few settlers in the next 100 miles and no one after that. After a hot morning for packing, we got on the way, following the creek up and crossing Montney Creek on the bridge where there was a small settlement and store. We were kept busy getting the horses lined out through Montney. Ernie asked me to slip into the store and pick him up some kind of a small mirror for shaving. All I could get was a lady's compact, powder puff and all, so Ernie got lots of teasing about his make-up.

Crossing Montney Creek. BC Archives B-07378.

We headed straight west and camped for the night on Red Creek. The camp was good for horse feed – pea-vine and vetch knee high, but a lot of second-growth poplar, so we had plenty of trouble wrangling the horses. We hunted until near noon, then started packing. When we were ready to turn loose and start out, we were still two pack horses short. Geake said to me, "I think you can find them, Bob. If you get them you can follow along, and if you don't find them by dark, come on into camp."

I tracked and hunted in that second-growth poplar the rest of the day but failed to catch up with them. With so much fresh sign it was hard to sort out the tracks, so at dark I gave up and hit the trail toward camp. After travelling several miles of wet trail I went over a height of land and dropped down into the head of one of the branches of Cache Creek. It was around midnight and I was damn cold. I saw a light still flickering so I rode over. There were some Indians camped there, with a couple bucks still sitting beside the fire. I asked them which way the big outfit went.

One Indian pointed up the creek and west and said, "Lots pack horses that way go. They lose one horse, we catch um and tie up." They showed me the horse and I found it was a little bay mare we called Daisy, a green horse but not too wild. I took her with me and about a mile along the trail I found her pack, so I tied it on, rode over a ridge down into another branch of Cache Creek, and into camp. I was pretty cold and as hungry as a bear. I hobbled my horses, grabbed a bite to eat, and climbed into my bedroll about 2:30 am.

I wasn't there long for camp was astir about 4 o'clock. Ernie, Art and Bob went out to wrangle horses and brought a bunch into camp an hour

Ernie Peterson.
Floyd Crosby photograph; LAC PA173916.

Art MacLean.
Floyd Crosby photograph; LAC PA171467.

and a half later. They were missing 20-odd head. After a quick breakfast Ernie and Art headed back to the Red Creek camp to try again for the missing horses there, while Bob and I went looking for the rest. We finally found 8 and while Bob took them into camp, I got on the trail of the 14 head still short, heading down Cache Creek. I caught up with them about eight miles down. It looked like they were trying to quit the country, for they were still going strong. I didn't have too much trouble tracking them since the ground was pretty heavy, and there was practically no other domestic stock in that vast country. Although hobbled, they had gone quite a distance. I unbuckled the hobbles from one front leg and buckled it onto the other so that they could carry their own hobbles back to camp.

We didn't intend to move camp that day for we wanted to try and simplify our packing method. We decided to bore holes in the ends of the wooden pack boxes, thread a rope through, and tie a knot, thus making a loop, so that we could hang the packs from the forks of the pack saddles instead of tying the basket hitch. We had begun to realize we were short-handed for such a sizeable outfit. Four of us – Art, Ernie, Bob and I – were doing most of the packing. The boss didn't have too much experience at packing, and invariably any of the horses he packed soon had to be adjusted on the way. Willard, the cook, had never packed before. He was supposed to pack his immediate kitchen horses but never got too far at it. I mentioned that I could rustle a brace and bit from a homesteader who lived about four miles distant. I knew this part of the country well for I had broke horses on this range for Billy Hill four years before. He had quite a bunch of horses that ranged along the head of Cache Creek and north toward the Blueberry River.

The land wasn't surveyed at that time and I had been one of six who had squatted on some land on these two branches of Cache Creek. The Peace River Block was under the Dominion government at that time and squatters' rights were recognized. When the BC government took over the Block in 1930 they discontinued squatters' rights, but sent a surveyor from Victoria to survey those claims already there. I had built a log cabin on a flat near one of the creeks, but had never lived in it nor done any improvements, for baching on a homestead didn't appeal to me. I had always been able to get jobs elsewhere. A chap by the name of Bohunk Ed (most of us never knew him by any other name) had located on the quarter section just south of mine. He was noted far and wide for the good moonshine he used to make. It was to his place I rode to borrow the brace and bit.

We had never met for he moved into the district after I moved out. After finding out who I was he said, "Well, doggone it neighbour, we just got to have a drink on this!" I was not much of a drinking man, though I used to hoist a few rum and scotch, but always stayed shy of home brew. So when Ed dug his crock from a hole in the ground and filled a mug near full of the stuff, I didn't know quite what to do. His reputation for turning out a good brew helped a lot so I started working on it and before too long had it all lapped up. I could sure feel it. After swapping lots of talk for an hour or more and turning down a refill, I headed the four miles back to camp. For two miles I cut across through scattered bush, then hit a trail leading up along a creek to camp. I was a pretty happy hombre and my vocal chords were sure working overtime. When the boys in camp heard me coming down the hill they thought the Grand Ol' Opry had strayed back into the bush.

After an hour or two working on the pack boxes to make for quicker and easier packing, we had our feed of good old macaroni. We were all hungry for fresh meat. The boss suggested I take the rifle and look around. Geake had his .303 British rifle with him and I carried the 30-30 Winchester Carbine, the company gun, on my saddle, and was the hunter whenever we needed meat. I rode down the creek a mile or two and was lucky enough to get a nice buck deer. This was when I found old Smoky, my horse, was game shy. I hauled the buck as high as I could over a tree limb, then blindfolded Smoky and led him around and around the tree until he finally let me lower the buck on him and we got it back to camp.

Crossing Cameron River. BC Archives B-07379.

It was getting late but there is lots of daylight at this time of year in the north country.

Ernie and Art had arrived back in camp in the late afternoon with the two missing horses, having had the good luck to pick up their tracks. Bob had spent most of the day herding horses and we all had come to the decision that from now on it would be necessary to night-herd them. This fell to Ernie, Art, Bob and I, so from that time on we were to be minus a lot of shut-eye.

Our nights being so short we decided to split the shift in half, one taking it to midnight, then the change taking it until four o'clock, the time we wrangled and brought them into camp. We would tie up and put the saddles on and leave the cinches just snug, eat breakfast, then start hanging packs. It would take us about 2½ hours to pack. Then we'd have a shot of tea and a bite to eat, turn loose and be on our way.

We climbed the hill out of the coulee and after a few miles crossed another branch of Cache Creek. Two of us managed to get away from the string to return the brace and bit to Bohunk Ed where we enjoyed another shot of his fire water. The serving wasn't as generous as I had had the day before, so we didn't get to singing any hymns. We continued past Stan Clark's (the old Billy Hill place), then on and down the steep hill into the Cameron River. Crossing that without any trouble, we went up the long hill on the other side, then along the top until we dropped down to the Halfway River, making camp on the lower Indian reserve. It had been a long day but the horses had behaved pretty good. Art and I split the herding. I took the first shift to midnight. This was a swell camp with all kinds of grass and big open flats. The only company we objected to was the mosquitoes. I counted up to a million, then lost count. We kept a smudge going for the only break we got from them was when we'd ride in and sit in the smoke for a while.

At midnight I hauled Art out – he just loved that – and told him there was a nice little job awaiting him. My old rabbit skin robe sure looked good to me. From midnight on the mosquitoes weren't nearly so bad for in the north the nights generally cool off. Art had no trouble getting the horses together and into camp shortly after 4 am. We got the saddles on, had our breakfast, went back to packing up, and were on our way.

It was good travelling, big flats and a dry trail over the hill dividing the reserve's two flats. We passed the Chief's cabin, went past Nels Wester-gaard's ranch, over another hill and down onto the Halfway River again, camping on a nice flat just above the Hudson Brothers cabin. These two old trappers had been in the country since 1919.

There was a lot of excitement that day – a horse stampeded and bucked his pack. This was one of Geake's own horses and he was to be turned loose on his home range that night. Geake, with his usual way of packing, didn't get the cinches tight enough. After a horse has been on the trail a few hours his stomach empties and the cinches get slack. The pack goes one side or the other, pinching the horse's withers, and then it does the only thing it can do – try and ditch the pack.

Art and I took after the horse. After catching him in the brush we started back to pick up the pack. Among other stuff he was packed with an extra case of jam. The horse made a job of scattering his pack. Of the 14 tins of jam 12 popped open, and since we were beyond any stores to replenish our supply, we had to save all we could. We scraped up what we could and ate so much jam that one of us got the brain wave to catch Midget, a little black horse that carried a box of pilot bread as a top pack. He wouldn't let us catch him so I said I'd rope him. Midget got into some brush and I couldn't get the rope over his head, so I roped the pack and held him until Art took hold of the halter. We weren't long getting our fill as it was pretty dry stuff. The box was broken so we put it into a bag to save the piece, for every time we tied the diamond hitch over it we'd make more pieces. After our little caper and a few laughs, Art and I got the horses on the trail and caught up to the main outfit.

Ernie and Bob had the honour of splitting the night-herding job. This was a swell camp, big flat, lots of good grass and water. They had the ponies in camp about 4 am, so we were on the trail in good season, travel-ling on a dry trail, crossing Grayling Creek, Iron Creek, then on up to the Forks of the Halfway River where the south fork [Graham River] comes into the main river from the mountains to the west.

We went north up the main Halfway River for the next 50 to 60 miles. It was necessary to ford the river just above the forks and the river was at a fair stage of water. We couldn't go straight across without swimming the horses so it was necessary to head and tail them into groups of four and follow the riffle upriver quite a distance to get across. We had to raise the more perishable packs on some of the horses for the water got quite deep, especially on the upstream side. We got everything across without any damage, then headed up the trail, crossing Dirty Creek and on up to Blue Grave Creek where we camped for the night.

The meadows were small with plenty of brush and all kinds of grass two feet high and more, a perfect breeding ground for mosquitoes. They must have had a 100 per cent hatch for they sure chewed us up. Art and I were stuck for the herding, Art taking the first shift, and I the graveyard shift until wrangling time at 4 am. It had showered off and on during the day, settling into a steady rain that lasted all night. We had all been running short on sleep since leaving Fort St John, so it didn't take long for me to start sawing wood in my blankets.

Next thing I knew Art had me by the arm and said, "Come on, pardner. How would you like a nice little job herding horses?"

I sure hated to leave those blankets after only two hours in them. But Art was real good. He had my horse in and saddled with my slicker over it to keep it dry since it was still raining, and some cocoa brewing over the fire. While I was downing a shot of that Art told me that the horses were camping pretty good but to watch for Spider and Red and their bunch that were on the downriver side. Art turned his horse loose and headed for the tent while I put on my slicker and rode off. It was pitch dark and mosquitoes so bad you had to have your hands going all the time. I eased through some horses as quiet as possible so as not to get them moving, and worked my way down through the brush until I was sure I was below them all, then spent the rest of the night riding the lower half of the circle.

When it began to get daylight the rain let up and by four o'clock I rounded up the bunch and drove them into camp, lucky to have them all. They had a good fill of grass. We tied up the 51 pack horses and five saddle horses while I turned Smoky loose to catch up on his eats. We saddled up before breakfast, leaving the cinches just snug. After eating we went to hanging packs, Art and Ernie packing together, along with Bob and I. Geake would pack a few by himself. Willard was supposed to pack his own kitchen packs, but we nearly always had to help him.

When we finished packing we had a spot of tea and food, then hit the trail, heading upriver. We crossed Horseshoe Creek coming in from

Christmas on the Trapline – 1930

Bob Godberson and I spent Christmas with the Brady family the first winter we trapped. Our trapping country was over on the Cameron River 20 miles to the east, while Brady had a spur line over to his cabin, also on the Cameron. Bob's territory was from Brady's cabin downriver, while mine was north to the watershed of the Cameron River, over to the Elbow of the Halfway, and up the Halfway to Two Bit Creek. We all used Brady's cabin on the Cameron and would leave notes to one another. One night we found a note from Brady, inviting us over for Christmas. That sounded pretty good to us.

Late in the fall of 1930 we had walked out from Hudson Hope over 90 miles to the south leading four pack horses, two loaded with traps and equipment, and two with grub and bedding. We were in a strange country and still lacking much experience at hunting and bush life in general. We unpacked our horses and headed them downriver hoping they would get back to their range lower down on the Halfway River. We were in for the winter or as long as our grub lasted. Our grub pile went down fast for we weren't too successful at hunting. Rabbits being scarce, we had to get out to our snares before daylight to beat the owls and hawks and many a time we would only get a piece of the rabbit. So when we got Brady's note we weren't long in deciding we'd be there. We arrived at Brady's shortly after dark on Christmas Eve after a snowshoe hike of 25 miles from my main cabin on the Cameron.

The first thing Brady did was to present each of us with a 40-ounce bottle of over-proof Demerara rum. "Now," he said, "you can treat the boys a little tomorrow," meaning the Indians, who always came in at Christmas time to get the odd drink and do a little trading. Since it was against the law to give an Indian liquor, we would all be in it together. We had a wonderful feed that night of bread, potatoes and roast beef, finishing off with pie made from dried apples. Our appetites were normally good, but spiked with that over-proof rum it took a lot to fill us up. Our trapline fare didn't include many luxuries – oatmeal and bannock for breakfast with bannock, beans and rice the rest of the day, and all the meat you want whenever you have it.

After our big feed we got out our T&B plug tobacco, filled our pipes, and smoked, drank rum and swapped yarns until midnight when it was time to blow the lamp and candles out. Brady said, "You fellows can roll in there," pointing to a bed in the corner of the big room. There wasn't a bought piece of furniture in the whole house: homemade tables, benches and stools made of split logs with augered-in legs, and bedsteads made of round poles with light poles instead of springs, or rope or rawhide laced back and forth. So with the lights out we climbed into bed. They had Hudson's Bay four-point wool blankets but no pillows, so we rolled our mackinaw coats up for a pillow.

When we lay down we smelled the damnedest stink. I said to Bob, "Where in hell is that awful stink coming from?"

He said, "Damned if I know, but it's sure powerful."

We got to investigating and found that the bunk had been made with the hide of the old shorthorn bull that Brady had butchered for his winter meat supply. They had laced the hide in between the pole frame and it made a pretty fair bed with the hair side up. It had dried good where it was stretched tight, but in the corners and in between the lacings on the side where there was some loose hide it hadn't dried but went rotten. We felt better when we found where the perfume was coming from.

Christmas morning arrived nice and bright, but quite frosty. Later in the morning quite a number of Indian bucks came up to the house from where they were camped down near the bank of the Cypress River. They were all dressed up in their new white shirts, ties, their best suits and moccasins. Brady invited them in and they squatted on their heels around the room. We took turns going around with our bottles of rum. When it was my turn I was amazed at how they could take their liquor. This was over-proof rum and would just about choke you to take it straight. I would ask them if they would like some water with it and they would answer, "No, that way good," and they would down it without batting an eye. These Indians were a fairly good lot and did pretty well trapping.

Brady nearly always managed to pack a Christmas turkey in on his last trip in with his pack train before Christmas and this year was no exception. We sat down to our Christmas dinner about one o'clock. Brady had cooked the turkey himself and a swell job he made of it too, while Bessie made the apple pies and had cooked the bread and potatoes. We enjoyed the meal as well as any we had ever eaten. The six boys were dressed up in their clean shirts. (The two daughters hadn't yet arrived in 1930.) The boys all got a packet of tailor-made cigarettes and a plug of chewing tobacco along with their Christmas present, even little Herby, who wasn't yet two. The constitution of those youngsters was amazing for I expected to see them keel over. Little Herby would wander around with a chew of tobacco in his mouth, then climb up on Brady's knee and say, "I want a 'moke." Then he'd take Brady's pipe out of his mouth and puff away on it and let the smoke roll out of his nose. Bessie also chewed and she surprised me by pouring herself a mug of strong black tea. She took one big spit into the woodbin, tucked the remaining cud over into one cheek and downed that tea, tobacco juice and all, without batting an eye.

We stayed over Christmas night and got an early start back to the trapline the next morning, loaded down with flour and other necessities. After thanking Brady and family for everything and a last drink of rum, we headed out. Because of the heavy packs it was quite a climb over the height of land between the Halfway and Cameron Rivers. We played out before we got through to the cabin. Rather than camp out without any bedding, we hung our packs in a tree and snowshoed on to the cabin in the dark.

the mountains to the west, then on upriver, crossing Stoney [Chowade] Creek, a good-sized stream also coming from the mountains to the west. There was quite an Indian camp at this place, but not too many here at this time. [This was the summer range of the Halfway Band.] A few miles above the Stoney we had to cross the Halfway River again at a fairly deep ford but not too swift. We had to raise the packs on a few of the smaller horses. A lot of our horses were green to these mountain streams and would drift with the water, so we would stretch a long rope between our saddle horses and keep swinging it on the lower side to keep them moving across. We moved up the east side of the river, quite a bit of timber along the way, making camp on McFarland Flats, a good camp with large dry meadows.

Bob and Ernie, the night herders, had a better time of it since the mosquitoes weren't quite as bad, the ground being drier and higher, and they had plenty of room to ride around the horses. They had the horses in camp around four o'clock, and when we went to saddling we discovered a little black mare called Ribbons had quite a swelling on the side of her withers. All our horses were soft when we started, and with a fair-sized outfit and small crew the packs were on the horses' backs longer than was good for them. The circulation would be cut off and when we unsaddled the horses they would welt up. We doctored them as well as we could by bathing their backs with cold water and rubbing.

When we told Nick Geake about Ribbons, he said, "Just put the pack saddle on my saddle horse and I'll ride Ribbons." We said that we didn't think Ribbons was broke to ride. "Oh, well," he said, "if I can't ride her Big Bob can." My packing partner's name was Bob, too. We had trapped together for the last four winters and were known all over the Hudson Hope and Fort St John country as The Bobs. We were distinguished by being called Big Bob and Little Bob. We both weighed the same, and the only difference was I had about an inch and a half in height over Little Bob.

When Nick mentioned that we might ride some of the pack horses that had developed sore backs, none of us were in favour of the idea. We were close to a hundred miles out of Fort St John by now and it would be an 80-mile ride over pretty rough trail to the nearest car road at Cache Creek in case of any injuries. I would have ridden Ribbons except for the fact that if I was riding her, my saddle horse, Smoky, would be carrying a pack, and I had become quite fond of my flea-bitten grey. I had made a good choice when I picked him out for my saddle horse. He had a nice gait, was easy to ride, and would stay put when I dropped the lines. He kept his head in fast water and, as it turned out later, was a good swimmer. Smoky had a good breadbasket, so he was a good feeder and stood the work well.

After we had got packed up Nick thought he'd better try Ribbons before we turned loose. He led the little horse away from the grove of trees where our horses were tied and climbed on. In two jumps Nick was on the ground. He climbed on once more and after four pretty fair jumps he was on the ground again. Nick didn't seem to mind since he had landed fairly easy both times, and he said, "Anyway, I didn't lose hold of my reins." Apparently in the old country it wasn't so much of a disgrace if you managed to hang onto the reins when you got unloaded. We all admired Nick's guts.

The cards were sure stacked against him, but give up, no sir, the bulldog determination of the Englishman was beginning to show through. He was using an English riding saddle, one of those pancake affairs with an English riding bridle and looped lines. He had a rifle on the left side, stuck back under the stirrup leather, and a trail axe on the right side with a two-foot machete hanging from the front of the saddle, a coat or two tied to the back of the saddle and his hat rolled up and tied on as well. Nick, an old Army man, wore his usual army shorts with his shirt sleeves above the elbows and no hat most of the time, a prey to the hordes of mosquitoes we had with us most of the time, but he was never one to complain. He finally climbed aboard Ribbons the third time. She bucked him off again, and when he landed it knocked the wind out of him. I went and got my horse and when Nick got his wind back I asked him if he'd like me to snub her to the horn of my saddle and take her for a whirl around the flat.

"We can try," he said, so he climbed on and we made a few circles out on the meadow. She behaved, so I asked him if he'd like to change back to his regular horse. "Oh, no," he said, "I walk most of the time anyway. All I'll need her for is crossing the rivers, and one of you can snub her and lead me across." So Nick walked most of the way to our next camp and Ribbons wasn't ridden any more that summer.

We finally got away. After a few miles we had to ford the Halfway again to the west side, then followed up that side about seven miles and crossed the Cypress River, a shallow but fast stream, coming in from the mountains to the west. On the north side of this stream B.C. [Bassiter or Baxter] Brady had a nice place about 100 miles from Fort St John and the end of any settlement. Brady had come from Missouri. After spending time in central BC he came to the Halfway country in 1916 where he started trapping and then ran a small trading post with the Indians. He took an Indian wife [Bessie was from the nearby Halfway reserve] and

A Visit to the Brady Ranch

Cecil Pickell, a cowboy who was initially on the trail-cutting crew but later joined Geake's freight supply group, wrote some of his memories of the Bedaux Expedition. While on the trail-cutting crew he and two other men were sent back to Brady's Ranch for supplies.

Tommy [Wilde] made the decision that he and I and Jerry would go back as far as Brady's Trading post that was about four days travel....We had killed a deer a few days before and the three of us lived on dried deer meat and tea until we reached Brady's. The boys and I were also nearly out of smoking tobacco. Brady was real low on supplies but was able to supply us with flour, beans, salt, rice, some coffee and tea and plug tobacco and only one pipe. By this time he had some rhubarb, lettuce, turnips and radishes in his garden so he sent his son Billie with me to bring the horses back and we took off to catch up to our axemen.

I might mention here that Mr Brady was a real old frontiersman. He had married a squaw and had about six children. The little kids would be playing around the yard. Then they would run over to him, stick their hands in his pocket, pull out a plug of chewing tobacco and have themselves a chew, even the three- and four-year-olds, girls and boys. Mrs Brady also chewed tobacco and I swear she could hit a one gallon can from 20 feet and never spill a drop. She was also a very good cook and you can bet I showed my appreciation in the way good cooks seem to enjoy. An 18-year-old boy who works and lives outdoors can be a godsend to a good cook's ego. Well, Billie and I left with three pack horse-loads of grub and full stomachs.

Charles Bedaux with the Bradys at their Ranch. Bedaux had also visited the ranch during his 1932 hunting trip.
LAC PA171679.

now lived here with their six boys and two girls. Brady raised a few cattle at one time, but being too far out, had settled to running a few horses and doing a little trapping for a living.

Bob and I knew Brady well and found him to be a very good friend.

We enjoyed seeing Brady again. After getting a few pair of moose-hide moccasins we continued up the Halfway for seven or eight miles and made camp at the lower end of Mosquito Flat, a three-mile flat on the west side of the river. A bay mare called Daisy stampeded as soon as we came out of the bush onto the flat and scattered her pack. Luckily no stuff was lost but some boxes were busted. This was a swell camp and since we were camped on the lower end of the meadow we only hobbled the worst horses for wandering, giving Art and I an easy night. The horses came into camp well filled and we got on the trail in good time, travelling over a fair trail up over the hills and down onto the river flat again. We then had to cross the river and had some trouble holding the horses on the ford. Again, we had to raise a number of packs. Then we proceeded on and around the Elbow where the river makes a sharp bend to the west. The Halfway comes out of the mountains almost straight west of here. We made camp just above the Elbow on a nice meadow. This part of the country was on my trapline. Bob and I had one of our better cabins here – a nice location in the timber on the river bank with plenty of dry wood, an open spring in the river bank, and lots of fish to get through the ice.

The horses camped good, so Bob and Ernie had no trouble getting them in camp on time. After we got packed we climbed the hill to the west, then down into the big flat, and on west through the mountain pass with Pink Mountain to the north. That big flat we came through today just east of the mountain pass would someday make a swell place. There were several sections of semi-open flats of good soil, but the country wasn't surveyed and the only way in was with a pack outfit on a trip of about 130 miles from Fort St John. A man could build up a wonderful place here if he had money enough: a splendid location at the entrance into the mountains, lots of good hunting around for deer and moose, lots of fish in the river, an unlimited supply of timber for corrals and buildings, and lots of range within easy reach. [After the construction of the Alaska Highway, access into the Halfway valley became much easier. Today there is a road that is paved past the forks of the Halfway and a large ranch has developed on the site Bob describes.]

We made camp on Two Bit Creek, a small stream coming in from the north. This stream was the western edge of my trapping area, and I shared a cabin on this creek with the Westergaard brothers, Nels and Einar, who trapped the country west and north of here. We had a good camp with

Nels Westergaard's ranch on the upper Halfway River. Left to right: Lyle Westergaard, Nels Westergaard, Gloria Westergaard, Bill Beckman, Bob White, Bob Godberson. The Westergaard family still lives in the area.
Rosie Westergaard photograph; Bob White family collection.

fair-sized grass flats, but the night was muggy with some showers and the mosquitoes were bad, so this kept Art and me on the go. I had the graveyard shift and had to keep riding all the time for the horses were hard to hold – on the move most of the time trying to get away from the mosquitoes. I was glad when daylight came so I could haze them into camp and get them tied up.

Into the Wilderness
(July 16–29)

After packing up we headed north away from the Halfway River, follow-ing up Two Bit Creek where we got into rougher going through some muskeg. After getting to the head of the stream we went over the water-shed leading down into Marion Lake and made camp at the north end of the lake. There was quite a bit of small bush around – not the best of camps, but plenty of feed for the ponies scattered through the bush.

Next morning we continued north toward the Sikanni River, hitting a bad stretch of muskeg as soon as we started. We had to help several horses that got stuck, including our jenny mule. I'll explain how we got stuck with the mule. Nick Geake, who spent a lot of time around Pouce Coupe, thought he'd help Bill Pickell pick up pack horses for the Bedaux Expedi-tion. He bought five head and had them trucked up to Fort St John. Only one of them turned out to be any good, and that was the bay mare that Nick rode quite often. The mule, which was good on dry trail but hope-less in muskeg, was old and some claimed she helped to put the railroad into Grand Prairie 15 to 20 years before. Nick took plenty of ribbing about his mule. The third head Nick chose was a light-built roan mare that showed thoroughbred breeding. She couldn't stand the packing so Nick ended up riding her sometimes. The last two, Rex and Spider, were the worst renegades in the outfit. They wouldn't camp, wouldn't let you catch them, and they weren't good in water. You had to corner Spider to catch him and he'd kick at you any chance he got. We had the hobbles off most of the horses by this time, but Spider was to still wear his for a while. I nearly got my head kicked off at Marion Lake camp. I had followed Spider for quite a while and was reaching for the halter when he wheeled and two hind feet clicked about an eighth of an inch from my nose. This riled me, so I got a switch and took after him, chasing him through all the windfalls I could find. He was in a lather and sweat was pouring off me. I finally got him into some higher windfall. In jumping over one his hobbles caught on a snag and turned him over on his back. He struggled but couldn't get loose. I sat there until he cooled off, then got him up and took him into camp. That run did him some good.

We worked our way north through more muskeg getting near the Sikanni. Following it up several miles past a few small lakes, we camped in a semi-open place a short distance from the river where there were a few sloughs with fair grass for the horses.

Next morning we continued up the Sikanni a few miles, then crossed at a ford where the water was very swift with a lot of big rock. We had to watch that the horses didn't stumble and go down. We angled away from the Sikanni River, going northwest, proceeding up Trimble Creek, which drains out of Deadman Lake. We followed Deadman Lake several miles along to the west end where we camped. There was a lot of ground birch bush, but lots of grass as well. There was a small trap cabin not far from the edge of the lake put up by Billy Neves. We waded and swam out into the lake to set a fish net, but when we pulled it in next morning found we had no luck. An old bull moose was standing at the east end of the lake on our way in, feeding on lily roots out in the lake. When he stuck his head down to get a mouthful all you could see was a bit of back. I could have shot him pretty easy, but I figured we didn't want to be burdened with that much meat for the horses had about all they could handle. When I mentioned it to Nick later he said I should have taken him for we could use some meat and that I better take the next one.

Deadman Lake is several miles long, lying between two mountains, and had got its name from two men shooting each other. Several years ago two fellows who had quite a bit of money came up from Texas to explore the mineral possibilities of this part of the country. Jack Thomas, a trapper and packer, had packed them out from Hudson Hope. He left them in camp and was to come back later in the season and pack them out. Jack said when he came out, "Those buggers will end up shooting each other," for they were on the prod with each other all the time he was with them. Sure enough, that's what happened, and they were buried there. Their graves were marked by a pile of stones at the east end of the lake.

Leaving this camp we immediately got into muskeg, which made travelling slow. The jenny mule had a rough time. We had to unpack and help her out more than once. We were heading through a pass for the Besa River, a swift rough stream. The trail leading down the river had several crossings that would be swimming and rafting propositions. After getting through the muskeg stretch to the river we decided to avoid the crossings by going upriver and behind Sheep Mountain, dropping down into a creek on the other side. We went up the Besa a few miles, crossed to the north side and continued on up, making camp just below Redfern Lake. Redfern is a very pretty, glacier-fed lake and the water looks quite blue. There were some high, rugged snow-capped mountains around us, and the night got quite cold.

After making the river crossing we spotted a moose and Nick dropped him with a shot from his trusty rifle. Nick and I stayed behind and dressed the moose out, packed it on our two saddle horses, and walked into camp. I tried to persuade Nick to leave some behind, thinking of the added weight on the horses going up the mountain.

"No," he said, "we don't want to waste any." And of course he was thinking of his two dogs, who could use a fair share. Nick had two pedigree dogs, Nigger and Garrett, that he had brought out from France when he was on one of his world tours. Nigger was a black German Shepherd with short, shiny black hair. Garrett was also a German Shepherd, a big tan coloured dog with longish hair and a big square-looking head, not as nice looking as Nigger, but the smarter of the two. If Nick lost his hat or gloves he'd tell Garrett to go and find them, and he'd find them and bring them back.

Next morning we angled up the mountain through some ground birch brush, then into timber, and back into more brush at timber line. Nick had forgot his hunting knife at the moose kill the evening before, so I rode back to get it and didn't catch up with the outfit until near timberline. While riding through the brush I noticed Nick's black dog, and he seemed to be hurt, so I called to him. When he came to me I noticed he had a bad cut on the side of his mouth. He had bled a lot and I figured he would bleed to death before too long. He wouldn't follow me, so I rode and caught up with Nick at the head of the pack string on top of the mountain.

Nick was very strict with his dogs and if they didn't obey, they suffered the consequences. It seems that when Nick was swinging his machete while cutting his way through the brush, the dog had got too close. Nick had caught him with his knife, cutting through both lips and halfway through his tongue. Nick knew he had hit him, but didn't realize it was so bad. He told Ernie and me to go ahead and lead the outfit while he would go back for his dog.

We had good going over the top of the mountain but had trouble when we started down the north side. We got down a draw when we came to a waterfall and had to double back. As we were working our way around the mountainside, Soapsuds, one of our gasoline pack horses, tried to cross a shale slide, lost his footing, and went rolling down the mountain side. We thought he'd end up in the canyon below, but he wrapped himself around a gnarled old spruce tree.

Art and I worked our way down and found Soapsuds on top of his pack, up against the tree with his feet in the air. We thought the horse and pack would be damaged beyond repair. We undid the ropes and cinches and finally got the horse on his feet. To our amazement we found him to be OK, only a few cuts and bruises, and the packs were also good. Aside from being dented, the gasoline cans showed no signs of leaking. We had quite a time getting the outfit back up the mountain. After getting Soapsuds packed up again and tightening the lash ropes on a number of the other pack horses, we worked around the mountainside toward Goat Creek.

Our situation was becoming a bit grim, with the showers now developing into a steady rain. It was getting late and we had to get down off this mountain and hope we could find some grass along Goat Creek. There was no trail down through the stunted spruce so the horses spread out and we had to watch that we didn't lose any top packs. Barging through the trees the horses would sometimes pull the ropes off the side packs. The top packs would then become loose and in some cases fall off. I spotted a top pack roll off and followed it down the hill and found it to be a 50-pound mat of figs. This happened again to a 50-pound sack of granulated rock salt that we had for our horses. The rest of the boys had the same trouble, but as we found out later, we were lucky not to lose anything. Eventually we slid and worked our way down to Goat Creek and followed it a few miles to a grassy side hill where we made camp.

Nick rode into camp just as we finished unpacking the horses. He looked glum, for his dog, Nigger, had died in the saddle, and Nick had buried him on top of the mountain. We all felt sorry for Nick for he thought a lot of his dog. We were a weary outfit, wet through, and it was still raining. We set to and made camp, putting up the tent and getting a good fire going. Eventually we got something to eat, including a fair portion of that good moose meat that we cooked on sticks in front of the fire, and we sure didn't need anyone to sing us to sleep that night.

Grass wasn't plentiful at this camp, so we had to wrangle early before the horses went wandering too far. It was a wet chilly morning. We packed up and headed down Goat Creek. After a few miles of rough going and crossing the creek more than 10 times, we came out onto the trail that went down the Besa River. The trail led away from the river toward Keily Creek, which came into the Besa from the west. We followed up

Over the divide to the Prophet River. White rides the trailing horse.
BC Archives G-02671.

Keily Creek a few miles before climbing the side of the mountain to the north.

After a long tough climb zigzagging up through the timber we came out at timberline on top of the Caribou Range. The trail led northwest for 10 miles along the mountain top. There were a few ups and downs, but on the whole we had good going and were lucky to have a bright clear day. We got a wonderful view of the surrounding country, a sea of mountain peaks, especially to the west. We saw a few Stone sheep to the east and several caribou as we plodded along. We worked our way down a steep draw leading to Richards Creek with a lot of mud holes that gave us some trouble. Finally we reached the valley and made camp.

It had been a long drive for the horses and they were beginning to show the strain of the steady going. A few cinch sores had showed up and we had to doctor them as well as we could. We hadn't had a day off since we started and all of us were showing signs of wear.

The boss decided that night that we would take the next day off since we had such a good camp. There were good grass meadows for the horses and we were camped on their back trail so there was no need to hobble them. We rolled out early just the same for we had plenty of chores to do – wash our clothes, sew up pack manties [canvas covers] and tarps, and overhaul some riggings. Bob and I took on the job of drying some of our moose meat, which wasn't keeping too good in the packs. We made a rack of light spruce poles, cut the meat into strips, and hung it over the poles. We built a smudge of dozy spruce wood below the meat to keep the blow

Crossing the Prophet River. BC Archives F-03739.

flies away. We hung pack manties around to keep the breeze from fanning the fire and keep the smoke going up.

It was necessary to watch the fire all the time to keep a uniform flow of smoke for the blow flies were bad and would dive in on the meat if the smoke let up at all. I was watching the fire when the rest of the boys were eating their midday meal. Nick came over and said, "You go and eat. I'll take over." He stirred up the fire too much and when he wandered off the fire broke into a blaze and burned up four of the five pack manties we had draped around. We were to miss those pack covers for we had been equipped with eight ounce canvas instead of the heavier twelve ounce. As a result we had snagged and torn a lot of the pack covers and it was necessary to double the covers on the more perishable packs. We spent considerable time sewing up tears and holes in those tarps. In the afternoon we went for a dip in Richards Creek to get cleaned up but didn't get too much swimming for that mountain stream was mighty cool.

The day's rest did the horses a lot of good, and they looked better when we wrangled them the next morning. There were a few saddle sores and Joan, the little roan blood mare, had quite a lump on her withers. Nick said that he'd ride her and pack his saddle mare. Joan was broke to ride so he had no trouble.

We followed up Richards Creek a few miles before heading north over a pass to the Prophet River. We travelled up a draw with muskeg. In getting through the best way we could we lost track of the blazes made by the advance trail cutters. When we got onto higher ground on the east side of a lake we lost all trail signs so Nick sent me toward the mountain and Ernie toward the lake. We couldn't find any sign of a trail so we came to the conclusion that the trail was on the west side of the lake. In order to get there we would have to back track and cross the muskeg at the south end of the lake.

Nick decided we'd take a chance on getting back to the trail further up, which turned out to be a bad mistake. The end of the lake narrowed but it was far too soft to get across. We entered a timbered rock gully with a stream leading down to the Prophet River. We had to do some trail cutting for we couldn't get across the creek. Eventually we got right into the stream and followed it for over a half mile until it entered the Prophet River. The river crossing was about three miles upstream. We couldn't climb the bank out of the creek so we followed up the edge of the river until we found a place where we could climb the bank. The water was quite fast and about two feet deep, but a few feet out from the bank it was swimming depth. We head and tailed a few of the horses until they got lined out. They all followed along and climbed up the bank except for one that strayed out too far, got into swimming water, and shot downstream with the current. He just managed to get footing at the mouth of the creek and climbed out. He had a wet heavy pack for the rest of the day. We were lucky that it wasn't one of the more perishable ones.

We worked our way up along the bank through the brush and small spruce, having to cut the trail at times. I was riding second from the lead when the boys relayed word up the line that they wanted Nick to go back for a horse had fallen into the river. Nick left me to find and cut a way across a muskeg that drained a small lake set back from the river. This horse was following along the bank when it went on the wrong side of a tree. His foot went through and he toppled over an eight foot bank into swimming water. He couldn't get out on this side so he swam across to an island. When Nick got there the boys decided it wasn't a good place to swim across. Ernie suggested building a raft, but Nick said he'd swim it. They dug down the bank and Nick and his little roan mare Joan went into the river. He made it across and got out himself but he almost drowned Joan before he found a place to get her out. After resting Nick worked his way up the island with the pack horse and put them both into the water. The pack horse came across and the boys hauled him up the bank. But Nick and his horse went further down with the current before he landed. The boys went down and hauled them both onto dry land. Nick was pretty cold but never complained.

It was getting late by this time and still no camp in sight. We got across the muskeg and up to the crossing where we found our troubles weren't

Willard Freer

Willard Freer, a well-known cowboy in northern BC, kept a diary for many years, including his experiences on the Bedaux Expedition. Freer worked with Skook Davidson at his ranch for many years and is featured in Clem Reierson's book, *From Vanderhoof to Lower Post*. While the other cowboys in the freight party got along well with each other and were able to tolerate Geake, Freer did not have a good relationship with him. As cook, Freer had the most contact with Geake, because White, Godberson, Ernie Peterson and Art McLean worked mainly with their partners. Freer was not hired to be a cook on the Bedaux Expedition and he did not enjoy having this job. In his diary, Freer confided his dislike for Geake several times.

Floyd Crosby photograph; LAC PA171477.

Monday, July 9 – We left Cache Creek and made the Indian Reservation on the Halfway River. Four packs came loose, rest went fine. Geake broke his rifle. His own darn fault. Peterson and Geake night herding. I am not a cook but not starving. Fifty-seven pack horses, six saddle horses. We forded Grahame River, quite a few hills. Rather pretty country. Weather fair.

Sunday, July 15 – We left Mosquito Flat at 1:00 pm and camped at Two Bit Creek at 5:10 pm. The outfit went along fine. None of us boys are getting along with Geake. He is too much of a slave driver. The weather fair.

Tuesday, July 17 – We left Marion Lake at 10:20 am and camped at the Sikanni Chief River at 2:40 pm. We hit lots of up and down hills and swampy country. The horses went good. Trouble brewing among the men. Too bad somebody wouldn't tie a stone to Geake's neck and shove him into the Sikanni River. The weather fair, strong westerly wind.

Wednesday, July 25 – We stayed in camp all day. Bob White cut up the moose meat and smoked it. Bob Godberson, Ernie Peterson, Art McLean and Geake looking over and repairing the pack outfit. I am still trying to do something I can't and don't like – that is, to cook. The weather very fair, hot.

Thursday, July 26 – We left Richard Creek at 10:00 am and arrived at the Prophet River at 7:30 pm. The travelling tough, lots of swamp. Geake lost the trail and never did find it. Ernie Peterson found the trail. Too bad somebody wouldn't brain Geake. He is useless. We saw three moose. Three horses swam the Prophet with packs and got them wet. Twenty pounds of sugar melted to nothing. We swam all the horses to north side for feed and we camped. Left packs on south side to be rafted. The weather clear, hot.

Friday, July 27 – We stayed at the Prophet River all day. Bob White, Ernie Peterson and Nick Geake rafted outfit over. Bob Godberson looking for horses. Art McLean packing outfit up the hill. Geake is not any good. The weather very hot and clear.

Sunday, July 29 – I stayed with Geake until noon and went with Earl Cushing back to the Lamarque party. Oh boy! Am I tickled. Cecil Pickell and I traded jobs. To hell with Geake. Earl Cushing and I started out for the Muskwa River and went about four miles and we hit it. We crossed about 20 back channels and swam one. We got wetter than hell. Geake and the boys are repairing pack outfit. The weather squally as hell for a few minutes, then comes up hotter than hell. The trail going up the Muskwa is pretty good. We camped at the Horse Corrals. No rest for the wicked (that's us).

Friday, August 3 – Earl Cushing, Jack Stone (Telegraph Creek Indian) and I cut the road to the Muskwa River west from camp. Lamarque went to the out-camp to see how things are running. He is the boss of the outfit. It is sure a great relief to be away from Geake.

over yet. There was no horse feed on our side of the river, so we had to swim the horses that night. There were no trees nearby to tie to so we ran a long rope around a clump of small willows and started tying horses to it. Old Dusty and Blue, two horses with kitchen packs, got into the river and swam across. Dusty, an old pack horse who had been up the trail before on a hunting trip, knew his supper was across the river.

The Prophet River makes a sharp bend at this point. The ford was just below the bend where the water was fairly fast and the river was at its narrowest. Nick decided that would be the best place to raft our stuff across, working the raft back and forth with ropes. We were sure it would be impossible for we would have to tie several of our lash ropes together to reach across. It would be doubtful whether they would be strong enough because when a raft comes to the end of a tight rope it has a tendency to go under the water. The rest of us thought the most logical solution was to load our raft at the bend, line it up the slow water on the outside of the bend, then go up the main current a short distance before shooting across

Jack MacDougall (left) and Willard Freer sawing deer roast. Bob White family collection.

and landing on the far side just above the bend. This is what we would do the next morning.

Willard was with me when we started to unpack. I said, "Willard, let's take a few at a time and unpack at the bend of the river. It will save packing up in the morning." We got eight horses unpacked before Nick noticed what was occurring. He worked me over and said he was running this outfit. After unpacking the horses we loosened the cinches, took off the blankets, and snugged the cinches again for we were swimming the horses with their packsaddles on to save extra rafting. We had to have a man across the river to catch the horses as they came across to take the rigging off. Bob swam his horse across and was kept busy catching horses before they headed out through the trees to the meadow.

Nick told us to keep our saddle horses and said we could swim across with our bedrolls on our shoulders. Ernie looked at me and said he didn't feel like taking a chance on sleeping in a wet bedroll. It was now well past 10 o'clock. We were tired and hungry, having not eaten since camp. We said we'd take time to put a raft together to get our beds and some grub across.

Nick said, "You can suit yourself, but I'm going to take mine across." He made it, although he almost rolled his horse. Only one end of his bedroll was wet. Nick had no faith in rafting for he had lost his outfit rafting the Graham River, and had a couple close calls on other rivers. We went to a logjam, cut a fair-sized log in two, got them into the water, lashed two crosspieces, laid a few more light poles on the crosspieces to hold our stuff, and got everything we needed across in two trips. It was after 11 o'clock when we tied into a feed of bannock and moose meat. It had been a long hard day for both horses and men. This was a good camp for the horses and they would have the next day off while we rafted our freight across.

We had a nice bright morning, and after a big breakfast of more of our moose meat, which was getting nicely aged and tender, we set to work cutting timber to make a decent raft. As soon as we started moving the stuff we realized we needed horses so we swam four back across the river to relay the packs up to where Willard and I had unpacked the eight head. We never said anything but thought that if we had unpacked there the night before it would have saved us a lot of work. Our rafting went well and we got everything across without any trouble. We had a good place to land for the water was up enough that the bank wasn't too high. It was a sizeable job getting our plunder across and the right packs all sorted out to their respective saddles, for each saddle had its horse's name on it. There wasn't much of the day left when we got everything covered up.

The horses were easy to wrangle the next morning so we got away in fair time. We left the Prophet River and climbed the long hill going north toward the Muskwa River, making camp at a small lake with fair grass just over the height of land. At this place Earl Cuishing and Cecil Pickell rode into camp. They had come down from the trail-cutters' camp on the Muskwa looking for us because their provisions were getting low. Tommy Wilde of Fort St John was in charge of the trail-cutting crew and had six men with him: Earl Cuishing and Art Paul from Edmonton; Cecil Pickell, 18 years old, raised in Fort St John; and the three Lundquist brothers, Bill, Bernard and Ingval, from Rose Prairie north of Fort St John. Tommy's job was to blaze and cut a trail six foot wide through any place there was timber. It was a big job and they had been out since early May. We didn't necessarily follow his trail all the way for he was cutting trail for the tractors that were to follow after us. He avoided the heavier timber and also the side hills wherever possible.

Several of us were glad to see our good friend Cecil, and before the night was out we decided to make a trade. Cecil would stay with us as cook while Willard would go back upriver with Earl as an axeman for the trail cutters. Willard had never been satisfied with his role as cook and had got the idea that if he served us poor grub that someone would take over. Willard had never got the knack of packing or some of us might have spelled him off at times. Down the trail he had deliberately dished up some half-cooked rice for our lunch. We were an easy bunch to cook for but sure didn't like the idea of eating raw rice. When Nick started on his plateful he looked at Willard and said, "Willard, this rice isn't cooked." Willard made the excuse that he didn't know how and had too much to do. Nick didn't say much, but what he said was to the point, and we had no more raw rice.

We had a pressure cooker that could cook beans in a short time, but it was a little tricky over an open fire. Willard generally forgot about it until it blew out the lead filing, which was the safety valve to keep it from blowing up. We used to replace the plug with lead from our 30-30 shells, but there was always the chance that we would get the plug in too solid and have the cooker blow up.

Misery on the Muskwa
(July 30 – August 23)

Earl and Willard left early with their two pack horses. We got packed up and worked our way toward the Muskwa. We crossed a few wet spots but our mule Jenny was the only one that needed any help. We went west up the Muskwa a few miles and camped at a little creek coming in from the south.

During the afternoon Nick had trouble with old Red. I was riding lead at the time and Nick was down along the line when he saw that Red's pack needed fixing. Red was a chunky little reddish chestnut gelding and plumb ornery. He gave us trouble all the way. He never got over his habit of pulling back, and if you didn't cinch him up right he would throw himself or try and buck his pack off. You had to watch him along the trail or he would wander off into the bush. Nick would say, "Just leave him to me." We didn't argue, so he packed Red quite often, but invariably Nick's packs had to be tightened during the course of the day. This day Nick had Red snubbed to his saddle. In the process of getting his rigging tightened he reared up and lunged ahead, breaking the stock off Nick's pet rifle. Old Red didn't know it, but he was almost courtmartialled and shot right there. But Nick said he'd try and even the score at a later date. Little did he know that Red was to meet his Waterloo in the river within the next few days.

We had a good camp here and all appreciated our new cook. Cecil was pretty good at building bannocks and he also dished out some tasty hotcakes. After travelling a few miles the next morning we crossed a shallow stream coming in from the south. This stream tumbled off the top of the mountain a few hundred yards from the trail. We gave the pack horses a breather and rode up to look. The waterfall was 600 to 700 feet high, and the noise was deafening when we got close to where the water landed in a pool at the foot of the mountain. You couldn't get too close without your slicker or you'd get soaked from the spray. There was quite a volume of water and that hole at the foot of the waterfall looked deep. We saw a few goats but they were too high up the mountains to shoot. There were all kinds of game animals through this country but we rarely saw them along the trail, for an outfit makes too much noise and the game gets spooked before we see it.

We continued upriver, crossed another creek, and made camp at a place we called Horse Corral Camp. The valley narrowed here, and a piece of mountain jutted out to within 10 feet of the river. All we had to do was put up a few rails and we had the horses' back trail blocked. There was a good grass meadow above camp, bordered on one side by the river, and on the other by a long narrow lake at the foot of the mountain. There had been some trouble along the trail during the afternoon. At a rocky patch we had to work our way down. After 20 or 30 horses had slid down they had cleaned off most of the moss from the wet rock. The rest of the horses had to slide down. Two tripped on some roots and rolled the balance of the way down. We were lucky to have no injuries and the packs weren't damaged too badly. Near our camp was an old trap cabin put up several years ago by the Sheffield brothers, Bert and Kelly. They had trapped this area for a number of years.

It started raining while we made camp, rained heavily all night, and continued the next few days. The next 10 miles led up through a canyon. We had to cross the river four times and the fords angled upriver, so it was impossible to raft across. The river was rising fast. We knew we had no chance of getting through the canyon and would have to sit out the rain. By dark the next night the river came over the bank near our camp and we had to move our tent and packs onto higher ground. It rained all the following night and when we woke before daylight the water was coming into the tent and had already surrounded some of the packs. We rolled out in a hurry and started carrying packs to higher ground. We had trouble finding space for our tent. In the dark it looked like the whole floor of the valley was under water, and we were very concerned about the horses for it appeared that the meadow would be flooded. It took us time to get a good fire going for it was still pouring rain and everything was soaked. After Cecil filled us up with a breakfast of porridge, bacon and hotcakes, we went out to see what the scene was.

It was now daylight but we couldn't see far for the clouds and fog were hanging low. We went up to a rock ledge and looked up the valley. It was all water and not a horse in sight. We got busy cutting down some dry

Bob White (foreground) and Ernie Peterson rafting freight across the Muskwa River in high water. BC Archives B-07382.

trees and lashed a raft together. Nick decided he and Bob would paddle up the dead water of the lake to see if there was any sign that the horses had swum the lake to the mountain side.

Nick said to me, "You better take your rifle and go out and look for some horse feed and maybe get us a piece of meat."

There was no horse feed near the camp other than the meadow. I got my rifle and axe and went downriver a few miles to a creek that was a little stream when we came in, but was now a raging torrent about 10 feet deep. I knew there was a little grass further down but wanted to see how much. I dropped a tree across the stream but the water caught the boughs, whipping the tree away like a match. I went upstream where the banks were higher and cut another tree. When it fell it stayed in place, but when I started across I realized that a fall into that boiling mass would be my last.

We couldn't get the horses across anyway, so I scouted around through the timber up the mountainside. It was still raining and I was completely soaked, so about midday I built a fire, ate my lunch, and dried myself a little. Then I continued up the mountain following game trails. There were lots of moose sign but I didn't get to see any. I wanted to get up to timber line and maybe get a chance at a caribou, but when I came out at tree line I saw the ground was white with snow with a driving sleet storm whooping it up. It was foggy enough that you couldn't see any distance, so I headed back down. Part way down I saw an animal's head above some brush. I brought up my rifle, then saw the head had a halter on it and I realized it was one of our horses. I found 17 of the bunch and backtracked them down to the lake shore. Apparently the horses had swum across the lake and with some difficulty worked their way up through the moss-covered rocks.

Along the lake shore I located six more horses that were trapped in a pocket of land. Working my way down through the rocks I finally found a place to get the bedraggled horses out. I left them up on higher ground although their prospects of getting filled up were pretty slim for I had seen very little grass all day. It was now near dusk, still raining, and I was soaked. I had a difficult time getting back to camp. I had to work my way along the mountain side for the water line was back up into the timber. I was a tired and hungry hombre when I finally saw the lights of the campfire.

Then I found out I wasn't the only one that had a rough day. Nick and Bob had taken the raft up the lake as planned that morning and had located a bunch of horses out toward the middle of the valley. They were in water about halfway up their sides. Nick and Bob couldn't get over to them for there were too many willow tops sticking out of the water, so they paddled back down the lake. Ernie, the best man with rafts in our outfit, said he and Art would go up. Nick said he'd go, so after a cup of hot tea to get warmed up, he and Ernie started up the main drag. There was a fair current so they had to work their passage and couldn't get right to the horses. They tied the raft to a willow top and decided they would wade to the horses. This was glacier water, so cold you couldn't stand your legs in it for very long. Nick and Ernie both knew it would be grim, but they slipped off their raft with the water coming up to their belts. They worked their way to the horses and each caught one. They put a bridle on and climbed aboard.

Ernie told Nick to take the lead and head downstream and he would try to get the rest to follow. They had nearly half a mile to go and had to swim and wade that distance. The boys counted 34 head as they climbed out of the water. They were a miserable looking bunch of ponies, some of them so cold they could hardly walk. Nick felt bad about the ones that were missing and he figured there was a fair chance that they had drowned. He was relieved when I came into camp after dark that night and reported that I had seen 23 head, which made up our full count.

Though lighter, the rain continued until about daylight when Cecil hollered out, "Come and get 'em you hungry hombres or I'll throw them out."

Our big square tent flap was pegged out in the front with the corners tied to trees. The rain water would accumulate in the sag in the middle, and Cec would generally lift it up in the middle and let the water run off the edges. This morning he had neglected to do this, so when he was by the fire working on the last of the hotcakes the rope broke and down came around a tub of water. It caught about half of Cecil along with the fire, porridge and hotcakes. Cecil's good nature was strained somewhat. We hollered out, "Don't let a little thing like that worry you Cec. Just sing us a song." Cecil had a fair voice and used to entertain at times with his singing. Cec managed to salvage some of the porridge, but the hotcakes and bacon were a total loss so he had to work on a new batch.

As the morning progressed the weather showed signs of clearing. There was no chance of getting up through the canyon and it looked like we would have to cross the river and make a detour to the north. It seemed like we would have to climb to the top of the mountain to do that. We built a bigger raft, then paddled up and retrieved the other raft. While Bob and Art went out to see the horses Ernie took me across the river where I was to look for horse feed, blaze a trail up to tree line, and pick up some meat if possible. I located plenty of grass but saw very little moose sign. There was no chance of hunting caribou for the mountain above timber line was all fogged in. I got a trail marked up the mountain.

When I got back to the river that night I was to fire a signal shot so Ernie would come across and get me. While making my way toward the river I spotted a coyote and drilled him with my signal shot. I took him into camp, tossed him down by the tent and told the cook that was the best I could do. We sure watched that coyote for we didn't put it past Cecil to stick a hunk of that old coyote in with the beans.

Our horses weren't faring too well for feed and were doing a lot of wandering. Later in the day the creek to the east had dropped enough to allow them to cross, but there was only enough grass to last a day. We decided to swim them across the river in the morning. The boys stayed with the horses quite late in case they took off downriver. They also hobbled a few of the bell horses and leaders.

The morning broke bright and clear and it was a treat to see bright sunshine again. We wrangled the horses early, then trimmed off all the sweepers on both sides of the river. We put the pack saddles on without the blankets and sent the horses into the river. They all made it across without any trouble except old Red. As soon as he hit the water he seemed to flounder, then rolled over, went under, and never came up. Later in the day we followed down the river and found his body grounded on the point of a bar. We waded out, salvaged the saddle, halter, and pulled off the horseshoes since we had lost several floundering through the muskegs. We had a busy day getting all the stuff across. The current was fast and we'd drift down the river quite a piece before we could land. Ernie made most of the trips across for he could handle the raft better than the rest of us.

As we were eating supper that evening we heard bells heading down-river. Bob and I took after the horses. We came to a large stream that came out of a canyon to the north. The water was fast and we had to get a pole to steady ourselves as we inched our way across. The water boiled up above our belts although it was just over knee deep. After getting around the 12 head of horses we started back and met Nick, who had come down to help. We followed them back but they got into the creek higher up before we could catch any to ride across. The water was deeper here and Nick started in. I thought we should go down to where we had crossed, but Nick thought he could make it. He got into deeper water and lost his footing. Luckily he made a lunge and caught a tree sticking out of a logjam in the middle of the stream. Bob and I went down to where we had crossed before. The horses settled once we got them back to the good grass.

The next morning we packed up and followed my blazes up to timber line. It was a long hard climb. We wanted Nick to make camp and scout ahead. "Oh no," he said. "There is no other way so we'll keep on."

We climbed about another 2000 feet and had quite a time keeping the outfit moving. It was all rock with a moss covering in places. Occasionally a sleet storm blew over us and we would have to put our backs to it for the duration, then continue on when it let up. We finally made the top and worked our way along for a couple miles. The prospects didn't appear good ahead, but we didn't have much time to look for the clouds settled down over us so thick you could hardly see your hand in front of you.

This condition lasted over an hour and the only way we could hold our outfit together was by shouting to each other. We realized we were in a hell of a fix with an outfit this size on top of a mountain. A few feet to the south was a sheer drop of over 1000 feet, while to the north a big basin cut into the top of the mountain with a drop of about the same depth.

When the clouds lifted and we could see a little, Nick hollered, "Let's get the hell off of here." So we weren't long in getting them lined out down the mountain. We went down to the tree line and made camp.

Next morning Nick told me to go back up the mountain to see if there was any chance of getting through, while he would take some of the other boys and search for a route below timberline. I barely passed the place where we had been yesterday when the clouds settled down again.

I just had time to line up a few rocks parallel to the top of the mountain for I thought it might help me get off the mountain if the weather didn't clear. Then I laid down in the shelter of a rock and had a snooze. We had lost so much sleep since we'd been on the trail we never missed a chance to get a few winks. When I woke up it had cleared. I walked along the mountain until I came to a dead end. There was no chance of getting horses through: a regular saw-tooth mountain in front of me; a sheer drop to the south; and a big glacier extending up the mountain from the north. While gazing out over the glacier I spotted an animal lying down but couldn't make out whether it was a sheep or caribou. It was a long way off, but I opened up on it. My first shots were short, but I finally hit it. The glacier was so steep that when he jumped he sailed down and out of sight. I thought "goodbye meat". I went away around the big basin and came out on a point where I saw the animal had sailed down over a thousand feet and got caught on the mountainside at a kink in the glacier. If it had stayed on the glacier it would have gone down at least another thousand feet. I scrambled down the mountainside and found I had a nice caribou. The worst part was that I was on the wrong side of the mountain. I dressed the meat out and decided to get the hindquarters and part of the back up the mountain. I was afraid to tie it on as a pack for fear of losing my footing and ending up at the bottom of the mountain. When I got on top I made it into a pack. After travelling the length of the mountain I signalled the camp below and Art came up with a horse to meet me.

I told Nick there was no chance of getting over the mountain and he said they had come to an impassable canyon in their attempt to find a way through below timberline. I mentioned seeing from the top of the mountain a place about halfway down where I thought there might be a chance of getting across the deep canyon that extended all the way down the mountain. Next morning Nick, Cecil and I struck out with saddle horses, taking a pack horse along with some grub and bedding. After some difficulty getting through the bush we found the place. On investigation we found we could get across with a little work. We felled some trees and slid them down to form a guard on a rock shelf. Then we dug out some rocks in places and built it up in others, and finally we got our horses over. It was a tricky crossing for a missed step would plunge you down into the canyon. Then we angled down through the bush and landed in the Muskwa River bottom just above the canyon, where we camped for the night.

Nick was quite relieved and satisfied that we had found a way through. We sat around the campfire late that night talking. Nick never talked much about himself, but he opened up that night and kept Cec and I

Crossing the Muskwa. BC Archives G-02264.

entertained with his experiences. After serving in the First World War he was with the British Secret Service on work that had taken him all over the world. Some of his missions in the Far East had quite an element of danger. Nick said he always had a well-trained dog or two along with him and they helped him out more than once. The dogs that he brought with him on this trip were valuable ones and that's why he felt the loss of Nigger so much. After listening to Nick that night our respect for the man increased considerably.

On our way back to the main camp we improved a few spots along the way. The next day we started back with the pack string. We had more trouble getting the outfit through the rock gulch than we anticipated. The horses had to work their way along rocky shelves, jump up and down two- and three-foot rock ledges, and pick their way through a lot of loose rock. We only had one mishap. Shamrock, a bay mare, cut her hind leg just above the fetlock. It must have cut an artery, and we were afraid she would bleed to death. Ernie suggested we sear the cut with hot grease, so we threw her down, tied her up so she couldn't move, and put a dab of hot grease into the cut. That stopped the bleeding. We bandaged the wound and it didn't seem to bother her much.

Our camp by the river had a lot of small brush and was short on grass. Nick made the mistake of giving the horses a ration of salt before they were turned loose. They came back during the night looking for more. When they couldn't find it they started pawing the packs. The horses demolished one flour pack and damaged another before we realized what was happening. After that we had the extra work of carrying all the flour and oatmeal packs to one place and fencing them off with rope.

After drizzling rain most of the night the morning broke cloudy and cool. We had to cross the river to the south side at this point. We found a place we could cross without swimming, but it was a very deep ford, so we had to relay the packs across and put them as high up on the horses as we could. We also had to head and tail them in groups of three or four so they wouldn't wander off the ford and get in deep water. My horse stumbled on one of the crossings and gave me a ducking above the waist. The first thing I thought of when Smoky came up was my camera. As it turned out it wasn't damaged. The canvas case a lady in Fort St John had made for me had proved true to its construction.

After getting everything across and all the packs sorted out and repacked, we continued up the Muskwa. Along the way we had to bridge a back channel of the river. Spider, the renegade pack horse of the outfit, slipped on the wet logs and toppled into the water. Bob and Art had to haul him out. Fortunately the packs that got wet were the less perishable ones.

When we came to a stream flowing in from the south that didn't look too promising we made camp for there was fair grass. After turning the horses loose and having a bite to eat, we decided to ride up and see what was ahead. This was a milky glacier stream that tumbled off the mountain not far back from the river. Nick was just going to ride over the bank and into the stream when Ernie said he'd better get a pole and test it for the water was so milky you couldn't see how deep it was.

"Oh, I'll try it," Nick said. When he put his saddle mare Jean over the bank the whole outfit went out of sight. By the time we got both of them pulled out they were cooled off plenty. It was a cold plunge for Nick so he went back to camp to get warmed up. We went upstream and chopped a big tree down, pointing it across toward two more big trees on the other side. We limbed the tree as we walked across it. Then we dropped the other two trees parallel to the first one, laid them in close, pegged them, filled in the cracks with smaller poles, and had a first class bridge. Most of our horses were getting used to walking on these makeshift bridges and didn't give us too much trouble.

The valley of the Muskwa River was very narrow at this place, with high mountains on both sides. Wrangling the horses was easy next morning for the only grass was right around camp. We packed up and crossed our bridge without any trouble. After travelling a few miles we met a rider leading a pack horse. This was Ingval Lundquist who had been sent downriver from the trail-cutters' camp up ahead. They needed a few items of grub, mainly baking powder. He had camped last night a few miles up the river at the lower end of the Big Bar, a six-mile stretch of river bottom. Since the valley is narrow the bar is submerged during high water. As the water lowers the river separates into several channels. These channels keep changing as the water zigzags its way from side to side down the bar, leaving a few spots of quicksand.

With Lundquist as our guide we started up the bar, crossing and recrossing these different channels as we went along. Everything went well until Nick had to stop and fix one of the pack horses. I moved up toward the lead. Lundquist was riding along the bank looking for a crossing since the current had changed from yesterday. Suddenly the whole bank gave way and shot Lundquist's saddle and pack horse into the river. Ingval's horse was in swimming water right away and heading downstream. The pack horse had a better footing. Ingval foolishly had the halter shank looped around his wrist. When he tried to slide it off with his other hand his black leather coat sleeve slid down over the rope so that he couldn't get it off. Luckily, just as his horse was about to be pulled over backwards, his pack horse got into swimming water and they both shot downriver, coming out on the far side lower down. It was a close call for Ingval, for if his horse had rolled we would have had a slim chance of getting him out of that fast glacial water.

As the pack horses started crowding along the bank I hollered to Ernie to give me a hand. Before we could get the horses away from the edge another section of the bank gave way and eight pack horses went into the Muskwa, shot downstream, and came out on the far side. Finally we got the remaining horses turned back and held them while we scouted around and found a place where we could ford without getting the packs wet. We had to cross the channels several more times, but didn't have any other serious trouble.

We travelled to the upper end of the Big Bar where the Muskwa comes out of a series of canyons. There the pack trail led up over the shoulder of a timbered mountain. We made camp at the foot of the hill. First we unpacked our wet packs to see how much stuff was damaged. The salt in the 2½-pound bags was a total loss, with just the empty sacks left. The sugar fared better for we had that double sacked in a canvas bag. Water had gotten in, so we hung them up and put some empty jam tins underneath to catch the syrup. We had several sacks of oatmeal that were just mush. The canned goods, of course, were fine. The flour packs weren't damaged too much for water doesn't penetrate flour readily. Since we were over 250 miles on the trail all the grub was valuable, for there was no way of getting any more. Nick's orders were to cook up all this oatmeal into some form of cookies, so Cecil got the whole crew busy mixing up different concoctions of that soggy oatmeal and using up some of that liquid sugar. Most of it was made into some form of cookies that we cooked in fry pans and reflector ovens and some over the open fire. These were bagged up for future use and were good.

Ingval got himself dried off and was none the worse for his dunking. Next morning he left camp while we were packing up. The trail zigzagged up through the timber, making quite a climb with rough going all day. It was good goat and sheep country on both sides of the valley and we saw a few moving up around the peaks. We made camp that night in a big burn. A fire had gone through the area many years ago. About half of the timber had blown down, and we had quite a time getting enough room for our packs. The ponies had to jump considerable windfall in the course of their grazing. There was fair grass over at the foot of a slide a few hundred yards from camp, and no shortage of wood for our cook tent. We cleared out as much as we could to make it easier to pack up the next morning.

It was threatening rain when we wrangled the horses at 4 am, but it didn't rain much until we were on our last packs. From the start we had tough travelling. There were lots of rocks to contend with at the beginning. Then we hit a snow-slide area where the slides over the years had stripped the timber off the mountainside and left it in all sorts of weird-looking piles. We had to cross some of these. At times our horses were 10 feet off the ground, so we had to do some patch work to make it safer for them. After a lot of axe work we got the whole outfit across and made camp.

It had been a wet, miserable night, and it was a chilly, damp morning. There was pretty fair grass at this site, so we had no trouble getting our horses into camp in the morning. We had more rough going and had to cross several rock gullies coming in from the north. At one that was quite deep (which we called Goat Gulch) we had to cross the horses one at a time so they wouldn't crowd each other off the ledges. (We lost one horse here on our next trip up.) About noon we came to the north fork of the Muskwa River, which came out of a big glacier field to the northwest. There was a natural bridge over this stream where it cut through a rock ridge. The whole stream boiled through this rocky gorge that was about 15 feet wide and about 20 feet down. We dragged a few logs to lay along the edge of this rock bridge to keep the horses from getting too close to the edge and perhaps falling to their doom in that foaming water. We followed up the west branch of the Muskwa River, which started from a lake on the summit (later named Fern Lake after Mrs Bedaux). It was a wet, drizzly day.

Just as we were making camp two riders arrived from down river: Jack Bocock, the second in command of the expedition, and Jack MacDougall.

The natural bridge. BC Archives G-02699.

They brought word that Bedaux had given up the idea of getting through with the half-track trucks. After a lot of difficulties the Citroëns were abandoned 80 miles out of Fort St John. Bedaux decided to get more horses and try to complete his expedition that way. Bocock and MacDougall were sent to catch up to us and have us return and join the main outfit.

After a wet night we had the day off to make a grub cache. We chopped the tops off three pine trees about 15 feet up and put a deck on the crosspieces. The grub packs were put up there with a tarp lashed over the top. Ten packs totalling 20 ten-gallon cans were stacked on two logs under a big pine tree. None of us were sorry to see the last of our packs. Those 200 gallons of gasoline were to sit there for 35 years. Don Peck, a big-game outfitter and very good friend of mine, had that country in his registered hunting area. He went in there with a hunting party in the fall of 1969 and used some of the gasoline in his chainsaws for cutting trail. In the next year Don packed out several of the tanks and saved one for me as a souvenir.

It continued to rain off and on and the mountain peaks were all fogged in. Jack Bocock and I went out hunting for a caribou for we were all hungry for some fresh meat. We climbed over the shoulder of a mountain and down into the north fork of the Muskwa, following up the river until we came to the foot of the big glacier that continued on up into the fog. Although we were in good caribou country we failed to see any, so in the fog and rain we headed back to camp where we had to settle for our usual sow belly and macaroni or rice and good old bannock.

That evening we sorted out supplies and rearranged our packs. We had been carrying four 50-pound mats of figs and several boxes of Florian chocolate, a very good French chocolate that came in squares like Baker's chocolate, except that it was sweeter. We found out later that it was wonderful for lunch as we rode along the trail. Nick Geake, our boss, wouldn't let us start in on these.

When Bocock showed up, we asked him and he said, "Hell, yes! That's what it is for." Bocock also took an axe and cut one of those 50-pound mats of figs in half. "Now," he said, "eat all you want."

Most of us found out that when you do, you are sure not bothered with constipation!

We awoke to another damp, chilly morning, but it cleared up and became a sunshiny day. The two Jacks packed up their horses and started back downriver to locate the main party. We put eight packs and the extra packsaddles and rigging on 26 head and let the remaining 24 run loose. A few horses had cinch sores and some sore backs, so this would give them a chance to heal.

We started back down the river to join up with the main party but we had no idea where that would be. With light packs we made good time, and on the second day reached the Horse Corrals Camp, where we had been flooded out on our way up. While coming down the Big Bar I got a dunking in the river, which sure cooled me off. I went to head off some loose horses that were following down the wrong channel. To get ahead of them I had to cross another channel. It didn't look deep, but it was hard to tell with that milky glacier water. I put my horse Smoky right into it and we went right out of sight. The first thing I thought of when we got out was my camera. Luckily, I had my camera on my shoulder strap. I emptied the water out of the case and the camera was unhurt. A short time later Ernie Petersen got his horse, Friday, into some quicksand, but with some help he managed to get him pulled out. We got across the two deep crossings in the canyon without having to swim and raft our stuff.

After leaving the Muskwa River we went over the height of land to the Prophet River. From the top of the hill leading down to the river we spotted two moose at the edge of a small lake on the south side of the river. Nick said to me, "You better go ahead and see if you can get one."

I was carrying the company gun on my saddle so I rode down to the river where we intended to camp. I had to swim the river and went down over a mile where I picketed Smoky by the front foot. Walking along the shore of the marshy lake I soon spotted a cow and calf moose. I didn't want to shoot the cow for Nick would want to pack all the meat along with us, and we didn't want any more packs. Besides, we couldn't use that much meat. I took a shot at the calf and down it went, out of sight in the tall grass and water. The cow got excited and made a dash for me. I didn't want to shoot her, so I started for some spruce trees. The cow turned back to her calf, then made two or three more starts in my direction before taking off.

I was glad, for I didn't want to shoot her, nor did I want her to catch up to me. After a while I started wading out through the bog to drag the calf in, and was surprised to see the calf take off through the tall grass. I threw two quick shots at it. I missed with the first shot and clipped the hair along its back with the second. Then I found I had no more shells. The moose went out into the middle of the lake and stood there watching me. There was nothing I could do but head back to camp. When I got to Smoky I put the bridle on him, jumped on him bareback, dashed back to the river, swam across, and went into camp.

The crew was just finishing their supper so I had a bite to eat while some of the boys rounded up a few horses. I collected some ammunition and Art MacLean went back with me. Bob Godberson was to follow with a pack horse. When Art and I got to the lake the moose calf was still standing out in the lake, but there were two big bulls and a cow standing at the edge of the lake. The bulls had good sets of horns and they stood there watching us for a while before taking off.

One shot dropped the calf, so we waded out and brought it into shore where we skinned and dressed it out. It was a big calf and would make a nice chunk of meat. It was getting late and Bob hadn't got there yet when we heard a "Yo-ho!" from the far side of the lake. Bob had got mixed up in the muskeg and the end of the lake and got on the wrong side. It would take some time to go back around, so Art and I decided we could pack the meat across the lake if it wasn't too deep. We started across with a quarter apiece. The water was up to our armpits but we made it. We also went back and made a second trip. Then we got the horse packed. By now it was getting quite dark. Art and I waded across the lake, packed up the rifle and got back to our horses. I saddled up Smoky and we met Bob at the end of the muskeg, then swam across the river and got into camp. Nick promised us the next day off. The horses camped good for there was all kinds of grass here.

After Cecil cooked a good breakfast of moose liver and hotcakes we got busy preparing to have a good bath and do our washing. We dug a hollow in the ground, put a good tarp over it. and filled it with water heated over the fire. This made a first class bathtub. We also sewed our pack manties and patched our tents. In the afternoon we wrangled our horses and doctored the ones with sores. We had mixed up a concoction of grease, pine tar, turpentine and camphor, which had some healing properties as well as keeping those pesky black flies away.

After dinner we rode up the valley a few miles to investigate a hot spring we had heard about. We found a fairly hot sulphur spring coming out of a gorge on the south side of the river. It spread out over a rock area that was built up by mineral deposits over the years and sloped down to a 10-foot drop into the river. The Stone Mountain sheep of this area had well-worn trails leading down to the spring from all directions. Their droppings started about the size of marbles on the top of the rock slope. Further down they got to be the size of golf balls, and when they reached the river the droppings were the size of baseballs. [In his memoirs Ernest Lamarque also recalled visiting the hot springs. "These springs have evidently been visited by wild sheep and goat from time immemorial, and there must be tons of their petrified dung nearby."]

Back in camp Cecil made us a supper of delicious moose steak. Then we took the packs we didn't need down to the river and rafted them across so we would have less to do in the morning. We wrangled the horses at 4 am and they looked better after their day of rest. We rafted the rest of the equipment across the river. The water level had dropped, so it was a short swim for the horses.

After packing the horses we travelled south over the low divide between the Prophet River and Richards Creek, followed Richards Creek down a short distance, and made camp along a creek coming in from the south. The next morning we travelled up this creek, then climbed up the mountainside through the timber, and came out on an open mountain top we called the Caribou Range. We followed this for 10 miles, seeing a few caribou along the way. Then we started down to Keily Creek. Before we reached timberline we spotted someone on foot and realized we might be nearing the main camp. We found them camped at timberline where they could look down into Keily Creek. The lone man we saw was the cameraman with his movie camera on a tripod. He had seen us coming and wanted to get some pictures of our outfit. As we rode into camp we had lots of help to unpack and turn our horses loose to join up with their 47 head.

This was a great day for us for we were to meet many of our packer friends from Fort St John and the Big Boy Bedaux who was responsible for it all.

Charles Bedaux
and the Bedaux Expedition

Charles E. Bedaux came out from France as a young man to the United States. He was fairly well known the world over as an efficiency expert. He made big money by selling his efficiency plan to the various factories, and ended up not being too popular with the labour unions. Bedaux had interests all over the world. Some of our boys were asked to continue on his payroll after this trip was over. This was the third expedition he had organized. The first was through the steppes of Russia, the second a motor trip across the Sahara Desert in Africa.

This trip was organized during the winter of 1933-34 and was advertised as going through unexplored regions of northern British Columbia with the final destination to be Telegraph Creek on the Stikine River. Bedaux had made a deal with the Citroën Tractor Co. in France, and had five half-track trucks shipped out to Edmonton. These trucks had a caterpillar drive on the back end with balloon tires in the front. There was a drum between the front wheels, which was supposed to help the vehicles through the muskegs. They were equipped with a 10-horse motor and their top speed was 20 miles per hour.

Bedaux's plan was to drive these trucks from Edmonton up to Fort St John, then follow the pack trail from there. That would be cut six feet wide by an advance trail-cutting crew. The route would take them up the Halfway River 130 miles, then over to the Muskwa River, up that river to its headwaters, over the main range of the Rockies, through what was later called Bedaux Pass. From the pass they would go down the Whitewater [Kwadacha] River to the Finlay River at Fort Ware. A few miles from Fort Ware the expedition would go up the Fox River to Fox or Sifton Pass. There Bedaux intended to follow the height of land northwest to Dease

The Bedaux Expedition departing from Edmonton. LAC PA 186071.

Lake, before heading southwest to Telegraph Creek on the Stikine River. At Telegraph Creek Bedaux planned to take a boat down the Stikine to the coast. But things didn't turn out as planned.

Ernest Lamarque, a BC land surveyor, left Fort St John in late April with a small crew and a string of pack horses to mark out the route with little red ribbons. A few days later Tommy Wilde followed with a crew of axemen and a string of horses. Their job was to cut a trail through the bush six feet wide, with stumps not more than six inches above the ground, and to avoid as many side hills as possible. Tommy's crew included Cecil Pickell, Art Paul, Earl Cuishing and the three Lundquist brothers: Bill, Ingvall and Bernard. They were using axes and Swede saws for there were no power saws in those days. It was a lot of hard work. When they hit a timbered stretch they would follow the edges of sloughs and muskegs whenever possible to try and avoid some extra cutting.

Bedaux's departure from Edmonton with his five trucks caused quite a bit of excitement with a lot of picture taking and well-wishing going on. They went north by way of Lesser Slave Lake, but with the wet summer, lots of mud, and a top speed of 20 miles an hour, they didn't make very good time. When the vehicles hit the Grand Prairie mud it proved difficult for them. The gumbo acted as a grinding compound and cut out the tracks on the trucks. Bedaux had to send out for new ones, which caused quite a delay.

When the Bedaux Expedition reached British Columbia they wined

The Citroëns at Fort St John. LAC PA171566.

and dined at the Hart Hotel in Pouce Coupe, then proceeded on through Dawson Creek and up to Fort St John where they made their final preparation to start out on the pack trails.

There was a passable road out to the Montney settlement about 20 miles from Fort St John. After that there was only a cut-out pack trail. Thirty miles out of Fort St John they started having trouble with muskeg and creek crossing, and more difficulty getting through rough country at the Cameron River crossing. When they made camp on a flat on the lower Halfway Indian Reserve, along the Halfway River about 50 miles out, Bedaux found they had used far more gas than they expected, so they decided to leave two of the trucks there.

At this camp Charlie Blackman created quite a stir. He had been sent back down the trail to retrieve a rope that had been left behind. However, he missed the trail into camp and went on upriver to the Westergaard Ranch where he stayed for the night. Back in camp search parties spent most of the night looking for him. Charlie didn't get too good a reception when he walked into camp the next morning.

Continuing on with the three trucks the Bedaux Expedition got to the forks of the Halfway River about 75 miles out after experiencing more difficulty along the way. Since this section of the pack trail was better than what lay ahead, Bedaux made the decision to abandon the idea of getting through with the trucks.

Bedaux had a movie camera outfit along for he intended to make a film of the whole trip. They decided to stage a few scenes, so it was arranged to roll two of the trucks over a high cliff into the Halfway River with Bedaux and his crew jumping for their lives just as the vehicles started to roll.

Northwest of Fort St John. BC Archives B-07519.

The Bedaux Expedition left Edmonton on July 6. The first half of the 1100-mile journey traversed dirt roads to Fort St John. Prevailing rain turned the roads into a thick mud ("gumbo") that slowed progress and cut the bands of the half-tracks. It took 11 days to reach Fort St John. At many of the small towns along the way, Bedaux made donations to the community or paid people to appear in his film.

He hoped conditions would improve when they entered bush country northwest of Fort St John, but it only got worse. Bedaux tried to maintain good spirits. He wrote: "Rough afternoon lands me stuck in a stream. We open the cheese. I entertain astonished cowboys." On another day: "We lunch 300 yards from breakfast!"

But less than a week from Fort St John, Bedaux admitted defeat in his diary: "We know we are beaten.... I think a lot & sleep badly." The following day, he wrote: "Fern grieves for me & revels for herself – a deadly combat in her nature.... Crosby going full speed – he has visions of tractors toppling down mountains."

They continued to the Halfway River, where on August 9, Bedaux wrote: "Cars condemned at conference.... Big preparations for pictures." From there the expedition continued on horseback.

These two trucks were given to the Westergaard brothers, Einar and Nels, who had a ranch a few miles downriver. They salvaged them from the river that fall when the ice got strong enough.

The third truck was cut loose on a raft and went down a rapid for the benefit of the movies. There again, Bedaux with others were to jump for their lives. Edgar Dopp, a big rugged cowboy, was to rescue Bedaux when he jumped off the raft into the river. A gust of wind blew Edgar's hat off,

The cowboys built rafts to transport the Citroëns across rivers.
LAC PA171663.

Al Phipps with one of the Citroëns. BC Archives B-07387.

The Citroëns frequently got stuck in mud holes and boggy ground, and the men had a difficult time getting them out. LAC PA171582.

Heavy rainfall turned the Peace River roads into a thick mud, called gumbo, that cut the tracks of the Citroëns. LAC PA186095.

Stuck in the mud. BC Archives I-57371.

so he forgot about Bedaux until he retrieved his hat, much to the disgust of the cameramen. Part of that scene had to be run over again.

The loaded raft was supposed to float down to a rock cliff at the bend of the river, where a large charge of dynamite had been planted to simulate a rockslide that would swamp the raft. But the charge failed to go off. The raft bumped into the rock wall, spun around, and continued floating downstream, lodging on a gravel bar three miles down. The truck was driven off the raft by Bill Beckman and a hired man putting up hay on a river flat. However, it didn't do them too much good for the nearest gas was 75 miles away.

If those of us on the freight pack train had only known we could have saved ourselves a lot of work, for we were still packing 200 gallons of gas up the trail until Jack Bocock and Jack MacDougall caught up to us near the head of the Muskwa. We were glad to see the last of the gas packs. The grub packs were piled up on a cache we built in the top of some trees. With very few packs our trip back down the trail was easy.

After abandoning the trucks Bedaux decided to try to complete the expedition with horses. This meant a lot of reorganization. They got a number of horses from the Westergaard brothers, a few more from the Hudson brothers, and then rented a pack string from Stan Clark who had bought Billy Hill's ranch. The radio man was sent back and quite a bit of surplus equipment was left. Bedaux's cowboys made up the packs, some of them pretty cumbersome, got them tied on the horses, and started up the trail. They received additional help from trappers in the area. The progress of the main party was slow.

While camped on a flat on the Besa River about 160 miles from Fort St John they had a very serious accident. Walter Thomlinson, one of the packers, got bucked off a horse while performing for the movie camera, tore the ligament loose at the knee, and opened up the knee joint. They tied his leg up in a splint, and he was faced with a 160-mile ride back down the trail. Charlie Hudson and an Indian helped bring him out. Charlie said it was a tough trip for Walter but he never complained. Walter went right out to Edmonton where he spent all of the next winter in the hospital. He finally recovered and was able to use his leg.

From their camp on the Besa, Bedaux's party moved up Keily Creek, then climbed up through the timber to timberline at the start of the Caribou Range. It was at this camp that we joined them. Charles Bedaux broke out a couple bottles of rum and we had a few get-acquainted drinks.

The two outfits together made a sizeable crew. The members of Bedaux's party included:

Charles E. Bedaux, leader
Mrs Fern Bedaux, his wife
Madame Bilou Chiesa, companion
Josephine Daly, maid
Big John Chisholm, a gamekeeper from Scotland and our policeman along with his other duties like Bedaux's valet
Balourdet, the expert French mechanic
Jack Bocock, second in command of the expedition
Bruce Bocock, in charge of supplies
Frank Swannell, B.C. land surveyor
Al Phipps, assistant surveyor
Floyd Crosby, movie cameraman
Everett Withrow, assistant cameraman
Charlie Blackman, camp attendant
Joe Weiss, a Swiss skier from Jasper (detailed to cooking)
Bob Beattie, head packer
Jack MacDougall, packer
Bill Pickell, packer
Edgar Dopp, packer
Einar Westergaard, packer
Henry Philpott, packer

With the Main Bedaux Party
from the Caribou Range to Fort Ware
(August 24 – September 14)

Since it was now well into August the cowboys lost no time in getting things reorganized. There were a lot of packs to be made up and sorted out. It was decided to split the pack string into sections of 12 pack horses with two packers to each section. Bob Godberson and I were to pack together and were allotted a dunnage section, which was difficult to pack, for the dunnage bags were all sizes and weights, and would vary in weight from day to day. There were suitcases and roll table tops, brooms, folding cots, and a number of big bed rolls. It was like tying on bales of hay to get those bedrolls on a horse. One of our bed horses was a chunky bay we called Socks for he had four white feet. When we would come to a mud hole that he thought he couldn't get through, he would try and go around through the bush and end up being stuck between two trees. We would holler at him to wait, then get our trail axe off our saddle and go and cut the tree down to let him get through. He was a great little horse. The bed horses had a tough time. We had to unpack them several times to get through the muskegs.

Bob Beattie and Jack MacDougall had the tent section as well as dunnage. The tents were a mean pack, especially when it rained or snowed. Bill Pickell and Henry Philpott had the kitchen section and some awkward packs. There were also three freight sections.

Leaving that first camp late in the morning we travelled 10 miles along the Caribou Range and down through the timber to camp on a little creek that runs into Richard Creek. It was a beautiful sight that day, travelling over the Caribou Range above timberline with the different sections of pack horses strung out for a mile or more. The air was quite clear and you could trace the different rivers coming from the west. To the

Crossing the Caribou Range. LAC e008300557.

north was Richard Creek, then the Prophet and Muskwa rivers. Directly
west was Keily Creek. South was the Besa River, Redfern Lake and the
Sikanni River, all heading from that sea of mountain peaks to the west.
One would think, to look at it, that it would be impossible to pick a route
through that jumble of rock, yet we were to take our outfit through the
main range of the Rockies at the head of the Muskwa.

Bedaux had an accident when he started down the mountain. At timberline his horse slipped on a moss-covered rock and tripped on a root,
rolling Bedaux a few feet down the mountainside, over a ledge of rock and
into a puddle of water, giving him an unwanted bath. The first thing he
did when we got the tents up in camp was to get a change of clothes.

The horse range here at this camp was across Richard Creek. Ernie
Peterson and I were out at daylight to wrangle the horses. When we got
them rounded up, lined out, and heading toward camp, over 100 head
made a great sight crossing the creek.

We had some rain during the night, still drizzling when we packed up,
but it cleared around midday. We followed up Richards Creek for a short
distance, then went over the low pass to the Prophet River. The water had
gone down so we were able to ford it with the pack horses, making camp
on the north side at a small lake.

The next morning we travelled through a muskeg or two, then down
to the Muskwa and up that river. Edgar Dopp, who was following our
section with his freight string, had a big sorrel Suffolk Punch horse in his
string. A funny thing about some horses – they like to travel up front in a
string – and this horse had got behind while getting through some of the
muskegs. When he got to a semi-open patch of timber he made a dash to
get ahead, but in going between a tree and the river bank his pack hit the

The landscape of the upper Muskwa River valley. LAC PA173833.

tree, knocking him off balance. His hind foot went through the overhang of the river bank and he fell eight feet into the fast-running river. Edgar saw it happen and went to the rescue. Not too much damage was done, but he had quite a time getting the horse back up the bank.

Toward the end of the day I was riding at the head of our string. The mountain comes fairly close to the river bank here. On our previous trip we swam the horses across here. Old Dusty, one of the better pack horses from our string, knew it was getting near camping time and that the horse feed was on the other side, so he decided to swim the river. He got into swimming water before we could stop him, followed by one of Edgar's freight horses that had got up into our string. Bob Godberson got down in time to prevent any more horses from following.

Edgar came along and hollered for us to go ahead with the pack horses and that he would swim across, get the two horses, and bring them into camp. There was a good ford half a mile further up. When we got there Frank Swannell, the surveyor, and his assistant, Al Phipps, were getting ready to wade across, so they were glad for us to relay them. Several members of the camp staff had to change off walking and riding for there weren't enough horses to go around. Camp was made just past the ford in a nice grass meadow.

Edgar came into camp with the two horses that had taken the swim, and there was considerable talk in French as to whether the dunnage bags had let water in. They were double tied and supposed to be waterproof, but when Bob and I unpacked Dusty we knew the bags had soaked up lots of water. These were the ladies' dunnage bags. They were quite disappointed to find that everything was soaked, so we had to get busy and string up some rope lines to hang out all their fancy clothing. But the ladies were good sports about it.

We were one horse short when we got into camp. It turned out to be a bay mare that Jack MacDougall started out riding. When we were picking our saddle stock in Fort St John Jack asked me to try out that bay mare that we called Slick. She had a trace of thoroughbred in her. Although a nice horse to ride I said I didn't think she would stand the trail too well. Jack started out with her but she finally gave out and developed a sore back, so when we left camp that morning all she was carrying was an empty army pack saddle. She strayed off the trail along the way. Although they went back and looked for her they failed to find her. About a month later two trappers, Bert and Kelly Sheffield, who were packing to their trapline on the lower Muskwa, found her. She still had the saddle on, but it had turned and was hanging under her belly.

Going up through the canyon we had to ford the Muskwa River twice. The river had dropped so we had good crossings. The cameraman, Floyd Crosby, was having a heyday with his movie camera. He would set himself up at bad spots along the trail. Sometimes you didn't know he was there until you heard the camera buzzing.

Above the canyon Jack Bocock was riding along with me through the pine trees along a rocky mountainside. We came to a place where the trail led down a moss-covered rock slope to a lower level. The horses ahead had slid off all the moss down to the wet slippery rock. The previous few had tripped on the roots and went head over heels, much to Floyd's delight. He hollered to me, "OK, Bob, start your outfit down." But Bocock spoke up and said, "No more of that." He was more interested in getting the outfit through than in getting pictures. We dropped a tree across the trail there and cut a detour around.

We travelled up the six miles of the Big Bar without incident. The quicksand spots had improved since the water lowered. We camped at the top end of the Bar, but there was poor horse feed since most of the valley floor was taken up with gravel bars. From there we climbed over the shoulder of the mountain and camped that night in the big burn area. We had a difficult time getting enough space to pitch the tents among the windfall. There was plenty of feed for the horses, but they had to jump a lot of windfall to get at it.

We saw several goats and Stone's sheep along the way. Balourdet spotted some sheep just above them as they were riding along and drew Bedaux's attention to them. Both men got out their rifles. Balourdet thought that Bedaux should have the first shot since he was the boss, while Bedaux thought that Balourdet should have the first shot since he saw them first. They both waited on one another long enough for the sheep to walk out of sight. They were still arguing about it in camp that night.

From camp Jack Bocock and his brother Bruce spotted a goat high up on the side of a deep gorge. They made quite a climb and got a shot at it

Shoeing a horse. LAC e008300553.

across the gorge. It went tumbling down but got hung up on a snag on the sheer side of the mountain with no possible way of getting at it. They were sorry to leave it there.

After this it was rough going to the head of the river. We got through the snow-slide area but had trouble getting through Goat Gulch. Bob and I got our outfit across and were helping Ernie Peterson. The trail angled down into the gorge on a shelf of rock and angled back up the other side. Two gray horses that always travelled together started across. The one in the lead hesitated a while as he was climbing out. The other horse tried to get by but lost his footing and fell 15 feet to the bottom of the gulch. He landed on his rump and injured his back. When we climbed down and got the pack off we found it contained a case of dynamite and a case of champagne. Both survived the fall. After hauling the packs up they handed down the rifle off my saddle and I put the poor horse out of his misery. We put the packs on Smoky and I walked the rest of the way to camp. Our camp was along a beautiful lake a little further past the place where we built the cache on our first trip up. Frank Swannell, our surveyor, named this clear blue lake Fern Lake (after Mrs Bedaux's Christian name). This is the head of the Muskwa River, which flows east into the Liard and eventually the Mackenzie River. After eating, Bob Godberson and I chopped down a few dry trees, built a raft, and paddled the length of the lake to the outlet where it tumbled over a rock reef into a gorge below.

We had a day off here and Floyd Crosby and his assistant Everett Withrow got some of us busy working on the movie. They spent all morning staging scenes around camp. Art MacLean and I were to re-enact the shooting of the gray horse in Goat Gulch. We picked out a similar gulch near camp. We were in the bottom of this gulch, and although there was no horse there, we were to look sad about what had happened. As we were helping each other climb out we started laughing.

Floyd said, "Hold it. We'll have to shoot that over." He said, "No laughing, you're supposed to look a little sad."

Cecil Pickell (right) and other cowboys drying dishes at camp.
LAC PA173883.

When we got out I was to walk to my horse Smoky and get the rifle and take a shot down into the gulch. Then the camera was set up a few feet away, and I had to take another shot and say a few words about how sorry we were to have to shoot such a good horse.

After dinner Cecil Pickell, Tommy Wilde and I were in a night herding scene. [Tommy Wilde came back from the trail-cutting crew to be the cook for the Dude section.] We rounded up about 45 horses in a shallow draw where the brush was fairly short. Although it was a sunny day, with a coloured lens in the camera it was to depict a moonlight scene. Tommy and I were to meet in front of the camera, roll a smoke and shoot the breeze. Then Tommy was to raise his head, sniff in the air and shout, "There's a fire coming! I'll go and warn camp, you fellows bring in the horses." Tommy was to go galloping off with the camera trained on him until he was out of sight. Then the camera was trained on me. I was to gallop off and "hollah" to Cecil and we were to round up the horses and chase them down the draw until we got out of sight of the camera.

A funny thing happened here – just before we got out of sight of the camera we met two fellows with a pack string. They happened to be people we knew from Fort St John – Ollie Southwick and his son Tud. They had to turn and go right along with us. He said, "I thought we'd run into a band of wild Indians when we saw that herd of horses coming." They had been out all summer on a prospecting trip and had been over around Fort Ware on the Finlay River. There had been a third member of the party, Otto, but he drowned in the Whitewater River. He went to swim the river and a piece of driftwood struck his horse, which upset him and

Bob White stands at the far right and Charles Bedaux sits in front pouring champagne into another cowboy's cup. LAC e008300558.

Celebrating at Champagne Meadows

Several camp scenes were filmed, then we were to depict a forest fire sweeping down on camp. We were to pack up and run for our lives. We got 25 horses saddled and hung anything on them for packs. We were to put them on in such a way that many would fall off with the first few jumps. There were flares and smoke bombs planted all over camp, and at a given signal they were all to be lit. The cases of dynamite were to be used to cause a fake landside that was to come down and demolish our camp, but that scene was never done. Then the show was on.

Camp attendants dashed around to take the tents down while we started throwing anything on for packs. The cowboys started firing off their .45 revolvers and got the horses stampeding in all directions, causing the darnedest mix-up you ever saw. It was all over in a few minutes. The flares burnt out and the horses ran to the dark meadows, trailing ropes, canvas pack covers, and the odd pack.

Then the job began to locate the scattered packs and equipment, and get the saddles off the horses. Bedaux's champagne, supplemented by the occasional shot of his overproof rum, had us all in a pretty fair mood. It was black dark and started to rain. We were riding around through the willows in the meadows armed with flashlights. When anyone spotted a horse with rigging on he'd yell and start after it. The horses were so spooked they were hard to catch. The night was pretty well spent by the time we got all the saddles off and the stuff all gathered up.

Cecil Pickell also had vivid memories of the celebration that evening:

Bedaux had us all sit in a horseshoe with a row of dudes on chairs directly behind us, that is the ones at the top of the horseshoe. He gave us a pep talk and started to serve the bubbly; all this was also being filmed. I think it was Einar Westergaard, Bob Godberson and I who were sitting directly in front of Mrs Bedaux, Madam Chiesa and Josephine. After the first round these ladies emptied their glasses into our cups after each round. By the time the juice was all gone everybody was feeling pretty gay and the three of us were naturally doubly gay. I don't remember much of what went on after that.... Once when I was being interviewed by John Fisher who then had a radio program called *Canadian Tales*, I remarked that I would bet that was the first time excellent champagne had been consumed by a bunch of packers and guides out of granite cups in the wilds of northern British Columbia.

separated them. The horse managed to make it but Otto didn't. Ollie and Tud had been lost for the last month and had only found the pass through the main range that day. They were happy to see us. They had two grizzly bear hides with them, shot a few days before. They camped with us that night, and we were interested to hear what they knew about the country that lay ahead.

Frank Swannell, who was making a rough triangulation survey of the route, climbed the mountain to the southwest with his assistant, Al Phipps, put a cairn on top, and took readings on the various peaks around the area. He later named some of the mountains and features after members of the expedition.

Edgar Dopp, John Chisholm and Balourdet went hunting on the mountain to the west. They got close to a big sow grizzly with two yearling cubs. When the sow charged them they shot her and the two cubs. By the time they had them all skinned out and brought back to camp they were tired but proud of their trophies, and well satisfied with such an eventful day.

Bedaux had a very expensive gun that he called his elephant gun. It was a double-barrelled rifle. I don't remember the size of the bore, but you could put your finger down the barrel. They tried it out on the lake. One cowboy took a shot, and the recoil spun him right around. He said, "The damn thing went off before I was ready."

We wrangled the horses early the next morning. Ollie and his son Tud left camp in good time on their 300-mile trip out to Fort St John. While we were packing up, Bob Beattie, the head packer, came to me and said, "I've got a job for you." We had two horses crippled with foot rot. Foot rot usually started from a bruise or a snag below the fetlock and was very painful. We doctored some by putting poultices on and washing the sores out with a solution of bluestone, but it didn't do much good unless we laid over. We led the horses away from camp and shot them. One of them was the nice bay mare that Bob had been riding. It seemed such a pity, but it was the most humane thing to do. Had we left the horses they might have recovered, but they would have had quite a time surviving the elements that high up in the mountains.

We rode west through what was later called Bedaux Pass, zigzagging through heavy windfall and muskeg. Crossing the head of the Kwadacha (Whitewater) River, we followed down Chesterfield Creek to a nice camp on Chesterfield Lake where there was lots of horse feed.

Bill Pickell and I took the rifle and intended to get to the end of the lake, hoping to get a shot at a moose. There was no shoreline so we had to jungle through the bush, which was tough going. It got late, and rather than go back through the bush, we decided we'd build a makeshift raft and float back. We chopped a dead log in two with our little trail axe, chopped a dovetail notch in the big ends, and fitted and wedged a crosspiece into the notch. With our belts we fastened the other end of the crosspiece to the smaller ends of the logs. With makeshift paddles, Bill perched on one crosspiece and me on the other, we paddled to camp. It was late and some were wondering what had become of us, until they heard us singing "Come a ti-yi-yippy-yippy-yay" out on the lake. When Floyd heard about it next morning, we had to go out in daylight for his movie camera.

Nick Geake was in charge of a freight section of pack horses with Edgar Dopp as his helper. He was still riding his little roan mare Joan, but she was showing signs of wear, so he decided to put a light pack on her and ride that black mare, Ribbons, that he had tried down on the Halfway River. He saddled her up, led her a short distance, then climbed on. She took off running. With lots of windfall around, she tripped and went down with Nick underneath. Had he been using a regular stock saddle instead of that army pancake saddle, he might have suffered considerable damage. Edgar, further up the trail, happened to see him and got back in time to pull the mare off. Otherwise it would have been curtains for Nick. Nick was a hardy soul, and didn't let a little thing like that bother him.

We moved down through more muskeg and windfall, making camp at a place later called Champagne Meadows, a nice grassy meadow with clumps of willow scattered through it. The horses were showing signs of wear, so it was decided to unload some of the excess baggage. We were still carrying a case or two of dynamite and several cases of champagne.

Floyd had big plans for some movie scenes that night. After demolishing a case and a half of champagne, we were in a pretty good mood to tackle anything.

We were out at the first peep of day, for we were worried about the horses leaving camp. They had every reason to, after the working over they had got last night. The rain had quit and it looked like a fair day coming up.

Jack MacDougall, Bill Pickell, Bob Godberson and I headed up the back trail. We rounded up the first bunch of more than 20 horses and Bill took them back to camp. A few miles further we caught up to about the same number. Bob started them back to camp. Jack and I could see two tracks still going up the trail. We were out six to eight miles when we caught up to one. We tied it up and kept on the trail of the second one. We knew which horse we were after. When we got to a crooked section of the trail that went through muskeg and windfall Jack said, "You follow the tracks. I'll see if I can get ahead of her." Jack made it and sure enough, it was the bay mare we called Pet. She was an old campaigner who had been up on the Nelson Trail many times in previous years. (That was the 300-mile freight trail from Fort St John to Fort Nelson.) Pet had her mind set on heading back out and was quite annoyed about turning around. She was to quit camp later, near Sifton Pass, and we never heard of her again.

When Jack and I got back to camp we were ready for a bite to eat. The boys had a lot of the packing done. Bob Beattie said to me, "Get your rifle. There's two more horses crippled with foot rot." We led them off and shot them. To lighten our packs we left some gear here. We travelled down Chesterfield Creek, then headed west through a series of small lakes, proceeded down and across the Warneford River at a fairly deep ford, and made a nice camp in the pines a few miles below the ford.

Along the trail Nick and his freight string had their usual trouble with the jenny mule. I had previously worked with Nick on the Halfway and he was the worst man I ever heard for swearing. When the jenny got stuck he really let loose. With Edgar's help they got the mule unpacked, pulled out and on the trail. Just around the bend in the trail the Dudes had stopped for their midday lunch. Bedaux said to Nick, "Is it necessary to carry on that way?" Nick gave him another sample of his swearing and said that instead of sitting there listening to him he should have come back and given them a hand. Apart from that habit, Nick was a fine man and a hardy soul. He slept in the tent with us and would sponge himself off every morning, even after the weather turned cold and he had to break the ice on the water pail. It made us shiver to watch him.

From Pine Camp we proceeded down the Warneford River to the Whitewater [Kwadacha] and followed it down to our Disaster Camp. When we reached the Whitewater Bob and I had the misfortune of one of our pack horses rolling down a mud bank, landing on her feet with water well up on her pack, and no way of getting down to pull her up. She took a step or two and was immediately in swimming water. The current took her down out of sight behind the trees. I hurried downstream to an opening in the bush and got Smoky out to the bank. When the horse showed up I called to her and she swam in. I was so anxious to save her from going further downriver that I piled in, chaps and all, and got a rope on her halter. When more help arrived we unpacked and dragged the packs up the bank – heavy as lead – and got the gray mare we called Bell out of the river. We split the pack between her and Smoky and walked back to camp. It was a sad day for Al Phipps for it was his personal dunnage and bedroll and some of Swannell's as well, that got soaked. It ruined Al's camera and field glasses and the exposed film that he valued so.

This Disaster Camp was a day's travel from Fort Ware, a Hudson's Bay post on the Finlay River, a short distance up from the mouth of the Whitewater. There were a lot of rolling sandy ridges around camp, but very little grass. The country had been burnt off many years ago, and was now covered with windfall and a scattered growth of young pine.

We were out at daylight, and as expected, had trouble finding the horses. After our first gather we were about 20 short. Some boys came into camp and said they had tracked some down to the river but were afraid to cross and had come back to get Jack MacDougall. I had been with Jack for several summers and found him to be the best waterman I ever trailed with. Jack rode downriver with them. After sizing it up he said, "We can get across down there." They rode across and brought 11 horses back. In those glacial streams the water is always a little milky and it is hard to tell how deep it is unless you understand water.

We were still nine head short. The Dude section had left camp earlier and given orders for none to leave camp until all the horses were found. We finally tracked them down, but it was three o'clock before we got packed and left camp. The trail led through sandy ridges with muskeg spots in between. Daylight ran out, it clouded over, and a drizzling rain started. In the black darkness the horses had become mixed up so we counted the horses as we unpacked and tried to remember where the beds and grub boxes were. The outfit was scattered and getting wet. Different groups of us got a fire going and rustled something to eat. We located some canned sausage and hardtack, which helped. Then we hunted up some blankets, spread them on the ground, pulled a tarp over us, and went to sleep.

When the Dudes left Disaster Camp they lunched along the way and debated whether to wait for us to catch up. They decided to go on to Fort Ware where they spent quite a night. This post was founded and named after James Ware, a Hudson's Bay man who established it several years before. His son, Jimmy, was running the post at this time. He was the lone inhabitant other than a few Indians and white trappers at odd times. When the Dude party rode in late that night and saw only three or four log cabins they knew they were in for a rough night. Jimmy didn't know what to do, so he turned his log cabin over to the ladies. The men found shelter in the store and other cabins. They put in what they said was a deplorable night and sure missed their luxurious bedrolls with their eiderdowns and air mattresses.

When we awoke at daylight everything was white and it was still snowing. We were so disorganized, with packs scattered for some distance up and down the trail, that we just had a makeshift breakfast. We were lucky to find all our horses. When we got them in camp it was snowing so heavy that we had to saddle and pack the horses at the same time to keep things as dry as we could. We had a big fire going so we could warm our hands once in a while. When we turned loose to hit the trail there was three to four inches of snow on the ground. We kept going until we rode into camp at Fort Ware at three o'clock that afternoon. We were a cold, wet outfit and were met by some boys from the advance trail-cutting crew. When we started catching our pack horses they told us they would unpack. The advance party, who were camped nearby, had put up a large tent where Bedaux set up a kitchen. They sent us down to the tent where Bedaux was presiding over a pot of hot rum. A round or two of that sure warmed things up on the inside and we worried less about the cold on the outside.

Fort Ware
(September 14–16)

Bedaux had arranged to have supplies brought up the Finlay by boat, but owing to the lateness of the season and the condition of our horses we had far more supplies than we needed, so Bedaux decided to put on a real spread. We couldn't have been in better shape to appreciate a big feed since we had not eaten too well for the last two days. After the rum they herded us into the grub tent. There was so much food there we couldn't believe our eyes. First, there was caviar and toast with dinner wines. We passed that up and went for the real grub. There was canned turkey and ham that was roasted, and different types of sausage. All kinds of vegetables, including sweet potatoes and corn on the cob were on the table. There were lots of flavours of pickles and cheeses along with a big variety of desserts – pies, cakes of all kinds, and the real old plum pudding. Oh yes, and fruit cake with a good layer of almond icing. With everyone in a happy frame of mind it sure was a day to remember. We ate so much we had to hunt for a place to lie down. We put our tents up and gathered a supply of spruce boughs for our beds, got a big fire going and started drying everything out, including ourselves. It was still snowing, and by night there was at least six inches on the ground.

It continued snowing on and off for the three days we laid over there until we had more than a foot of snow. We had a lot of repacking to do and some members of the expedition were sent out from here by boat down the Finlay and Peace Rivers. There was no further use for the axemen, so they went out. In the boat that went downriver were Nick Geake, Earl Cuishing, the three Lundquist brothers, Art Paul, Charlie Blackman, and Joe Weiss. With all this snow coming down it began to look doubtful whether the Bedaux Expedition would be able to get through to its destination of Telegraph Creek, still another 250 miles away. However, Bedaux

Fort Ware was a Hudson's Bay Company trading post on the Finlay River.
LAC PA 173957.

decided to go north 60 miles to Sifton Pass, which would take us to the Liard River watershed, and see how things looked from there.

Floyd got us busy on a few scenes for the movie. He wanted Ernie Peterson, Cecil Pickell and me in a swimming scene crossing the river, so we packed a string of ponies with fake packs, mostly empty boxes. There were two cameras, one taking us going in, the other coming out. I was to lead. When that cold river water hit up around the belt you could sure feel it. I looked back and saw Ernie entering the water. I said, "Come on in, Ernie, the water's fine." He didn't look very happy. We swam out part way, then swam back and headed for the tent and a drink of rum. We had taken our underwear off so there were less clothes that had to dry out.

We staged another swimming scene near here a few weeks later, on our way back. It was in October with quite a bit of snow around. Floyd wanted two men in a horse-wrangling scene. He wanted me to swim out in the lead, part way across, then come back lower down the river. It was pretty chilly and the water looked cold.

I said to Floyd, "Take Edgar there and let him lead. He needs a bath more than I do."

By gosh, Edgar said, "Sure, I'll do it if you get Colonel for me to ride."

Colonel was a big bay and one of our better swimming horses.

Edgar and I were to be in this scene with 40 head of loose horses. Edgar peeled off his clothes by a good fire and just put on his coat and overalls. We had a few natural-looking windfalls to make a bit of a wing. With Edgar in the lead I chased the horses over the bank into the river. When Colonel got into the water it must have been one of his off days, for he kept going down until his nose, eyes and ears were level with the water and Edgar was in up almost to his armpits.

He said later, "I thought the son-of-a-gun was going to walk across on the bottom." There was some hot rum waiting for us when we got back to the fire. Edgar got more for getting extra wet.

There was one cowboy in the outfit who never learned to get his directions right in the bush: Henry Philpott, or Hardluck Hank as we called him. We never let him wrangle any more than we had to for quite often we ended up looking for him. One day, at the Fort Ware camp, Bob Godberson and Art McLean followed some tracks quite a distance from camp. They heard bells and headed in their direction. They didn't seem to be getting any closer, so they started to run and finally caught up to Hardluck Hank. He had caught a horse and chased the other horses several miles up the Whitewater before they could catch him. Bob and Art had quite a time convincing Hank that he was going in the wrong direction.

During our stay we wrangled the horses every day, but we had a lot of trouble keeping track of them. There was a wide flat in the valley east of the river covered with pine and poplar. The grass was patchy, so the horses did a lot of wandering. With all the snow there were tracks all over the place. A few more cases of foot rot showed up and these horses had to be shot.

The weather got worse with more snow coming down but Bedaux decided the expedition would pack up and move north. We were still going to be heavily packed. Bedaux hired three horses that belonged to a trapper near Sifton Pass. He rented these horses to trappers to relay their supplies from Fort Ware over the pass and into the Liard watershed. These were the only horses available in the area. When I saw the horses, one looked familiar. She was a very light sorrel mare with a silver mane and tail. On checking the brand I found she was one of a bunch I broke to ride on the Billy Hill Ranch in 1930. Billy had outfitted some prospectors who had trailed in over the mountains that summer. This horse was one of a few that had survived the winters.

North of Fort Ware
(September 17 – October 6)

It was snowing like the dickens when we packed up to leave and we had a lot of trouble finding all our horses, so it was after mid-day when we got away. The snow was getting deep, which made for heavy going, and we hit some bad muskeg places. When we stopped after about 10 miles we had to shovel quite a bit of snow to get spaces for the tents. Since it was still snowing, it was a good night to use a lot of wood. The horse feed through this part of the country was grim, so we were lucky to have a grassy slough near camp that held the horses most of the night.

The Dude section complained about the noise the horse bells made. They said it kept them awake most of the night. Not so with us, for the bells were music to our ears. As long as we could hear bells we knew we had horses in camp. It's when you can't hear bells that you get an uneasy feeling and start wondering how far you might have to walk to find them.

It snowed most of the night, with a light snow still falling in the morning. Packing up with all the snow was a miserable job. We were late leaving camp, for some of the horses had strayed and were hard to find. We had lots of trouble in some bad muskeg. Several horses got stuck. They had to be unpacked, their packs carried out, and then the horses had to be pulled out. Floyd was having a heyday. He would station himself at the worst places with his camera. We only made about 10 miles because of the deep snow and wet spots. Once again we had to do lots of shovelling to make space for the tents. The horse feed was poor, so we were late finding all the horses. It was a hard, miserable day getting through to our camp in Fox Pass. We travelled through up to 18 inches of snow, which made tough going for those who had to walk. Edgar lost a big sorrel horse out of his string. The horse crippled himself in a bog and had to be shot.

We had been following up the Fox River since a few miles from Fort Ware. The river comes from the north and the valley is quite wide. Big fires had gone through the area many years before. The rolling sandy ridges were covered with windfall and second-growth pine with very little grass, so our horses didn't fare too well.

We laid over a day here, expecting to meet Ernest Lamarque coming in from the west. Lamarque's job was to pick out a possible route from either Fox or Sifton Pass through the height of land between the Finlay and Liard watersheds to Dease Lake. His party managed to get through but had some rough going. When Lamarque arrived that day with his helpers Bill and Henry Blackman they had quite a discussion. Lamarque advised against taking his route so late in the season for he said some of the passes that we would have to go through already had considerable snow in them.

Instead, Bedaux decided to go north over Sifton Pass, down the Driftpile and Kechika rivers to the Liard, then follow that river up to Dease Lake. But the planning was a lot easier than the doing.

Our next drive, up to a camp just short of Fox Lake, was one of our worst. The weather had cleared and the snow was settling, but there was plenty of tough travelling and we went through several muskegs. Bob and I had trouble getting our bed horses through a muskeg and had to cut a way around. Most of us got wet up to our knees wading through the snow so we built good fires to dry things out.

Camp at Sifton Pass. LAC PA209630.

Everett Withrow, the assistant cameraman, had been detailed to help Edgar Dopp with his freight string. Edgar had lost two horses out of his string, so they only had one saddle horse between them. Edgar had the only mule in the outfit and had to help her out of several mud holes. They arrived in camp late that night. Everett was in tears, wet through to the hips, and pretty well played out. We sent him to the tent and said we'd unpack his horses. Then Edgar found he was missing two pack horses. It was dark by this time and too late to go looking for them.

Edgar was a hardy soul; when he straightened up he stood over six feet. He rolled out early the next morning, got a cup of coffee, put some bannock in his pocket for lunch, and headed back down the trail to look for the two missing horses. He thought they could be near a muskeg about six miles back, and he found them not far from there. They still had their nose nets on so weren't able to graze. Edgar took them up the trail until he got to some grass, then took off the packs and nose nets and let the horses graze while he ate his lunch. He arrived back in camp toward evening. We didn't move camp that day.

We did a lot of walking to gather our horses the next morning. Still, one was missing, the mare Pet, who had tried to quit camp at Champagne Meadows. We never saw her again. Normally we put the bells on the leaders of the different bunches of horses, but with a shortage of grass they scattered in all directions. Bedaux bought all the sleigh dog bells in Whitewater (Fort Ware) and made up a number of so-called bells out of milk tins, but they proved useless.

Bedaux was in quite a dither over the delay in finding the horses. He said, "You know, outside they consider me an efficiency expert, but back here in the bush there is no way you can make any plan work."

Then we moved up to Grave Camp. [The grave of a man who died en route to the Klondike was found at this site.] We had gained a little elevation and were getting into the bunchgrass country, so our horses fared better. Next morning we continued up to Sifton Pass where we stayed for several days. This was a good camp and had the best horse feed that we'd had for quite a while. The weather changed for the better, and some bare patches of ground began to show.

When they arrived in camp the Dudes were short two dogs. They had brought three dogs with them. One was a female mongrel collie they had picked up at the Halfway reserve. She had one front foot off, but Mrs Bedaux felt so sorry for it that she had to take it along. The other two were black Scottish Terriers, little long-haired fellows who had a difficult time through the snow and mud. Tommy Wilde, who had been detailed to do the cooking for the cowboy members of the expedition since leaving

Whitewater, arrived in camp ahead of us and said he'd ride back down the trail to see if he could find the dogs. When he passed me he said, "Lend me your gun, I might see something to shoot at." He never found the dogs, but did shoot a moose on his way back to camp. When he returned to camp he got busy with his cooking and we went back for the moose. We were all happy to have fresh meat.

The next morning, Jack MacDougall and Bill Pickell were sent back down the trail to round up the dogs. They found them at the last campsite. Jack said later, "You know, those buggers didn't talk my language and wouldn't let us anywhere near them."

Bill nearly laughed his head off watching Jack crawl around under the small spruce trees with his chaps on, holding a piece of bannock out to the dogs and calling, "Here puppy, here puppy."

Then it was Bill's turn. They finally caught them and had to lead them back at the end of their saddle ropes. By the time they were pulled through all the mud holes they were a sorry-looking sight.

Jack said, "When we got near camp we had to hunt up a good-sized puddle and pull them back and forth a few times to clean them up a bit." But the Dudes were glad to get their pooches back again.

Floyd Crosby got busy catching up on his movie scenes. He wanted to complete the scene that Tommy, Cecil and I did at Bedaux Pass, where Tommy left our night herding scene and went galloping into camp to warn about the fire. Tommy was to come right up to Bedaux's tent shouting "Fire!" He had to have the same horse and wear the same coat. Bedaux put a pyjama top over his shirt, and was to stick his head out of the tent, sniff the air, and sound the alarm. The camp attendants were to dash around, start taking down the tents, and get things packed up to vacate camp. Getting the packs on the horses had been staged at Champagne Meadows.

Floyd wanted us to buck a few horses for the movies, but I said, "Nothing doing, we are too far back in the bush for that sort of thing."

Hardluck Hank thought he'd like to perform on a bronc.

Tommy Wilde said, "You stay out of this. With your kind of luck, we'll be taking you out on a stretcher."

We rigged a dummy bronc by using a big dunnage bag with a saddle strapped on. Suspended by ropes to four different trees, and with a man on each rope, you could make that thing buck as bad as any bronc. The next scene was to depict cowboys at play. Some were to ride this dummy bronc and some were to get bucked off. Tommy, the cook, was to come up and make fun of us. He had his spurs and chaps on, a white apron, and a big white chef's hat. We were to sneak out and bring in a real bronc

Josephine Daly riding the dummy bronc. BC Archives C-08431.

and say, "OK, Cookie, making fun of us. Let's see what you can do."

Einar Westergaard and I were the pick-up men. We had seen a horse we called Frank buck pretty good. When Tommy got on, Frank made several good jumps, then ran, going under a big spruce. The dry limbs brought blood to Tommy's face. When we got out into the open to do it again Tommy was willing, but Bedaux noticed the blood and said, "No more of that." That ended the bronc riding.

One night Tommy said, "I'm going to give you boys a treat." He had found some canned tomatoes in the packs. They were supposed to be reserved for the Dude section.

While Tommy was busy in his cook tent, Bedaux picked that time for his tour of inspection. He said to Tommy, "Where did you get the tomatoes?"

"Oh," said Tommy, "we brought them with us," and smiled. Bedaux was satisfied with the answer and didn't say anything more.

Einar and I were out checking the horses that were ranging about two miles north one day. After locating all the horses we were wet to our knees. We came to a big lone spruce in the middle of an open flat. It was dry under the tree, so we got a fire going to dry out our socks. We were sitting there eating our lunch and enjoying life. The tree was heavily limbed with branches close to the ground. We kept breaking off branches and feeding the fire when suddenly the fire went up the trunk of the tree with such a roar, as if you'd thrown a pail of gasoline at it. We had to grab our socks and rubbers and step out into the snow. When the whole tree got ablaze, it was quite a sight, flames roaring up the tree and smoke billowing off into the sky. We stood and watched it awhile, then put on our still-wet socks and hiked back to camp.

We told Floyd about it and he said he should have been there with his camera. He said, "I want you two to find two trees and set them up for tonight." When it got dark we set fire to them. It made quite a sight in the dark night, the glowing cones falling against the dark sky. They used several hundred feet of film with their two cameras. Floyd said it would come out on the film as a big forest fire.

We staged other scenes at this camp before it was time to move on. A few more cases of foot rot developed here. It was hard to do away with those horses after they had worked so hard all summer.

We travelled north through Sifton Pass. As I was leading our string Smoky started snorting and sniffing the trail. I looked down and saw tracks of a big grizzly bear. It had stepped into the trail and was going ahead of us. I took my rifle out of the scabbard, made sure I had enough shells, and carried the gun across my saddle. Grizzlies are very unpredictable and I was worried about Bruce Bocock who wasn't too far ahead, walking behind a section of pack horses. I got word back to my partner, Bob, to be on the lookout for some company. The bear followed the trail for quite a distance, then stepped off into the snow for a while, and then headed west into thicker bush.

After leaving Sifton Pass we hit the Driftpile River, following it down several miles before we made camp. This river runs into the Kechika, a tributary of the Liard River. Our camp on the Driftpile was in the line of travel that the trappers would take, trapping north of here. They were a rugged lot. One fellow, originally a cowboy from Texas, George Myers, I got to know and trailed with later. We laid over a few days at this camp. Swannell and Al Phipps climbed some mountains to tie in their triangulation survey.

Bedaux held a big conference one evening to talk things over and decide whether to continue or turn back. Bedaux had picked up two Indian guides in Whitewater, Jack Stone and Joe Poole. Joe Poole was out of his country after coming through Sifton Pass. He said, "I guess me get lost that country," pointing north. "Me go back now."

Jack Stone knew a little about this area and agreed to go two more days. He said, "Maybe, pretty soon lots of snow come."

Bedaux asked how many of us knew how to make snowshoes. Most of the packers had run traplines so they were no strangers to making and using snowshoes. We were all anxious to continue on, but we couldn't overlook the fact that if winter did set in early it would create a tremendous problem of getting the three ladies out to civilization for we were still over 200 miles from our destination at Telegraph Creek. Now, if and when we got to Telegraph Creek, the river would be frozen and it would mean an

Movie Stars at Sifton Pass

Floyd got busy arranging a scene that was to depict the failure of the expedition. The first thing was to choose the setting. Floyd settled on a place a short distance from camp where there were some low sandy ridges with a few windfall and scattered stunted pine. This was to show the expedition on its last legs. We were all to come walking out through the ridges with big packs on our backs. First came the Dudes, all carrying various-sized packs, followed by the cooks with their pots and pans hanging from their packs. Next were the camp attendants with great big packs; the surveyors with their instruments; and finally the cowboy packers with packs on their backs, leading the thinnest horses in the outfit with big packs. It was quite a decrepit-looking outfit wending its way through the sticks and helping each other over the larger windfalls, most of us having big walking sticks. Floyd wound up taking several camp scenes, using up quite a few flares.

BC Archives G-02703.

In his diary Willard Freer also described the filming the cowboys did for Floyd Crosby:

September 29 – We did not move today. We are working for the movies. We are all movie stars now.

September 30 – We are having forest fires, the camp burning and everybody leaving in a hurry, horses stampeding with the packs and I don't know what. It snowed last night. The wild west pictures!

additional trek of 100 miles or more to the ocean. A decision was made to continue on and try to get through.

When Bedaux was asked by people about the feasibility of the expedition he would always answer, "I'm a man who likes to do the impossible." I think most of us realized there was an element of risk involved and that we might get stranded someplace. Nevertheless we were happy that they had decided to continue, although there were a few who wondered whether he wasn't stretching his luck to keep going so late in the season.

We wrangled the horses early the next morning expecting to pack up and start north, but found two more horses crippled with foot rot. When word got around they called another meeting and weren't too long in deciding that it wouldn't be advisable to continue. There were a lot of long faces in camp that morning for we were disappointed in having to turn back from here. It was Bedaux's responsibility. As he said, we had lost several horses recently and could lose more in the days ahead. On September 30 they definitely decided to call the trip off and start back south.

One of the two crippled horses was a nice little brown gelding called Brownie that Madame Chiesa rode. Madame Chiesa was a friendly person, and we had got to know her quite well, for Bob and I packed the Dude beds and dunnage on our string. She came to us and wanted to know if there was anything she could do. "You know," she said, "I could make a poultice and put it on the horse's foot." To humour her we helped tie a poultice on, but it didn't do much good.

Frank Swannell went to Bedaux and begged to let him go through to Dease Lake. Frank said, "Give me Bill Blackman, Jack MacDougall and Bob White as packers, Henry Blackman as cook, and Al Phipps, my assistant. He said, "I'm sure we can get through and I would very much like to complete this work."

Bedaux said, "No, if I don't go through, nobody goes through."

Frank was really put out. It was a glum camp the rest of the day.

Toward evening I was chopping wood when Bedaux came over to me and said, "Let's sit down. I want to talk to you." He said, "What are you going to do this winter when you get out?"

I said, "I guess we'll go out on our trapline for the winter."

He said, "How often will you get your mail?"

I said, "In the spring when we come out."

He said, "You know, you are in this movie film and we have picked out five of you boys: Bill Blackman, Tommy Wilde, Jack MacDougall, Edgar Dopp, and you; and if things work out, you will all go to France and help complete the picture there. You will take your saddle and riding outfit with you, and we'll tie the picture in with some professional actors. We won't know anything definite until Christmas."

I asked him about horses and he said, "We'll use those two I took over in 1932." Bedaux had taken a hunting trip to the Prophet River country in 1932 and at the end of the trip bought two horses, a steeldust and a buckskin. They had cost him quite a bit of money before he landed them in France. He said to me, "We'll use them and if we need more we'll ship some over."

Bedaux said to me, "I want you to keep this quiet. Only you five will know for the time being, and there's a chance that Bill Pickell will be asked to go. We should be able to let you know one way or the other by Christmas."

I said, "It sure sounds good to me. In that case I won't go out to our regular trapline, which is over 100 miles north of Hudson Hope. I'll trap around Hudson Hope where I can get my mail every week."

Then Bedaux went on to say that he intended establishing a location out in the Sustut River country, which is on the Pacific watershed near the headwaters of the Skeena River. He asked me if I knew anything about that part of the country. I said that I'd never been out there but had heard it was a very deep snow country and hard to get in and out of in winter. He said, "We'll raise horses and cattle, and if we can't trail the cattle out, we'll build a canning factory and can the meat there. We'll set up school for the families that might be working there." He said he liked the way I handled horses, and I could have the job of looking after them. I thought, what a pipe dream! But he was to make a start at developing the location in 1935, and I was to be a part of the action in 1936. More about that later.

The next morning we packed up and disposed of the two horses when we were ready to leave. Floyd took pictures before and after the shooting. I was sorry to see little Brownie go. We made camp that night back at Sifton Pass and stopped there for two days to work on the movies.

Floyd was a likeable chap and nobody minded doing anything for him. One time we were having a poker game in our tent when he sneaked up and put a smoke bomb under our tent, then had the camera ready to get pictures of the commotion he had caused.

After Sifton Pass we moved south to a camp at Fox Lake. From there we travelled to Fox Pass where we laid over for a day. Then we moved down to Fort Ware, making one camp on the way. A lot of the snow had melted, but the muskeg stretches were wetter than ever.

At Fort Ware Bedaux intended getting enough trappers and boats to take the outfit downriver. He also had the idea that he would arrange a horse sale and sell off as many horses as he could, preferably the poorer ones. Bedaux had Balourdet make some branding irons in the form of Roman numerals, and we hoof-branded all the horses with numbers.

There was only a few days' notice for the sale so there weren't many buyers. Bedaux tried to sell the poorer horses to the Indians, but they wanted the good ones. The few trappers around weren't interested in horses so late in the season, so only one or two were sold.

One night Bedaux broke out a few bottles of rum and had a bit of a party along with singing a few songs. Some of us ended up at the Indian chief's cabin half a mile downriver where he lived with his wife and three teenage daughters in a nice log cabin. They had a phonograph and we taught the ladies how to square dance. The mother did well, but when the girls got mixed up they would say, "That dance crazy," and go sit down. When the dance was over we would sit on our heels along the log wall.

Hardluck Hank was wearing a new pair of pants he had bought at the Hudson's Bay store. They were Indian trade goods and not too substantial. When Hank went to slide down the wall and sit on his heels his pants hooked on a knot and ripped a gaping hole in his seat. We were all feeling pretty good for one of the boys had got hold of a bottle of rum, so we asked the chief's wife if she would sew up the hole if we laid Hank on the bed. "Sure, I sew him," she said, but Hank beat us to it and headed back to camp.

The chief was a nice old fellow and offered his oldest daughter, who was about 17, to Cecil Pickell and said, "You marry my daughter, I make you chief."

On our walk back to camp we finished the last of the rum and none of us was feeling any pain. I had trailed with Jack MacDougall quite a bit and never saw him feeling as good as he was that night. He had a good voice and could let out some great wolf howls. When we got near camp Jack said, "I'm going up the hill to the Indian cemetery, that's where the wolves howl." Bill Pickell and I went along to help him serenade the stars with some God-awful wolf howls. The Dudes complained about wolves keeping them awake most of the night. If they ever found out who it was, they never complained to us.

During our days at Fort Ware we found time to have a bath, get our washing done and do some mending on our clothes. Jack Bocock, Big John Chisholm, Floyd Crosby and Everett Withrow were the only ones to let their whiskers grow. The rest of us shaved as regularly as we could.

The River Return to Fort St John
(October 8–21)

At Fort Ware Bedaux had spread word to any trapper along the river who wanted a job with his boat. He decided that the main party would wait for boats to arrive while the horses were to be taken downriver and turned loose at Police Meadows just out of Fort Grahame. [The Northwest Mounted Police had wintered their horses at this location during construction of the Moodie Trail in 1905–6. This trail was one of the federal government's overland routes to the Yukon.]

We had to cross the Finlay River and go down the west side. We had 16 horses with packs and about 70 that would be driven loose without their nose nets, so they would be off the trail a lot of the time trying to graze. Ernie said to me, "Let's you, Jack, Bob and I take the pack horses. We know what it's like to drive loose horses down the trail, especially as hungry as ours are." We said it suited us. Some of the boys thought that it would be a cinch driving loose horses, but they found out different.

Jack, Edgar and I were having a smoke and talking when Floyd came over and said, "Which one of you is going to swim the river ahead of the horses tomorrow morning?" Jack was the best waterman and I think Edgar was the hardiest, but none of us was fussy about the job, so Floyd said, "We'll draw straws," and I got elected. We went over to the river bank and Jack pointed out where I could get across most of the way before we would have to swim, and that would only be a short piece.

The next morning we had trouble finding all our horses. There wasn't much grass left and they had scattered all over. We found all but one, a grey horse called Chief, so we decided to leave without him.

The packs and saddles were taken across by boat and Henry Blackman, our cook, got a fire going so he could give us lunch before we hit the trail.

When we got ready to cross the river I took off my underwear, got the horses lined out behind and crossed the Finlay without too long a swim. It sure was wet and cold. After getting our 16 horses packed Jack, Ernie, Bob, Henry and I got started down the trail. We had a good day's travel and a nice camp along the river. The loose horses came into camp shortly after us. The boys reported quite a day, for the horses wanted to graze off the trail so the riders spent a lot of time off the trail jungling through the bush. Hank and Bill Pickell were at the tail end.

Hank had quite a temper, and he lost his hat so often going through the trees he began cussing it and said, "If you son-of-a-b—— go off again, you can just stay there!" When it went off again, Hank told it to stay there in no uncertain terms and rode on without it.

Bill happened to see it all. He slipped in, picked up the hat, and rolled it up in his coat on the back of his saddle. Bill laughed when he asked Hank where his hat was.

Hank said, "It wouldn't stay on, the son-of-a-b—— is back along the trail." Bill didn't give his hat back to him until the next day.

Bill and I went down the trail looking for horses the next morning and we found one bunch, but a few had gone further on, so we both went after them and found the animals. I said to Bill, "You take these on in while I get the others."

The bells seemed to be getting further away. When I got to the place where we had seen the horses the bells were still quite a ways off. I started running and getting nearer when I heard shouting and swearing. I knew it was Hank. He had found the horses and was taking them into camp, except he was going in the opposite direction. I asked him where he thought he was going with the horses. He said, "Where do you suppose? Back to camp."

I said, "Where is camp from here?" He pointed in the direction he had been going. I said, "It's back behind us, and you're quite a distance from it." Hank finally admitted being a little mixed up in his direction.

We got the horses back to camp. This camp was used by the river boats, and there were pieces of board lying around. Bob Godberson had the misfortune to run a spike into his foot, so he was hobbling around camp.

After gathering the horses we had lots of help to get packed up. We started down the trail ahead of the loose horses and had a good dry trail most of the way. That night we made camp on the river bank opposite Del Miller's cache where we intended swimming the horses across in the morning. (Del Miller was an old-time trapper on the Finlay River.) We were all enjoying this part of our trip – good camp, good weather, a good bunch of boys, good cook and the best of grub.

Cowboys at Del Miller's cache. On the roof (left to right): Art MacLean, Cecil Pickell and Bob White; Bill Pickell in the cache; and in front (left to right): Jack MacDougall, Einar Westergaard, Bob Beattie, Henry Philpott, Ernie Peterson and Willard Freer.
BC Archives G-02706.

The boats were to come down and help us across in the morning but they didn't show up, so we built a raft. After we got one load across the boats came around the bend, so we had lots of help to get the saddles and packs across. We rounded up the horses (our count now stood at 99) and drove them into the river, and they swam across without any trouble. We laid over the rest of the day and the horses had lots of grass to graze on.

Bob's foot was pretty sore so he went with the boats. They were to go down and camp above Deserter's Canyon. With all the heavy growth of grass the horses didn't wander far, so we had no trouble getting them rounded up.

Ernie Peterson and I decided we would ride a new horse this morning. Until now, Ernie and I were the only ones still riding the same horse we started out with. They were getting trail weary so we thought we'd give them a rest. Ernie's horse, Friday, was a raw-boned bay with a crooked blaze down its face and one china eye, rather homely to look at, but he and Ernie got along well all summer, while my horse, Smoky, was everything you needed in a good saddle horse. Ernie picked a fair-sized bay called Shorty that came from the Stan Clarke ranch. He was a good horse and had been ridden some during the summer. I picked a bay with a narrow blaze who was one of the Frank Wolf string. Frank was a noted horseman who shipped a bunch of horses up from the Brooks area of southern Alberta, and we had seven or eight in our outfit. The horse hadn't been ridden all summer, but we thought he was broke to ride. He had a good saddle back, turned out to be well broke, and was about the easiest-gaited horse I had ever ridden. But we were only to ride these horses for another three days.

We had good travelling down the east side of the Finlay, crossing several creeks coming in from the east, and made camp after crossing the Akie River, a fair-sized stream coming out of the mountains to the east. Einar Westergaard had an unwanted bath while crossing one of the river channels. He went to head some horses off when his horse dropped into a deep hole and went right out of sight. Einar came out of that cold water with a big grin on his face.

Alex Pierre, a French trapper, had a log cabin on a nice flat near where the Akie runs into the Finlay. He had married a native woman and had a nice family. Alex came to our camp and invited us over to their house. He could really play the fiddle so we did a little square dancing and had a real good time. Their boy, Billy, who was about 15 years old, had arrived home a few days before, having run away from a mission school. He had come back 200 miles on his own with no blankets and only the grub he could get along the way. I said that it must have been a tough trip.

Billy said, "Yes. Long way, but me want to come home."

Alex was busy whipsawing enough lumber for a new house. He had quite a pile finished and said he just needed a few more. He had built a stand about seven feet high. He would square the log with the saw, then cut off the boards. It was some job, with one man on top to follow the line while the other person (usually one of his boys) was underneath. They would pull and push that long saw up and down until they got to the end of the log. Alex said, "I'm getting tired of the job." I was through there two years later and he still hadn't started building the house.

The grass was good here too, so we had no trouble rounding up the horses in the morning. We had a good dry trail most of the way and a fairly short day, making camp above Deserter's Canyon on a level up from the river. We turned the horses loose to graze on the grassy mountain side.

The boats were camped on the west side of the river above the canyon. They intended getting movie pictures of the boats going through the canyon. For years the early trappers and traders considered it to be impassable by boat. With better boats and engines people were now running the canyon quite regularly. Bob Fry, at 72 years of age the oldest trapper on the river, and considered the most experienced boatman, was given the privilege of taking the Dude boat through. Floyd was to follow with his camera set up in another boat and try to get pictures of the entire trip through the canyon.

Going down the Finlay River. Bob White is in the middle facing the camera and holding up a frying pan. BC Archives G-03418.

Bob must have been a bit excited with his boat full of Dudes, for when he got to the chutes between the rocks he got too close to the big rock and slid partway into the well below the rock. The boat shipped some water, splashed and soaked some of the passengers and gave them quite a scare. But there was no serious damage and Floyd got some very good pictures.

Since we had our horses on better grass and we were a little bit of our own boss we hadn't been getting out as early in the morning. This morning, while looking for horses on the mountainside, we took our time. We thought we might see the boats go through the canyon below us. I had my camera, so Cecil Pickell and I climbed further up the mountain and got a good view of the canyon area. We saw some boats enter the canyon, then lost sight of them as they entered the gorge. While climbing the mountain Cec and I remarked to each other how short of wind we were getting from smoking too many tailor-made cigarettes. We were all issued sealed cans of 50 Lucky Strike cigarettes every so often, and when one of us wasn't passing a can around, the other fellow was. We ended up smoking too much, and sure noticed it running after horses.

Later that day we found out that we wouldn't have to run after those horses anymore, for we were to turn them loose. We thought that another day's travel would get them nearer to Fort Grahame, but when we angled down the mountainside below the canyon the boats were tied up along the bank. They called us in and said they had decided to load all our saddles and packs on the boats. They were going to turn the horses loose here for they thought they would drift downriver on their own to where the better feed was located. We had to catch all the horses and take the shoes off those that had any left on. We had lost a lot of shoes floundering through the muskegs. The bells were left on the horses. Several of us packers were sorry to see the last of the horses. We had a few misfits in the bunch but on the whole they were a pretty good lot of horses. Of the 99 head turned loose here only 34 would survive the winter. The sad part was that there was no need for the loss.

Henry Blackman had been our cook since leaving Whitewater and Tommy Wilde had been cooking for the Dude outfit. We had been living high on the hog for there was no need to go easy on the grub so near to the end. After a good midday meal everyone got busy and carried the packs and saddles down the bank to the boats. There were six boatloads. Bedaux intended storing the bulk of the equipment at Fort Grahame.

At the foot of Deserter's Canyon the valley was quite narrow. Ben Cork, a trapper, had a log cabin on the river bank just where we were camped. He had lost a leg in the First World War but could navigate quite well on snowshoes with his wooden leg. He had the reputation of being hard to get along with, so he lived alone. The Indians going up and down the river used his cabin as a stopping place in the winter when travelling was tough. Ben got tired of having them there, so one winter's night, with the Indian bucks and squaws rolled in their blankets on the floor, Ben stomped over to his bunk, doing some cussing, took off his pants, jerked at his wooden leg, unhooked it, and threw it into the wood box. Then he jerked at his head as if he intended to unhook it. The Indians were watching all the while. Then he blew out the lamp and rolled into his bunk. The Indians still went by but never stopped. They said, "I guess that man, he crazy."

When I packed up there two years later I got to know Ben. How he stuck it out along there I don't know. He set up a trading post there a year or so later. When they put the W.A.C. Bennett Dam on the Peace River it backed up the water to Ben's place and it flooded out the site of Fort Grahame.

It was now the middle of October. The weather had been holding good but was threatening to change, so winter could set in any time. We finally got everything loaded in the boats and were ready for our run down the river to Fort Grahame. The men running the boats were: Bob Fry, Del Miller and his son Don, trappers on the upper Finlay; Shorty Webber, a trapper on the Ingenika River; and Art Van Somers and Carl Davidson, boatmen from Prince George. Carl had freighted in the supplies to Fort Ware for Bedaux.

Bob Fry was the lead boat and the rest were to follow. Art took us cowboys. We enjoyed the ride but it was cold on the river. Poor old Bob Fry got himself into a bind. He underestimated the depth of water in a cut-off back channel and he had to tip his kicker up and pole over the gravel bar. One boat followed but the others went around. When he got into good water Bob started the kicker and away he went only to run out of gas. He had to drift with the stream while he filled his tank. Art was right behind and drove around Bob. We started yelling for Bob to get that tub out of the way, and did he want a tow. Bedaux didn't appreciate it too much. Bob finally got going and had no more trouble.

When we rounded the bend in the river and came in sight of the few log buildings that made up the post of Fort Grahame the river was fairly wide. We got a race going. Bob Fry had the edge for a while. Then Art pulled up. We were waving our hats and cheering Art on. Some of us had our legs over the side spurring hell out of the boat. We all came into the landing with a roar about the same time. They were all experienced river men and all in good spirits.

We got busy unloading the boats, carrying everything up the bank. We stored the saddles and pack equipment in a log building belonging to the Hudson's Bay. The only white inhabitants in Fort Grahame were the factor, Larry Kemple, and his young wife, and another old chap, a retired factor who was content to live there in a neat little log cabin. It was a chilly night so we got big fires going in front of our tents.

King Gething had arrived from Hudson Hope with the mail boat and a few passengers. Bedaux pulled the cork on a couple bottles of rum so we had quite a lively time that night. There was a lot of good fellowship among us. We all knew it wouldn't be long until we would be going our different ways.

Floyd was busy that afternoon getting last-minute pictures. We would be doing something around camp like chopping wood or wrestling around and we could hear his camera buzzing. I would give a lot to see some of these pictures now.

The plan arrived at that night was that Jack Bocock would start down-river in the morning with the cowboys in Art Van Somers' boat to make arrangements in Hudson Hope for a big banquet. The rest of the crew would follow at a more leisurely pace.

Hardluck Hank took a fancy to a black and white dog an Indian had at Fort Grahame. The Indian wanted 40 dollars for it and Hank had only 15. He went around trying to borrow 25 dollars but everyone turned him down. He got to me. I tried to talk him out of it, but he really wanted that dog for a pack dog to take to his trapline that winter. None of us had much money on us but I knew I could get more in Hudson Hope. I felt a bit sorry for Hank, for everybody seemed to pick on him, not that he didn't deserve a lot of it. "Sure," I said, "Hank, I'll give you the 25 dollars."

Then he had more troubles. A dog that has been tied up all summer stinks like the very devil. When we got on the boat Hank had to sit with his dog. Art Van Somers, the boat driver, said, "Get that stinking thing away from me!" We didn't want that pair anywhere near us, so he had to pick a place among the bed rolls and ride there alone with his dog.

Some of the boys said I'd never get my money, but the first thing Hank did when he got to Hudson Hope was to rustle some money and pay me back. He got home with his dog and got good use of him on his trapline that winter. A few years later he got married and started a ranch on the upper Halfway River. He took his last ride a few years ago.

The six boats travelling downriver were to go down to Rocky Mountain portage and then bring a load of oats back to Fort Grahame. They expected to get most of these oats from the Jim Beattie Ranch at 20 Mile (20 miles up from Rocky Mountain Portage and 40 miles from Hudson Hope), and some from the Turner farm near Hudson Hope.

The boatmen had a tough trip back upriver. It was a slow trip going upstream against the current. The weather turned cold and they had to contend with ice. Some nights the men had to break ice to get into shore to make camp. I don't think there is a colder job than driving one of those river boats that late in the season, but that 72-year-old Bob Fry took it all in stride. The men were glad to end their trip at Fort Grahame where they unloaded the oats and went their different ways, some to their traplines for the winter.

The oats were stored in Fort Grahame to be rationed out to the horses when needed. Bob Beattie and Carl Davidson were to have dog teams and keep track of them. However, the horses scattered up and down the valley and some followed up the creeks to the east where many got trapped by deep snow. There was lots of grass at Police Meadows above Fort Grahame and with a ration of grain toward spring the horses had a good chance of surviving the winter.

We put on all the clothes we had, as well as our chaps, piled into the boat, and left Fort Grahame behind. It would have been a nice trip if it hadn't been so cold. We made about 40 miles downriver, then pulled ashore to have a bite of lunch. We got a good fire going on the gravel bar. This was Pete Toy's Bar where quite a bit of gold had been panned out over the years.

After getting the chill out of our bones we climbed aboard and continued down the crooked Finlay past a dead-water section of the river that

Homesteaders on the Upper Peace River

We knew most of the trappers in this area for they outfitted in Hudson Hope. Leo Rutledge trapped on the Clearwater that enters the Peace River from the south above the rapids. Fred Chapman and Bill Kruger trapped the west side of the Ottertail, which comes in from the north below the rapids. Dick Hamilton and Stanley Wallace had a cabin on Henderson Creek and trapped the east side of the Ottertail. Further down the Peace on the north side, Bill Mahaffey, a white-bearded Englishman, trapped on Schooler Creek in winter and panned for gold there in the summer.

Further down on the north side was the Jack Adams place, now abandoned. Jack, an early trapper and able axe man and his wife, Lucille, first located at Finlay Forks. Lucille had been an actress and spent a number of years on the stage. From Finlay Forks they moved down the river to Adams Creek, 50 miles upriver from Hudson Hope, where they built an elaborate log house. Jack passed away and Lucille went out to Victoria but would still make the periodic trip back to the country she loved.

Charlie and Madge Jones lived at the mouth of the Carbon River on the south side of the Peace.

Below the Adams cabin was Jim Beattie's Twenty Mile Ranch. Jim, one of the pioneer settlers of the Hudson Hope area, married in 1914 and settled at Twenty Mile. He and his wife, Elizabeth, raised a family of eight children as well as building up a wonderful ranch. Jim also developed another place eight miles downriver on Twelve Mile Creek that took in over a section of choice river bottom land. In the early 1930s Jim built a new log house on the home place, 40 feet square, with big logs hewed inside and out. Jim passed away before BC Hydro bought all the land that would be flooded. It was a real heartbreak for Mrs Beattie to see them put the torch to the buildings they had worked so hard to construct. All you see now is a big lake where those nice places had been.

Charles and Fern Bedaux visited the Beattie family on their 1932 hunting trip and the expedition stopped at the Beattie Ranch for a meal.
LAC PA173988.

was always the first to freeze over. We reached Finlay Forks, where the Parsnip River from the south joins the Finlay to become the Peace River, which flows east through the main range of the Rocky Mountains. A few miles down the Peace the river tumbles down the Finlay rapids. After their near tragedy in Deserter's Canyon Bedaux gave orders for all personnel to walk down, and only the bowman and driver were to run the rapid. It is a pretty wild-looking rapid, but those that are used to it go up and down without much trouble. We proceeded another 10 miles and made camp at the mouth of the Wicked River.

Buck Buchanan had a trap cabin here for this was his registered trapping area, but he summered in Prince George and hadn't come out to his line yet. We rolled out our bedrolls on the ground and pulled a tarp over us to keep the frost off. Henry did his cooking in the cabin. As a token of appreciation he left some items of food, including some vinegar in a Hudson's Bay rum bottle.

The next night King Gething camped there with his passengers on his way downriver. When he saw the bottle King said, "That's sure mighty nice of the boys to leave us a drink." He poured drinks and went to drink a toast to the Bedaux crew, but was terribly disappointed to find it was vinegar.

We awoke to a cloudy, frosty morning, and it was still chilly when we put on our chaps and climbed into the boat. For the first 10 miles we travelled between very high mountains. Then the valley widened out, although it was still mountainous until we got to the portage above Hudson Hope. About 45 miles below Finlay Forks we came to the Ne Parle Pas rapids. We unloaded there and walked down. The boat had no trouble going down for the water was at a good stage to run the rapids.

After the Ne Parle Pas rapids we went around a few more bends in the river before stopping for lunch and building a fire on a gravel bar. We were glad to get out, stretch our legs and get warmed up. Late in the afternoon we landed at the Portage cabin where we unloaded all our goods. Then we made up some backpacks with blankets and whatever we needed for the night and got started on our 18-mile hike over the portage to Hudson Hope. We were to get a team and wagon in the Hope the next morning to come over and get the tents and the rest of the stuff.

Our packs got pretty heavy by the time we reached Hudson Hope late that night. But those of us from the Hope were glad to see our friends. We spent the next day getting cleaned up and doing some washing.

In the afternoon we got a baseball game going. The next day, when the boatmen arrived, the cowboys challenged the boatmen to a ball game. It was a real good game with lots of cheering for both sides, with the cowboys finally edging out the boatmen.

Jack Bocock got busy making arrangements with Bob Ferguson, who owned the log hotel here, for a big banquet. The main party arrived and the banquet turned out to be one of the biggest celebrations Hudson Hope ever had. Bedaux still had some rum left, and had a rum punch mixed up, which was passed around with caviar and toast as an appetizer, not that there was anything wrong with our appetites. There were several toasts proposed. Big John Chisholm proposed a toast to all concerned and wound up saying, "Let's give a cheer the like that Hudson Hope has never heard before and maybe never hear again." Believe me, it must have been heard all over the settlement. We really enjoyed that good roast beef from the Joe Turner farm and the fresh vegetables from the gardens, a welcome change from the canned goods, macaroni and rice we had been living on all summer. The meal finished with real homemade ice cream and pie, making it a meal to remember.

Bedaux took a fancy to two boatmen, Art Van Somers and Donald Miller, both experienced river men. He offered them a job as boatmen on the Congo River in central Africa. The boys would have liked to have the job, but they thought it was a little too far from home. Bedaux also reminded the five of us about the trip to France to work on the movie. He said he would let us know one way or the other by Christmas. Jack Bocock and Al Phipps were both kept on as Bedaux employees. Jack went over to South Africa and spent more than 40 years associated with the gold and diamond mines there. Al didn't like the set up over there so he resigned and came back to Victoria.

It turned cold that night and started to rain. Next morning was cold and wet. Bob Godberson and I decided we would go downriver with the Fort St John boys. The cowboys who came down to Fort St John were: Ernie Peterson, Art McLean and Tommy Wilde who lived at North Pine; Bill and Cecil Pickell from Fort St John; Hank Philpott, who had a place at Montney; Edgar Dopp from Cache Creek; and Einar Westergaard from the upper Halfway. We were to ride in an open boat with only a few pack manties [canvas covers] to try and keep the rain off. The Dude boat had a tent put up on it, which would keep them dry. We packed all the Dude luggage down and loaded it on the boats.

It was a cold trip down the Peace 60 miles to Taylor Flats. There the Dudes were to catch some trucks that would take them out to Dawson Creek where they would catch the train to Edmonton.

Those that were to go out on the train from Dawson Creek were: Charles E. Bedaux, Mrs Fern Bedaux, Madame Chiesa, Josephine Daly, Jack Bocock, John Chisholm and Balourdet. From Edmonton they were to continue to New York. They were to see the uncut film there and they said there were some wonderful pictures. That was all we ever heard of that film, although there have been several attempts to track it down.

[About a month after the end of the Bedaux Expedition Bob White received a letter from Bedaux telling him the filming had been postponed. Bedaux tried to sell the footage to Hollywood film companies, but not surprisingly, no one was interested in making a movie of the expedition. The original footage was stored in France and located in the late 1980s, after Bob White died. Most of it was damaged, but the surviving sections were copied and are now housed at Library and Archives Canada.]

Frank Swannell, Al Phipps and Ernest Lamarque were to go out to Victoria. Bruce Bocock was to stay in Edmonton. Bill and Henry Blackman were to go to McBride. Floyd Crosby and Everett Withrow went to New York with Bedaux, then back to Los Angeles.

It was a wet miserable afternoon when we shook hands all around and bid each other goodbye. It had been an interesting summer: some tough times, but also some good ones, and we had made many life-long friends. We got four dollars a day straight time all summer, which was more than we could have got outside in those years, and we sure had no place to spend it.

We managed to get a cup of coffee and warmed up some at Howard Feeney's at Taylor. Then we found a truck to run us up to Fort St John. We had some trouble getting up the Peace hill, for that gumbo mud gets pretty sticky when it gets wet.

Bob Godberson and I spent several days with friends in Fort St John, then walked back the 60 miles to Hudson Hope.

Part Two:
Empire Ranch

Bedaux's Empire Ranch

Jay Sherwood

On the return trip down the Finlay River, Charles Bedaux began plans for the development of a ranch in the northern BC wilderness. He hired Bob Beattie, the head packer on his 1932 and 1934 trips, along with Carl Davidson, one of the boatmen. In his instructions to Carl Davidson, Bedaux listed his criteria for the ranch.

> Specifications for ground to be located for ranch purposes within space marked on map and tinted in red.

- Pacific waters.
- Salmon run.
- Open tops flattened out (such as Caribou flat).
- Winter range capable to accommodate 100 head.
- 200 acres capable of giving good results in cultivation (oats).
- Mineral possibilities within 50 miles.
- Good country for big game within 3 days pack train.
- Suitability to access through Hazelton.
- Near good timber for building.
- Fair trapping through purchase or sharing an existing line.

Bedaux also had specifications for the location of his future lodge:

- Good view over large open territory.
- Running good spring or creek water not spoiled by salmon & susceptible of being piped to house.
- Near to a waterfall if possible (for future power).
- Plentiful wood near at hand for fires (could haul 1 mile).
- Good shelter from hard wind.
- Dry ground.
- Gravel nearby for concrete.

In a letter to Carl Davidson, dated December 10, 1934, Bedaux stipulated his terms of employment:

From October 20th you have been receiving and will continue to receive a salary of $90.00 per month, payable at the Royal Bank, Prince George. Your food is paid for by me for one year beginning October 20th. After that date you will be expected to be settled enough to provide your own food without change in salary.

All the buildings you will put up while employed by me will be my own property, as well as all improvements you will make on the land. To facilitate purchase, if the land is purchased, you will be authorized to make the purchase in your name but after purchase has been effected, you will transfer the title to me.

All the live stock we now have and that we will acquire in the future will also remain our property. If a trapline is purchased, it may be purchased in your name but it will have to be transferred afterwards to me and I will be the owner of all furs you catch.

I am putting these hard conditions down only to remain business-like, but you may be sure that if things work out well, I will prove generous enough to give you a happy life and entire satisfaction.

Although Bedaux wanted a wilderness ranch he also wanted relatively easy access to the place. He envisaged a location that could be reached from the railroad station at Hazelton on the Skeena River. From Hazelton Bedaux wanted to travel up the Skeena by boat as far as possible and then by pack train no more than a few days to the location of his ranch. He had particularly fond memories of the area around the Sustut River, a tributary of the Skeena, that he had visited during the 1926 hunting trip.

Carl Davidson. Carl Davidson family collection.

From the beginning Bedaux's proposed ranch encountered difficulties. Although Davidson and Beattie were competent men in the outdoors, they had no experience in developing a ranch and they had limited skills in handling finances. There was no action plan for the two men to follow. Bob Beattie lived in Hudson Hope while Carl Davidson resided in Prince George so there was limited communication between the two men, and there was no division of duties. Bedaux's criteria for the ranch were not very practical. Although he was wealthy and had spent $250,000 on the 1934 expedition Bedaux was reluctant to spend much on the ranch, and he demanded strict financial accountability for all the expenses. Both Beattie and Davidson had families and were reluctant to move to the ranch location until there were suitable accommodations for them. Although he had been to northern BC on three trips, Bedaux did not seem to appreciate the difficulties the men faced, especially since he started the ranch at the beginning of the 1934–35 winter.

Bedaux stored much of his equipment at Fort Grahame, and the horses had been left above Deserter's Canyon in anticipation that they would make it to Police Meadows and spend the winter there. Bedaux ordered feed for the horses and had it shipped up to Fort Grahame during the fall of 1934. Beattie and Davidson's first priority was to ensure that the horses survived the winter.

Bob Beattie.
Floyd Crosby photograph ; LAC PA 171460.

Of the 99 horses Bedaux left for the winter, only 34 survived. In a letter dated April 10, 1935 Bedaux wrote to Carl Davidson, "I know you did the best you could in trying to save the horses, but at the same time we must remember there is an 'empire' somewhere in the circle that I have traced the map for you. I rely on you and Bob Beattie to build up that 'empire' and to take into it whatever we have left of horses and equipment."

In a letter written on May 14 to Beattie and Davidson, Bedaux noted the disagreements that appeared to exist between the two men:

> I ask you here to adjust your differences and to make friends again. You know I want to bring something worthwhile into your country. I have already spent money in that direction and I am prepared to spend more, but I want to see progress. If you fight among yourselves, progress will be prevented and everybody will lose hereby.
>
> I am told that Carl Davidson has gone West to find the location for the ranch we are going to build – this within the circle I have marked for him on the map. As soon as he has found the place and as soon as a good winter range has been discovered close by, I want you to move the horses and all of the equipment we have at Fort Grahame, at Prince George, or at Edmonton at Mr Bruce Bocock's if he still has anything. In other words, I want you to move every animal and every article to the spot that Carl Davidson will have then selected, building of course a cache for those articles which may be perishable.

The next step will be for Carl Davidson and Bob Beattie to start building houses for themselves and families and the step after that will be the building of our house. Carl Davidson has the rough plan and the work can be started. In connection with this you must find your way out via Hazelton and thus locate the easiest route in and out of the place and to the nearest railroad point.

Bedaux ended his letter by reminding Davidson and Beattie to "adjust your differences, make friends. Otherwise I shall become discouraged and give up the whole thing and thousands of dollars which would have found their way into your country will be going elsewhere." In a postscript to the letter Bedaux commented that he was going to spend two months in India and Tibet during the summer of 1935 and use Chinese Tibetans as guides. "We will have a fine chance to compare their qualities with the qualities of the men we had last year."

During the summer of 1935 Davidson and Beattie selected a location along the Sustut River as Bedaux suggested and began work on the ranch. In a letter to Bedaux's secretary from Fort Grahame on September 9, Carl Davidson described what had been accomplished during the summer:

I beg to report that in March I started out on an exploration trip to the site of Mr Bedaux's location. Returning on May 26, 1935, I was obliged to make to trip to Prince George, B.C. because of the unpaid accounts of $450.00 and $564.00. I made another exploration trip in June. After finding a place suitable to Mr Bedaux, we started in packing the outfit and cutting a trail for the expedition from Fort Grahame to transport the supplies required to erect buildings and to cut hay for the winter. The task just mentioned requires the additional help of two men as packers and three men to put up the hay; included among these services is the river freighting.

I wired to Mr Bedaux informing him that further progress required machinery and money.

I have received the machinery, but as yet, I have no word concerning the money.

On September 21, Bob Beattie wrote Bedaux from Hudson Hope explaining his work during the summer:

I came down here on the 18th and am going back today with the equipment that was left here last fall. I have made two trips to the location, one cutting trail with two men, and the other with a load of freight. The location is on the Sustut River about three miles up the river from where Johanson Creek runs in. The land is on gravel, not the best of farming land. There are approximately 40 acres with an average of eight inches of soil which should grow crops. This land in a dry year will have to be irrigated and from a creek running through this can be managed alright. It is out of the question as a range for horses finding their own living during the winter months; as a summer range it is good.

Last winter there were five feet of snow. I made a trip over some of the trail you were on in 1926. As a matter of fact I was to within five miles of McConnell Creek and saw two fair locations on this trail, but these locations would be awfully frosty as they must be 1,000 feet higher than the Sustut location. On my last trip in I saw quite a lot of game – 35 goats, 5 rams, 1 black bear and 2 fresh grizzly tracks – these within a day's ride from the location. The scenery is beautiful and the flats are about two miles long. These flats are long enough and wide enough to allow planes to land if necessary. I am sorry to say we won't be able to get our families in this fall as the buildings are not up. My wife and family are awfully disappointed for they have been packed all summer expecting to go.

Bedaux replied on October 17:

I have seen Bob Beattie's letter to me of September 21st and Carl Davidson's letter to Miss Lubowski of September 5th.

I have checked the location as described by Bob Beattie, i.e., the Sustut River, three miles up from Johanson Creek. It is within the circle I had specified on the map last year and from that angle at least, it should prove satisfactory. Bob Beattie tells me that the scenery is very beautiful and of course my wife and I are very glad of that.

I am still waiting for the complete inventory including tents, horses, equipment, etc., that we left last year either in Hudson Hope or with Bruce Bocock, or sent to Prince George to Carl Davidson. When you can gather the entire list, you will send me a complete copy, showing where everything is.

I notice that Bob Beattie has been breaking a trail to the location so as to move the freight in from Fort Graham. That is very well but I want you to know right now that my wife and I will never go to the Empire location by the way of Fort Graham. We want to go there next year, in August, but we will go from Hazelton, so you had better get busy this winter and pick out a trail that will connect with the Thutade trail which falls into the Hazelton trail. As you get organized, your business should be conducted entirely from Hazelton and in time we should have flat boats with kickers plying between Hazelton and Babiche Hill. The horses should be met at Babiche Hill.

In addition to your wages you have received this year, $1,014, plus the cost of the agricultural machinery. I know that $450 of that was to settle to account of the river men for last year's work. I can let you have another $500 this year toward paying men who have been doing the haying and to buy small supplies such as nails to help you put up your houses, but for this year I can do no more.

I do not want you to think of our starting the Empire location as something like the sending of Santa Claus. Men like you who have been picked as the best out of thirty, go into the Cassiar country often without a cent, just a little rice, salt and tea and through their mastery over a difficult nature, their great skill and strength, manage to develop a small ranch. Such men do not get $90 a month wages, they get only what they can pull out. I want you to live up to that reputation. I want you to get along with your wages and the farming machinery you now have and the few extra hundred dollars I will send you from time to time. Out of that I want you to start a ranch, show me what you men can do out of sheer strength and when you have definitely convinced me, it will be time for me to invest real money in the shaping up of the Empire ranch on a large scale.

In another letter to Beattie and Davidson later in the fall Bedaux repeated his opinions on the development of the Empire Ranch:

I cannot say as yet that I am satisfied with the work that the team, Carl Davidson and you combined, represent. I know it has taken months of idle time of Carl Davidson waiting on machinery and payroll. It seems to me that too much time is wasted but I will not be able to tell positively until I go to the ranch site myself.

Later in the letter Bedaux commented:

I fear you and Carl Davidson constantly going back either to Prince George or Hudson's Hope will not have the way marked from the Empire Ranch to Hazelton. As I have made up my mind not to go back to the Cassiar country except through Hazelton, I am afraid this is going to prevent our going to the Empire Ranch next summer.

If you and Carl Davidson had from the first started working from Hazelton, then you would have had the way marked and you would know all the difficulties. I hope I am unduly pessimistic and that the two of you will succeed in building your own homes to move your families in as you planned in the month of May and yet make the trail to Hazelton so that we can come and see the work you have done next August.

During the winter of 1935–36 Carl Davidson worked on locating the route for Bedaux while Beattie and a couple men did as much work as they could on developing the Empire ranch. Bob Beattie made a trip back to Hudson Hope. While he was there he hired another person, Bob White, to help get the ranch ready for Bedaux's planned visit in August.

On February 26 Bedaux wrote a detailed letter to Davidson and Beattie. He told the men, "I have no objection to your getting the seeds and other materials needed to start a farm," but he also cautioned them to "continue to be very economical – it is necessary."

Bedaux also discussed the planned trip for the summer:

Have you gone over the route from Hazelton to the location? Is it a hard route? How must it be travelled this summer? Will boats be needed? How far down can the horses come to make up the pack train? How many packers will be needed? Those we will want back are Jack McDougall, Bill Pickell and if more are needed Bob White, Robert

Godberson, Tommy Wilde and McLean. I will advise these men directly, when you tell me how many will be needed. We will probably be three, my wife, Josephine and myself. We will probably remain a month, just long enough to make plans for a real development of the place if we like it and if we feel you have gotten far enough in the first two years.

Do not forget to send me that inventory and all the information necessary for the trail, Hazelton-location.

That same day Bob Beattie and Bob White left Hudson Hope on a trip to the Empire Ranch.

Travelling to the Location, Winter 1936

After the Bedaux Expedition, Bob Beattie and Carl Davidson were kept on the Bedaux payroll. Their job was to look after the horses for the winter, take a trip out into the Sustut country, and start some development work there on the location. The Police Meadows above Fort Grahame had a lot of grass, and with a ration of grain, the horses had a good chance of making it through the winter. However, Davidson spent quite a bit of his time in Prince George, while Beattie spent much of his time in Hudson Hope, so the horses were, more or less, on their own. In the spring of 1935, when Beattie and Davidson went back up there, they found that only 34 of the 99 head had survived the winter.

In the spring and summer of 1935 Davidson and Beattie got busy and ordered a mower and rake shipped in from Prince George to Fort Grahame, along with some tools. They hired three more men to help with the packing: George Meyers, an old-time Texas cowboy and trapper; Lou Gerlock, a farmer from the Prairies who had gone into that country to pan for gold; and Ed Bird, who had married Alex Pierre's daughter.

George supervised the packing of the mower and rake on the horses for 140 miles over the mountains to the location on the Sustut. They had to take it all to pieces, but the main frame of the mower and rake still made awkward packs. But they managed to get every piece out there, the machines set up, and quite a bit of hay cut. There was lots of fine slough grass and red top, which they cut and piled up into good sized coils. There were some nice bunch grass flats but they were too rough to cut.

As the winter of 1935-36 approached Bob Beattie and Ed Bird went out to Fort Grahame and on to Hudson Hope. Davidson went to Prince George, saying he'd be back. George and Lou were to stay at the log cabin they built at the location and look after 15 horses as well as get out logs for more buildings. George, an old trapper, could read sign pretty well. He noticed where the rabbits had chopped the brush off quite a distance from the ground, which meant they could get lots of snow in the country. When the snow started piling up George and Lou went around putting long sticks in the top of the hay coils, but it was no use. The hay musted and soured under the snow and all 15 horses were dead before New Year's. George, an old horseman, felt bad about the whole thing, but by the time he realized that the hay wasn't fit for horse feed it was too late to get the horses back over the summit.

Davidson was to make a trip and blaze a location from Hazelton, but he never showed up, and when their grub started getting low toward the end of January, George and Lou snowshoed out to Fort Grahame. That 140-mile trip during a cold spell was a tough one with lots of snow. We were to know all about it later for Bob Beattie and I would make that same trip, but we went in a different way. The mail came into Fort Grahame once a month during the winter, by backpack and dogs. George and Lou waited around Grahame several weeks expecting to get word of Davidson. Finally they decided Davidson might have gone out to the location and they went back.

I will do some backtracking to show how I got in on this deal. The winter of 1935-36 started early and was a cold winter with lots of snow. After getting in from a big game hunting party that fall I took what was left of our grub supplies and went out and trapped alone until Christmas. Bob Godberson and I had sold our traplines. Since Bob had a job in Fort St John, I went out to gather our traps, which were cached in various places on our line. The fellow that bought the south end of our area was to buy our traps. He didn't intend to go out that winter, so I decided that while I was going out to gather the traps I would trap until Christmas. Before going out early in October I had arranged with Joe Turner that Bob Godberson and I would help him trail out some cattle to the railroad at Dawson Creek. Joe had tried for two years to get these cattle out but had run into difficulty crossing the rivers each time. After talking it over, Joe decided we would wait until the ice got strong enough to cross the rivers.

The weather moderated while we were in Dawson Creek so we enjoyed our ride back to Fort St John where we managed to take in a few parties. Bob stayed in Fort St John while I started back for Hudson Hope, picking up a cow at Cache Creek that we had left there on the way down. The weather had got very cold again. I was walking, leading my horse to keep warm.

A Cowboy on the Peace River – 1936

Before going out early in October [1935], I had arranged with Joe Turner that Bob Godberson and I would help him trail out some cattle to the railroad at Dawson Creek.

I arrived back in Hudson Hope from the trapline a little after New Year. Bob Godberson rode up from Fort St John, and we got started on our 120-mile trip with the cattle about the 20th of January. We had 97 head, all over two years old and many four- and five-year-old steer. Joe went ahead with the team and sleigh, grub box and bedrolls. Bob and I did the riding with the help of Pup, a big collie who was as good as two riders. The weather had settled in really cold. It took us 11 days, with 9 days travelling, and it was from 40 to 65 below zero the entire time.

They were all black cattle but with the intense cold the frost gathered on their coats until there wasn't much black showing. These cattle weren't grain fed but were given all the good brome hay they could eat, so they were carrying good flesh. Some of the big steer would make 1400 pounds or better.

It was 60 below when we pulled into George Daniel's place at Taylor Flats, and still 60 below the next morning when Joe took a load of feed south of the Peace River to Eight Mile Creek, our next stop. The next morning it was 65 below so we laid over an extra day.

The following morning it was 60 below. Joe said, "Well, boys, it's warmed up some, so I guess we'll move out." We camped that night in a log cabin on Eight Mile Creek. It was cold and we didn't do much sleeping, but we burnt lots of wood.

The cattle were shipped through the Pool at Dawson Creek to Toronto. After the overhead was taken off Joe only cleared 19 dollars a head. Joe said, "Well, I got rid of them anyway." I was to take another cattle drive from Joe's place in the fall of 1938. It was as hot that September as it was cold that January of 1936.

Guy Robison stepped out onto the trail and turned the cow into his yard. He had seen me coming up the back channel of the Peace. When I got up to him he said, "Get into the yard, it's too damn cold to be on the trail." He had just finished his chores, gone to the house and looked at the thermometer. It said 55 below zero. I was happy to oblige. Guy and his wife, Myrtle, were a grand old couple, real pioneers, who had located at the Gates 10 miles below Hudson Hope. I got the cow home to Joe Turner the next day and was glad to be off the trail.

The weather settled in colder than ever and the smoke from the chimneys in the settlement went straight up. Nearly everyone was kept busy

Bob White cutting ice on the Peace River near Hudson Hope. Bob White family collection.

on the wood pile. Our local trader, Henry Stege (the opposition to the Hudson's Bay Company), wanted someone to fill his ice house so Donny Peck and I decided we would take on the job. It was sure cold down on the river but it wasn't too bad once we got a hole started. It was 68 below by the thermometer when we went to work at 8 o'clock one morning. We didn't sit around in the shade that day. We got the job done and Henry paid us off at three dollars a day.

Using lumber from our local sawmill, Henry had put up a big two-storey building, which was later used as a store and post office on the ground floor, with a dance hall and rooms upstairs. The building was quite a piece from being finished, but we talked Henry into giving an opening dance, which turned out to be the usual good time. Whenever there is anything on in Hudson Hope people all turn out like one big happy family.

It was at this dance that Bob Beattie came to me and offered me a job to go back into the Sustut country with him. He said, "I'll give you 40 dollars a month and supply the grub." It wasn't too much money, but I wanted to see that wilderness country at the headwaters of the Skeena River. I figured we would be back before many other jobs opened up, so I agreed to go.

Bob Beattie wanted to get started right away, so before daylight on the morning of February 26, 1936, we had our packs made up and ready to hit the trail. We were to travel over 800 miles before we got back the 3rd of May. We travelled on snowshoes with backpacks and two pack dogs. Bob had his dog Peggy, and I had my dog Jip, a black curly-coated spaniel-and-collie cross.

Bob's brother, Jim, had been in town and was pulling out to go upriver with his team and jumbo sleigh that morning. It was 45 below zero when we started. We put our packs on Jim's sleigh and walked behind. It was too cold to make very good time and we thought it was too cold to stop and make tea along the trail, so we went right through 18 miles to the Portage cabin where we spent the night. The old log shanty was pretty chilly, so we had to do some firing up during the night.

It was still 45 below the next morning. We threw our packs in Jim's sleigh. He went around by the road, which was back from the river, while we followed the snowshoe trail up the river. At Six Mile Creek we came upon three Englishmen, Bob Clarke, Percy Stamp and Bill Jones, who were wintering together and had denned up during the cold spell. They hadn't been far from the cabin for some time. There was a trail to the creek for water, a well-worn trail to the wood pile, and a trail to their open-air privy out under a big spruce tree. Jim had brought their mail and we gave it to them, so the boys were glad to see us.

We got into Jim's cabin on Twelve Mile Creek and made tea and lunch before going on to the Twenty Mile Ranch where we enjoyed the hospitality of Jim Beattie's family. Jim was quite proud of their 40-foot-square log house. He had a big cistern upstairs that was kept full of water by a hydraulic ram installed in the basement, with the water coming from Twenty Mile Creek. They had the first house in the country with running water. We spent a very enjoyable night with the Beattie family.

Breakfast was over before daylight and we were on our own from here. We made up our packs, as well as packs for each of our dogs. We were hoping the weather would stay cold for it would make better travelling, but during the night we had a drastic change. A real chinook had blown up, and although we were on the trail early, the snow was sticking to our snowshoes, making heavy going.

We travelled up the river to Billy Mahaffey's cabin on Schooler Creek. He was a white-bearded Englishman who ran a short trapline in the winter, and spent his summers panning out gold at Gold Bar. Many years ago a company set up a gold mining operation at Gold Bar, but when it didn't pan out it was abandoned. Mahaffey took over what was left of the outfit, and with a few men each summer managed to get enough gold to keep going for a few years. He was a pretty lonely man and glad to get the mail we had for him. He gave us lunch and wanted us to stay longer, but we had to be on our way.

The going got so heavy after we left Mahaffey that we had to get sticks to tap our snowshoes and knock off some of the snow every time we picked up our feet. It didn't take many miles of that kind of travelling to play a man out, so when we got to Stanley Wallace's and Dick Hamilton's place just below the mouth of the Ottertail River we were glad to call it quits for the day. We had their mail, so they were happy to see us. They were both veterans of the First World War and trapped on the east fork of the Ottertail River and Henderson Creek. They were glad to have us stay with them and to get some news from the outside. We spent a comfortable night in their log cabin playing cards and talking until late.

When we were getting ready to leave early the next morning it started to rain. It eased up around noon so we started out. The snow had settled some. It was heavy going without the snowshoes on, but the snow would stick to them until we could hardly lift them. We plugged along with them on, then off, past the mouth of the Ottertail River up to Fred Chapman's trap cabin.

Fred was an old-time trapper and we were lucky enough to find him home. His trapline took in the west fork of the Ottertail River and a stretch of country up the Peace on the north side of the river. Fred was glad to see us and to get his mail. He asked us to stay overnight. Had it been better travelling we would have made a few more miles, but we were glad to stay. Fred was also a veteran of the First World War, and during that long cold spell he had stayed pretty close to the cabin. He had Bill Kruger as a trapping partner this winter and Bill had been on the outer line cabins for the last 10 days. Fred was a bit worried about him. Fred was plenty lonesome. We were playing his favourite card game called Fan Tan when Bill came in. He had waited for the snow to tighten up before travelling the last several miles.

About midnight Fred said, "I'll make cake and we'll have lunch." Fred was a good cook and had run the restaurant in Hudson Hope for a time. These river trappers lived better than we did. We had to pack everything to our trapline on horses while they were able to bring in anything they wanted by boat. They had coal oil lamps while we used candles, and they were able to bring in eggs and vegetables while we had beans, rice and macaroni. Fred's cake turned out good with lots of raisins in it. He said, "Eat 'er up, that's what I made it for." So we didn't leave much.

We wanted to hit the hay but Fred said we'd play a few more hands of cards. The four of us ended up playing cards until nearly daylight when Fred told us, "You fellows lie down and have a little rest while I get some breakfast." It had frozen pretty good during the night and we wanted to get an early start for we were afraid of overflow on the river.

When we were getting ready to leave Fred said, "I'm going to travel with you for the company. I'll go as far as my Weasel Creek cabin about 12 miles upriver."

We each put the packs on our dogs, shouldered our packs, went down the bank, and started upriver. The snow had settled some so it wasn't bad

Bob Beattie (left) and Fred Chapman on the frozen Ne Parle Pas rapids.
Bob White family collection.

snowshoeing. We passed the Ne Parle Pas rapids, which were frozen tight.

About 10 miles up we came to Leo Rutledge's trap cabin at the mouth of Point Creek entering the Peace River from the south. Leo's line was actually on the Clearwater River. Leo wasn't in so we left a note along with some mail we had for him. We went around the bend to Fred's Weasel Creek cabin on the north side. His cabin was up from the river, so we bid farewell to Fred and continued on, stopping to make a pot of tea at an open spring along the bank. We were in the high mountains where they crowd in close to the river.

We made Barnard River cabin for the night. I got busy and cut some wood while Bob Beattie got some rice on to cook and made a bannock. It was a nice warm cabin with lots of slough hay on the bunk, so we put in a comfortable night. This cabin was on Buck Buchanan's trapline.

We got away early the next morning, making 12 miles to the Selwyn cabin, another of Buck's trap cabins, where we made tea. We were travelling through the heart of the main range of the Rocky Mountains at this point, the mountains reaching up for thousands of feet on both sides. The chinook wind that whipped through here took all the snow off the ice in places, leaving patches of glare ice, which made it hard to walk with our packs. There were some patches of overflow as well so we got our feet wet.

We were pussy-footing our way along on the glare ice under a bank when a voice hollered out of the timber to the north, "Wait until I get out there." It wasn't long until a man came out of the bush wading through the snow carrying a pack, rifle and snowshoes. It was Andrew Jorgenson, who was trapping on Buck Buchanan's line. His main cabin was at the mouth of Wicked River several more miles upriver, where we intended camping for the night.

Travelling up the Peace River north of Ottertail River. Bob White family collection.

Andrew was on his way to the Selwyn cabin and preferred jungling through the bush to walking on the glare ice. He said he hadn't seen anyone for ages. "I'm so damn lonesome for someone to talk to I'll turn and go back with you." He slid down the bank and stepped onto the ice. His feet shot out from under him and down he went, his rifle butt hitting the ice so hard that the gun went off with a loud bang that startled us and scared the daylights out of Andrew. "Jesus Christ," said Andrew. "I could easily have killed someone."

Bob had met him before but I hadn't, so after introductions and a little visit we went on upriver. I carried his rifle for we weren't heavily packed. Our rifle that we were to take with us was up at Fort Grahame. The miles to Wicked River were tough going, with glare ice a lot of the way and patches of overflow. It was a treat when we hit a patch of hard snow. But we made it in before dark.

I got busy getting some wood while they took care of the eating end of things. Andrew had lots of wood cut, but it is always the custom of the north to leave a little extra wood for the use of the cabin. South of the river and a bit east Mount Selwyn stuck its head into the sky. Years ago hardrock gold was discovered up near the top of the mountain. They had to get the ore down the mountain, so they decided to rawhide it; that is, they built a series of log chutes down the mountain. By putting the ore in rawhide bags they could slide them down these chutes. The scheme worked after a fashion, but the mine was never a success and had long since been abandoned. It was a lonesome-looking, snow-covered mountain when I looked up at it that night while I was chopping wood.

Wicked River is a fair-sized stream that runs into the Peace from the north. This was Buck Buchanan's main cabin. He also had a nice grub cache on stilts. Buck had rented this trapline to Andrew on a share basis while he went on a job as caretaker of the Ingenika Mine up the Ingenika River. We will catch up to Buck later.

Andrew had been a silversmith in Holland. He ended up looking for gold on the Peace and Finlay Rivers. He didn't have much luck on the gravel bars or the trapline, although he managed to get a few skins and a little more than his grub stake. He was really glad for the company and we once again played cards most of the night. When we mentioned that Fred Chapman made us a cake at midnight Andrew had to do the same. He did a good job of it, and there wasn't much left when we got through working on it.

Before we went to bed the wind started to blow up a chinook. When we got up for an early start there was a wind howling down through the gap from the west, with sleet and rain. We were 90 miles upriver from Hudson Hope and 10 miles from the Forks [Finlay Forks]. We wanted to travel but it didn't look very promising for it would be ice most of the way, with a lot of water over it in places along with a howling wind. Bob and I decided to stay the day with Andrew, and he was glad that it rained.

We got busy working on some ice creepers that we brought with us. We had to rivet in more ice caulks and put on some moose-hide thongs so we could tie them on our rubbers. I rigged up some dog harnesses for we intended using our dogs on a toboggan when we got to Fort Grahame. We also spent time visiting and playing cards.

Early the next morning we bid goodbye to Andrew. The wind was still blowing but it was a lot colder. Our ice creepers worked slick so we were able to walk right along on the ice, only breaking through the overflow a time or two. We camped for tea at the Forks in an old log cabin that used to be the Hudson's Bay Company trading post, but had long since been abandoned. The current trading post now run by Allan McKinnon was six miles up the Finlay.

At Finlay Forks the Parsnip River flows through the Rocky Mountain Trench from the south, joining the Finlay River flowing from the opposite direction. Here they become the Peace River, which flows in an easterly direction, breaking through the main range of the Rockies. We were now 100 miles from Hudson Hope with 65 more to Fort Grahame.

We crossed the mouth of the Parsnip River and followed a good snow-shoe trail through the bush to McKinnon's where we spent the night. The game warden had a cabin close by and there were other trappers and pros-pectors staying at the post. Several of these men had put in many years in the north prospecting and trapping, and it was interesting to talk to them. Allan McKinnon had a good-sized log house and the walls of one large

King Gething the Mailman

King Gething of Hudson Hope had the contract to deliver the mail to Fort Grahame, once a week during the summer by boat, and once a month during the winter, by dog team, pack dogs or backpacking, which could be quite a job when you're battling the elements. On his last trip by boat late in October he ran into heavy slush in a slow or what they called dead-water stretch of the Finlay River. King had two men with him. They rocked the boat and did everything they could to keep moving, but it was no use. The boat got stuck solid in the middle of the river. It was a cold night and after spending most of it in the boat the ice was strong enough that they could get to shore and get a much-needed fire going. The three men got busy and built a rough cabin out of green poplar logs, then carried all the contents of his 36-foot boat up and stored it in the cabin. They made up packs of all the important stuff, including the mail, and backpacked down to McKinnon's.

Cecil's job, when he got to the cabin, was to chop the boat out of the ice and have it ready when King arrived upriver on his next mail run so they could drag it to shore and have it anchored when the ice went out. We could see that Cecil was in for a tough job chopping that boat out of the ice in the middle of the river. As it turned out, that old boat was to carry us downriver on the last lap of our journey.

room were decorated with every type of fur that was caught in that part of the country. The most recent addition was a mountain lion skin caught by a squaw in one of her lynx snares on her rabbit snare line, not far from the post.

After a comfortable night we hit the trail at daylight, wanting to take advantage of any ice that had formed that might hold our weight. People said there was quite a bit of overflow in places going up the Finlay. Our good snowshoe trail only lasted for a mile. Then we dropped down to the river ice where we took off our snowshoes and tied on our ice caulks. Our good walking on the ice only lasted a few miles when we stuck patches of overflow, which in some cases was a foot deep. In those places we had to take the packs off our dogs and put them on our own to keep them dry. We tried jungling through on the bank, but with the brush and deep snow we couldn't make any time. The open channel of the overflow zigzagged from one side of the river to the other. We had to cross and recross it, hitting a few places where we had good travelling.

After making about eight miles our feet got cold and we were wet to the knees so we stopped and built a good fire on the sunny side of the river bank. We wrung out our socks, dried off a little, and had a pot of tea. Then we continued on, getting wet all over again. We came to an old trap cabin along the bank where Bevel Creek comes in from the east. On entering the cabin we found a man still in bed on the bunk. It was Cecil Aubry, a brother-in-law of King Gething. He had been working his way upriver, got into this cabin about midnight and played right out. It was a nice day so we made our tea over a little fire outside the cabin. Cecil had tea and lunch with us. We said that he should travel along with us but he said he was still too tired from the effects of last night. We continued on, getting our feet washed again. On the west side of the river we passed Pete Toy Bar where prospectors still panned for gold every year after high water. We went by the Omineca, a good-sized river flowing in from the west, passed the Ospika, which came in from the east, and then arrived at King Gething's cabin.

The cabin was a crude affair, but it was better than camping out. We moved some of King's stuff to make room to spread our bed tarp on the frozen ground. We had a junior eiderdown to put over us. The cabin had been put up in a hurry and had a flat roof so it had been leaking and was wet and damp. There was a ragged tarp for a door.

After a rough night on that frozen ground we got an early start. The overflow wasn't as bad and we only got our feet wet a time or two. The dogs were able to carry their own packs and we were able to make good time. We stopped at Jim Holland's cabin for our noon lunch. Jim was out on his trapline but Bob Beattie knew him well, so he dug out one of his home-cured bear hams, which was really good eating. I've never eaten any pork hams that I liked better than those black bear hams.

We continued until late that night. It was good travelling and we were able to use our snowshoes quite a bit. Bob and I camped at an unoccupied trap cabin. Though an old cabin, it had been well built, so we spent a comfortable night. There had been a sweat house built near the cabin that had been used by a lot of trappers along the Finlay.

We started early in the morning, using our snowshoes most of the time. What a treat to travel all morning with dry feet. We stopped at Mr and Mrs Jensen's place about noon, enjoying their hospitality and a good meal. They were glad for company and to get some news from down river. The Jensens had a growing family that were going to school in Prince George. Mrs Jensen was a big jolly woman who was well liked and respected by all, and well remembered for her good meals. She would give to all that came along.

After our good meal and visit we started upriver, wanting to make Fort Grahame that night. We had our snowshoes on nearly all the way and were glad to get into Fort Grahame at dark. Bob and I went to the little cabin belonging to the Hudson's Bay where we were to spend the next couple days. The Hudson's Bay Company manager, Larry Kemple, and his wife lived in a log house beside the store, and a retired Hudson's Bay factor was spending the winter here in a neat little log cabin. The store and other buildings were all covered with whitewash. With their red roofs they showed up nice against the white snow and green of the timber.

My boss, Bob Beattie, expected to get some work of Carl Davidson, his co-manager, here. Before we got there George and Lou had left Fort Grahame to return to the location. They were going in by way of Aiken Lake [a gold mining area] thinking they might get some word of Davidson there. The only word they were able to get had come in by moccasin telegraph that Davidson intended going out to the location from Hazelton with a dog team.

We spent the next couple days hunting up a toboggan and getting it fixed up, hooking up our dogs, and hauling in wood for our cabin. The dogs worked out real good. Larry and his wife were very nice people and we had good visits with the retired factor. He dabbled in shortwave radio, sending and receiving, and at times could raise people staying at Aiken Lake. Through him we learned that George and Lou had arrived there, then gone on to the location, and that they didn't get any definite word of Davidson.

Bob Beattie was anxious to see how the horses he had left to winter in the Ingenika valley made out. He had not seen then since turning them loose up the Ingenika last fall. Instead of going out to the location by way of Aiken Lake as George and Lou had done, we would continue up the Finlay and Ingenika Rivers and over the Wrede Creek summit. We got our toboggan loaded and the dogs hooked up, went down the bank, and started up the river. We were lucky to have no overflow, but there was quite a bit of snow. We took turns breaking trail and driving the dogs. It was a treat to walk along without packs on our backs. About 10 miles up the Finlay we stopped for a pot of tea at the mouth of Big Creek, which came in from the east. There were some bad logjams in the river at this point, of which we will hear more later.

It was a little over 20 miles to the mouth of the Ingenika River flowing in from the west. We camped in an old log cabin that was in pretty rough shape, but there was lots of dry wood handy. The next morning we started up the north side of the Ingenika. After about seven or eight miles we saw some horse signs. We scouted around and finally found 12 head. We had brought some granulated rock salt that was in a cache at the Forks. The ponies were salt hungry and in surprisingly good shape for wintering on their own. It looked rather odd to see horses all alone in that wild country.

Beattie sledding to the Ingenika mine. Bob White family collection.

Three of those horses were part of the string Bob Godberson and I packed on the Bedaux Expedition. It was like meeting old friends to see them again.

After leaving the horses we continued up the river, making camp in some timber along the banks. The weather had turned quite a bit colder and it must have been at least 20 degrees below zero. With lots of wood we made out pretty good. The next morning was a nice sunshiny day and cold enough to make good travelling. Breaking trail ahead of the dogs was difficult, so we changed off quite regularly. Fires had swept through parts of this country many years before, so we had to contend with some windfall.

Bob and I arrived at the old Ingenika mine site that evening. The Ingenika Mining Company had gone in there many years ago and ran a shaft into some hardrock gold-bearing quartz. It didn't prove out, so it was abandoned, but they kept Buck Buchanan as caretaker of the place. He had a young German lad staying with him who had walked in over the Rocky Mountains through Laurier Pass last summer to hunt for gold on the Finlay River. With no gold and no way to get back out he was wintering with Buck. He had been a butcher in Germany. He and Buck were lucky enough to get a big moose who wandered too close to the cabin one moonlit night. The German lad was going to cure and make sausage out of some of the meat. Buck had a big Saint Bernard dog that he used on a toboggan, and the two of them ran traplines that radiated from their cabin.

Buck didn't have to twist our arm too much to get us to camp with them for the night. The moose steak proved good eating and they gave us

White mushing up the Ingenika River. Bob White family collection.

a piece to take. Buck and the German lad had only been out once to Fort Grahame all winter, so they were glad for some company and to get some news of down river.

The next morning we left early, travelling up the north side of the Ingenika to the mouth of the Pelly River. It was a rough day breaking trail through over two feet of snow, and we were glad to make camp on the bank of the Pelly. The following day we made 20 miles to Shorty Webber's main cabin at the mouth of Wrede Creek, where we camped for the night.

Shorty was out on his line but Mrs Louis Albright was in. With her seven-year-old son she lived in one of Shorty's old cabins close by. The poor woman had put in a terrible lonely winter. Louis, his wife and son had spent the summer prospecting for gold on the Finlay and Ingenika Rivers with very little luck. Finally they made a deal to winter with Shorty and take part of his line on a share basis. Shorty, as we got to know him, could be an ornery pelter, and he put Louis up his Wrede Creek line where there were no cabins. Poor Louis put in a hell of a winter, camping out during some of that bitter cold weather in February. Mrs Albright was so glad to have someone to talk to and get some news from the outside. She thought her husband was up near the head of Wrede Creek and that Shorty would be at his first cabin up the creek.

We struck out the next morning up Wrede Creek, making 12 miles to Shorty's cabin. We could have made a few more miles but the weather was pretty cold and we decided we'd camp with Shorty and have the benefit of his cabin. Around dark Louis Albright came down from the high country. He had been camping up in those mountains for the last two weeks and was going down to see his family and get cleaned up. He looked pretty rough but was glad to see someone to talk to. I had met Louis Albright in the Fort St John country. His family had had a rough time homesteading in the North Pine district with no market for their grain. They fed out a bunch of pigs, butchering them and curing the meat into bacon and hams and they peddled it to the trappers and prospectors. That's when Louis got the idea of trying his luck at prospecting, starting up the Peace River and ending up on the Finlay and Ingenika. Shorty didn't give him a very fair deal, so he was putting in time until the ice went out.

Shorty had shot a moose a few miles up the creek so we all took on a big feed of moose steak. We had given Shorty quite a scare when he saw us drive up to his cabin with our dog team. I was wearing my Stetson hat. He thought I was the game warden, and that he would be pinched for killing a moose out of season. Shorty was quite relieved when he saw it was me. I was wearing my hat because there was a chance I would be out in this country for the summer. Quite a few trappers wear wide-brimmed hats all winter to keep the snow off their necks.

Shorty's cabin was too small for four of us to bed down, so Bob and I got a pile of spruce boughs and made our bed outside. Shorty and Louis were anxious to hear news from the outside, so we talked until near midnight, drinking lots of tea. When we crawled in under the tarp it was snowing pretty hard. By morning there were four inches of snow over us, which helped keep us warm.

We headed up the creek, stopping at Shorty's moose kill to pick up some meat for the trail. Shorty had dropped small pine trees from different directions on to the meat to keep the wolves from getting at it. Bob and I got into some rough going and made camp at the lower end of a rocky canyon. This was one of our worst camps. Good dry wood was on the scarce side and it had turned cold, down to at least 30 below zero. After a miserable night we started up the canyon, very cold with fine snow falling. We had a difficult time getting the toboggan up through the canyon, crossing back and forth across the creek. Finally Bob and I took the dogs off and hauled the toboggan up the different ledges by a long rope. After sneaking along the mountainside we let the toboggan down the same way.

The snow got deeper above the canyon, and deeper still as we climbed toward the summit. We wanted to get as close to the [Wrede Creek] summit before we camped so that we would have a whole day ahead of us when we went over the top. As the trees thinned out the snow became so deep the dogs were nearly helpless. We had to help them with the toboggan. When we got to where there were only a few trees sticking out of the snow, we picked out a gnarled old spruce that had quite a struggle with the elements to survive, and we dug down six feet in the snow beside it, using our snowshoes as shovels. We quit digging when we thought we saw a blade of grass but found later we were still far from the ground.

The snow became so deep and soft it was impossible to travel with the dogs. We left them at the tree and broke trail toward the summit. We would have to step aside occasionally to let the other person ahead to break trail for we were sinking in two to three feet even with snowshoes on. We struggled along for a few miles until we got to the beginning of the wind-swept summit, where the snow held us up better. What a sight to see, with mountains all around and everything a sea of white. It was snowing a bit and hazy so we couldn't see the peaks too clearly. We back-tracked to our camp, knowing that our trail would set with the frost and make good travelling in the morning.

We finished digging out our hole under the tree, lined it with spruce boughs, made a hole in the side, and got a fire going. While Bob got busy working on a bannock, I searched for dry wood, which wasn't too plenti-ful. The few gnarled dry tree tops sticking out of the snow were tough cutting with our little trail axe. We were a pretty tired pair, so any kind of a camp looked good to us. By the time we bedded down that night our fire had melted down in the snow and was four or five feet below us. We were afraid to stoke it up too much for fear of setting fire to our spruce boughs. The next morning we had to tie a green stick on the handle of our fry pan so we could reach the fire to cook hotcakes for breakfast. We cooked our moose meat on sticks over the fire.

After a fair night we loaded our toboggan and had good travelling over our broken trail to the summit. Then we travelled 10 miles of open sum-mit, the snow holding the dogs up fairly good. When they got too close to a submerged tree top the dogs would drop through. This happened several times. It was quite a job getting them back on top without the whole works falling in, including us. We might not be enjoying our trip much, but we admired and enjoyed the beautiful scenery that day; absolutely white, mountain peaks all around us and the lower ridges and basins as well as the summit a sea of white. We had no idea how deep the snow was at the top, but when I packed over that same summit with horses in the summer we saw rock ridges, gullies, and small lakes that were covered with snow when Bob and I went over it. I guess it snows nearly all the time there during the winter. The sun did shine long enough that day for us to see and admire the beautiful scenery.

As we started down Johanson Creek the going became difficult. Break-ing trail was heavy going, and we had to help the dogs by pushing on the handle bar of the toboggan. Fine snow fell most of the day. We travelled later than usual for we wanted to reach the location the next night, so we were pretty tired when we made camp in some thick half-grown pines along the creek. We had to do a lot of shovelling with our snowshoes to get down near the ground. With lots of small dry wood handy we put in a fairly good night. It was heavy going all the next day as we followed Johanson Creek down to the Sustut, then up that river to the location. Snow fell most of the day, but the sun broke through at times, giving us a splendid view of the snow-covered mountains to the south, with Sustut Peak sticking up higher than the rest.

When we arrived at the location that night, pretty well played out again, we looked around for the lone cabin. All we saw was a bare spot, slightly below the level of the snow, which turned out to be the roof of the cabin. George Myers and Lou Gerlock were in, and glad to see us. George got busy working on a bannock for us, and started a pot of rice boiling. The cabin wasn't exactly a palace, with the ground for a floor, no windows, and a tarp hung over the opening for a door. The cabin had an overhang and we had to slide down the snow bank to get in the door. The heat from the cabin melted the snow on the roof, which dripped through and made everything damp. Away from the small tin stove the drops had frozen in little cones of ice that never melted while we were there.

The meat they were living on was some of the four caribou that George had shot early in the winter and buried in the snow. While he was waiting for the bannock to cook, George said, "I think we have a potato or two left." He lay down on the floor, stuck his long arm down a hole as far as he could reach, and came up with two potatoes they had packed in last fall. They were frozen solid but when cooked were edible, with a sweetish taste. George and Lou were disappointed that we didn't have any definite information on Carl Davidson's whereabouts. They had picked up a rumour at Aiken Lake that Davidson planned to blaze a trail from Hazel-ton, by way of Babine and Bear Lakes and get to the location around the middle of February. Now it was already March and no word of him. We talked it over and decided that we would all go down the Sustut River and see if we could find some track of him.

Bob and I would rest one day, then we would all get an early start the following morning. Dry wood was scarce around the cabin, so Lou and I took our dog teams and went looking for dry wood. We came in with two large loads. The cabin was damp and chilly. Not having enough spruce boughs handy, we set up Bedaux's canvas folding cots, which were cold to sleep on, but we dug out more saddle blankets and made out all right.

A Trip to Bear Lake

George was our elected cook, and after an early breakfast of hotcakes and caribou meat, we hit the trail in good time, heading down the Sustut River with two teams of two dogs each. George and Lou had a Yukon sleigh that George had made, while we had a toboggan with handles on it. We had to change off quite regularly breaking trail. We were a little anxious travelling along the foot of Sustut Mountain, which is a bad snow-slide area, for this was the time of year when slides generally took place. After getting by we were glad to stop for a pot of tea. Continuing on, we came to a waterfall in a canyon that dropped 300 to 400 feet. Gazing down into the canyon we could make out the tracks of a dog sleigh. The tracks were snowed over but you could still see the imprint where it had turned around and gone back downriver. We assumed they were Davidson's and found out later that they were his.

We had quite a time getting our outfits down to the river through the snow and scrub spruce on the steep sides of the canyon. It was difficult to keep our sleighs from falling off the ridges of snow between the trees, or sliding into the holes under them.

We made camp a mile below the falls. The weather had turned much colder, and we found out later that it was 35 below zero that night. We picked a place with lots of dry wood and got a fire going against a big back log, scooped a big hole out of the snow, and lined it with spruce boughs. George got busy on his bannock and rice, while we piled up our night's supply of wood. With a good backlog for a fire George turned out some good bannock, and with the rice and caribou meat that we cooked on sticks by the fire, we had a pretty good meal, not to mention good old tea.

We knew we were in for a cold night so we took off our socks and mitts and dried out everything as well as we could. Bob and I made our bed of boughs back from the fire so that the sparks wouldn't burn our bedding. When we rolled in for the night we put on all the clothes we had and pulled the tarp up over everything. Generally we would sleep through most of the night before we froze out. George and Lou wrapped themselves in their blankets and slept beside the fire.

It was really cold when we left camp the next morning, George and I went ahead, taking turns breaking trail. A slight breeze coming upriver froze our faces a few times. We passed the mouth of the Asitka River coming in from the east. Late in the afternoon we spotted some tree blazes on the east bank of the river, with more blazes leading away from the river. They looked as if they might be heading up a valley between two mountains. Up to this point we had been following down the winding Sustut River. None of us knew this part of the country and we had no accurate map of the area. We hoped those blazes would lead us to Bear Lake and decided to follow them.

We camped a short distance up that trail. Although not as chilly as last night it was cold enough. Lots of good wood helped a lot. We were on the trail in good time the next morning. It was still heavy going, with everyone taking turns at breaking trail and driving the dogs. When we camped for lunch we still had no idea where we were. Since we were travelling through small pine timber most of the way we couldn't see much, but figured we couldn't be far from Bear Lake if we were on the right trail.

Just before deciding to camp for the night we came out on the lake. We drove up to a log building, which was the Hudson's Bay post, but it was closed for the traders would only come up from Takla Landing on Takla Lake and open the post for a few days every month. An old Indian in camp said there was a free trader a mile down the lake, so we went on to his place.

Karl Hanawald was the only white man at the lake. He had been an officer in the German Army during the First World War. He was so fed up with the Kaiser's rule that when the war was over he wanted to get as far away as he could. He came out to Canada, and after working here and there, he opened this trading post away back here in the bush. Trade goods had to come from Prince George by way of Takla Landing, and up Takla Lake to where the Driftwood River comes into the lake. Then Karl would get the Indians to line his freight up the Driftwood to Bear Lake in their smaller boats, a difficult job.

Karl had a neat little log building back from the lake that was a store and living quarters combined. He made us welcome, but you could see he still had that military bearing. His stock was almost empty, so we couldn't get all the supplies we wanted. But we did get word of Carl Davidson. He had a hell of a trip coming in from Hazelton by way of Babine Lake, then got on the wrong trail and ended up at Takla Landing. He left there with a young chap that was to open the Hudson's Bay store at Bear Lake. They were on the trail during that bitter cold spell in February, got on the wrong trail, and got lost. The young fellow didn't have too much trail experience. While drying out his moccasins and socks by the fire one night he burned some of them and ended up freezing his toes quite badly. They both ended up back at Takla Landing. After resting, Davidson started out again and made it to Bear Lake. From there he started for the location, going up the Sustut River. On getting to the falls he figured that there was no way he could get up them. (Those were his tracks that we had seen from the top of the falls.) Karl backtracked to Bear Lake where he found there were some Indians down from the Kitchener Lake area to the north. They were almost ready to leave, so Davidson decided to go north with them and get to the location by travelling southeast from Kitchener Lake. As it turned out he arrived at the location the evening of the day we left. Had Bob and I rested another day, as we very nearly did, we would have saved ourselves a gruelling trip.

Karl was a little odd in his ways, not the free and easy way of the usual trader of the north. When an Indian came in with furs he would have us all go back into the storeroom until the Indian had gone. He seemed to have his own way of trading. We enjoyed our day of rest there but not the nights. With only a few blankets that board floor was mighty hard and also damn cold for Karl would let the fire go out early. We had quite a laugh at Lou Gerlock. He had to answer the call of nature and went to the

Near the junction of Johanson Creek and the Sustut River. Glenbow PA750-18.

George Myers (left) and Lou Gerlock at Karl Hanawald's trading post at Bear Lake.
Glenbow PA750-19.

little privy at the back that was built of logs only notched enough so that they didn't roll off, more like a corral. The seat was two poles, wider at one end than the other, so you could pick the size you wanted. There were several half-starved Indian dogs hanging around and they tagged after Lou. When he got settled on the poles the dogs got to fighting. The logs were far enough apart that a dog could reach through. Poor Lou thought that the dogs might take a bite out of him. When he came back to the cabin he said, "My God, I nearly got chewed out there." From then on we took a stick with us. It gave you a funny feeling to be sitting there and having dogs fighting below you.

The only grub we could purchase from Karl was flour, oatmeal, a little rice and sugar, but no bacon or chocolate bars, which we would have liked. The only sweets he had was some sugared ginger. It was pretty hot, but I liked the stuff so I got all he had, for the rest of the boys were not too keen on it.

We hooked the dogs up the next morning, bid goodbye to Karl, and thanked him for his hospitality. He said he was glad for the company. We went up the lake to the still-closed Hudson's Bay store. The Bear Lake waters are on the salmon run, so on our way in through the village we stocked up on salmon for our dogs. There was no good salmon available for our own use. The only difference between the two is that the Indians take more care in drying the salmon for human use. Some of the dog salmon was pretty rancid and full of holes, with parts eaten away where the maggots had got into it. We picked up more dog salmon on our way out.

A Letter from Bear Lake

March 27, 1936

My Dear Mother,

Just a few lines to let you know we are O.K. There is a chance of sending out a letter from here, so am taking this opportunity of sending one out, as I do not know when I will be out again.

We have had quite a trip. Just got in here (Bear Lake) tonight and starting on our back trail in the morning. We had been hunting down a Carl Davidson who hadn't been heard of since the middle of Jan. But we have got word of him here and he is still O.K. so we are satisfied to that extent even if he did cause us a considerable mileage on snowshoes. He had made three different attempts to get from here to the Bedaux location. He is out in that vicinity now and we intend going back there and will stay there and work on the buildings until the rivers break up.

We have seen quite a bit of country since leaving the Hope. We hiked the 175 miles from the Hope to Grahame. There we hooked our two dogs to an Indian toboggan, went up the Finlay and then up the Ingenika to Wrede Ck and up that and over the summit and down on to the head of Johanson Ck, down that creek to Sustut River and up that river a few miles to the Bedaux location. From there we came back down the Sustut River to Bear River and up Bear River to Bear Lake where we are now. It is about 150 miles from Grahame to the location and about 60 from there to here. We picked up two fellows at the location who came down here with us, so we had the two dog teams of two dogs each. It is certainly a dandy country to travel through as for scenery as it is all rugged mountains, but the snow, man oh man: about seven or eight feet deep in the high passes. Following the summer trails the blazes are nearly all under the snow. A plane flew over today but didn't land but the trader here thinks he will land here soon so there will be a chance of getting these letters out.

Well here's hoping you are all OK down there. I suppose you will all be busy planting gardens and crops soon, it sure doesn't seem much like break-up here. We snowshoed in here today over about five feet of snow. – The snow is a little higher here, and every indication of staying with us for awhile yet.

We might possibly get out to Grahame early in May so might get some mail then so will say bye-bye till then.

This is not very good writing paper but it is all they have here, and no more within 80 miles,

So will ring off for this time with
Heaps of love to all,
Your loving Son, Bob

George Myers, Cowboy and Trapper

George was one of the best men I ever trailed with. He started out life as a cowboy in Texas. Coming up north he took up trapping. George lived in Prince George and packed his grubstake over Sifton Pass, whipsawing out a boat on the Driftpile River. He would float down to the Kechika or Muddy River and continue down that river to where the caribou migration crossed the valley. George would follow the caribou east over the mountains to his trapping area on the Rabbit River on the Liard drainage. George said he rarely had to shoot a caribou for meat for he could get just about all he wanted for himself and his dogs from the wolf kills.

George was a pretty handy boy. He made his Yukon dog sleigh and shod the runners with strips of tin cut from tin cans and soldered the joins with solder he salvaged from other tin cans. He also made a cap and jacket for himself out of a Hudson's Bay blanket with only a needle and thread, and a jack knife.

George didn't mind cooking so we were willing to let him make the bannocks on the trail. The trouble was that he would never make any ahead. When we would stop for a pot of tea and lunch George would have to make a bannock. Lou and I were generally the wood cutters and we'd have a good fire going when George was ready. The snow was six to eight feet deep on our trip so George just had so long to cook his bannock. When the fire melted the snow underneath enough, the whole works would drop out of sight.

We discussed the idea of eating some of the dog salmon. George said, "Golly, I think I'll try some of that fish. I'm so hungry all the time I could eat pretty near anything."

I said to George, "If you are going to try it I will too."

We cut a couple of squares out of the best part and put it on a stick with the skin side to the fire so the oil from the skin would soften the fish. It was quite rancid but we had no ill effects.

The next night George said, "That's good stuff," and cooked a couple bigger pieces. So did I. The next afternoon, when we were plugging along upriver, George started cussing with his little laugh. "That goldarn fish anyhow," he said, and headed for the river bank. He had a good case of the trots, which lasted until we got to the location. It bothered me some but not as bad.

When we got back to the location, Lou and I were cutting wood when George came up in a hurry out of the hole in the snow that was our cabin, heading for our privy. He trotted out on the packed snow without snowshoes. He just got bent down over the hole when he fell through to his armpits. He cursed and laughed at the same time. Not being able to reach the ground, he had quite a time scrambling out.

George had been a pretty rugged boy in his time but had roughed it a little too much and now he was having trouble with his stomach.

The view south from the cabin at Bedaux's ranch. Bob White family collection.

On our return trip we had a broke trail and it was cold enough to make the travelling easier. The first night we made camp in the timber before we got to the Sustut River. In the morning we drove a short distance, then came out on the river and followed it north, stopping for tea where the Asikta comes in. As we went upriver to the canyon we wondered how we were going to climb up the canyon wall to get above the falls. We unhooked the dogs and started up, pulling and pushing, cussing some, pulling and pushing more, until we finally got up on top. Our toboggan was easier to handle than the Yukon sleigh.

After leaving the falls we travelled upriver and made camp before we got to the snow-slide area. It was a nice camp with lots of dry wood and a big back log for our fire, so we were able to get everything dried out. We had given some thought to these slides for the mountains on each side of the river were steep-sided, with lots of evidence of slides in past years. On our way down we had noticed one that had come down Sustut Mountain last year, went right across the river, and started up the mountain on the other side, leaving great piles of trees and sticks of all sizes. The weather had been staying cold but it was now almost April and would warm up soon. Bob and I were to witness several slides from a distance sometime later.

We were on the trail early the next morning, wanting to get by the slide area before it warmed up and to reach the location that night. We passed the slide area without incident, but saw where there had been several small slides in the last few days, although they hadn't reached the river. After seeing the evidence of past slides you marvel at their power, moving a path right through the trees, taking everything with it, some of it good-sized timber. It makes you want to stay clear of those mountains when the weather warms up. We stopped for tea at Johanson Creek, then went on to the location, where we met Carl Davidson. We had been gone a week. Carl was getting restless and was almost ready to pull out for Takla for he had arrived on the same day we left. We were all glad to see Carl. I hadn't seen him since the expedition.

Carl had a real tale of woe to tell, getting lost in the Babine Lake country, then getting caught in the February cold spell, lost again, ending up back at Takla Landing, back to Bear Lake, then up with the Kitchener Indians to Kitchener Lake. From there he had to go southeast to the location. He was on his own, with no trail to follow through a strange country, getting lost, breaking his snow glasses, going snow-blind, falling over a bank and half crippling himself. Carl landed at the location with his three-dog team and a Yukon sleigh in pretty rough shape, but he was in good condition again after a week of rest.

Bob Beattie and Carl Davidson didn't have much to show for their winter's work, just a leaky cabin and a small cache. The horses they undertook to winter at the location were all dead, and no building logs were cut as planned. Carl said he wasn't going to try and cut logs in that snow. Our grub supply wasn't too plentiful, and the caribou meat was getting low. Since it was stored so far down in the snow that it wasn't really frozen, it had a tendency to be sour and we were going easy on it.

George cooked us some of what he called "alfalfa", dried spinach in bags – a carryover from the expedition. It wasn't bad if you got the good stuff, but it had got knocked about, getting damp and wet. You had to pick out the mildewed parts, so we had to go sparingly on that. Going short of grub is bad enough, but getting sick on it is a lot worse. I hunted a little but only saw one moose track. He was heading southeast and I never caught up to him. There were several flocks of ptarmigan and I managed to get some of them. They are a pretty, white bird and real good eating.

After finally meeting their boss, George and Lou were anxious to get started on the trip out to Prince George. They decided to have a day's rest before getting away early the following morning. After the layover, George, Lou and Carl headed for Takla Landing on Takla Lake, almost 150 miles away. The weather was warming up but still snowing quite often, with the sun breaking through at times. We should have left then and saved ourselves a lot of grief, but Bob and I wanted to look over the log situation, and if we couldn't cut logs, perhaps we could split some shakes for the summer's building.

We spent several days scouting around but it was hopeless to cut logs in that deep snow. We did manage to split quite a few shakes. We would dig down around a likely-looking tree, cut it down, then cut off a block and test it for straight grain. If it twisted we wouldn't use it. The normal shake is 30 inches long, but with this poorer timber we cut the blocks into two-foot lengths. We hauled the shakes up from down near the river with the dog team, putting them on higher ground.

Return to Hudson Hope

The days were getting much warmer, with more sunshine. The snow was getting softer, so we thought that we should be starting back out. On April 18 we loaded our toboggan with the little grub remaining and left the cabin in the snow.

It was a warm bright day and the glare from the snow bothered our eyes. We only made about nine miles when we bogged down. About 11 o'clock we dropped through the snow in the middle of an open meadow. The snow, being more granulated underneath, would cave in on our snowshoes and the only way you could get them out was to reach down, tip the snowshoe sideways and pull it up. It took us two hours to make it to two pine trees on the mountainside about three hundred yards away. When we got to the trees we dug down between them and cut some of the limbs off to line the hole. There were a few dry snags close by that lasted us the day.

The weather stayed warm and we were held in camp for three days. We tramped a trench in the snow further up the mountain for more dry wood, which was scarce around there. Finally we cut down the two pine trees we were camped under. In the afternoons, from where we were, we saw several snow slides come down the sides of Sustut Mountain, as well as on the mountain on the opposite side of the river. There was no danger where we were. We rationed the dried salmon out to the dogs and had to save on our own grub. We had nothing to read so I drew out a makeshift checkerboard on the canvas back of my pack board with charcoal from the fire, and whittled out some square and round men. Bob wasn't too good at the game. I would have to let him win at times, or he wouldn't play, saying you always win anyway.

The third day was quite warm and there had been no frost the last two nights. The snow was settling some, but at that rate it would be a long time before we could travel. We had to laugh at our dogs. When they wanted to leave camp to answer the call of nature they would only get a few yards before breaking through the snow. Sometimes they went out of sight or just their tail stuck out, and then they had to struggle their way back into camp. Our tea was running out. We had to boil it over and over to get all the flavour out of it. Then I would dry the tea leaves and mix it with the little tobacco I had left. I smoked a pipe and cigarettes and had left Hudson Hope with plenty of tobacco. Lou Gerlock had gone out with no tobacco saying he was going to quit, but when I came along he ended up smoking more of my tobacco than I did so I was running out.

In the evening of the third day it started to freeze a little so our hopes picked up. We kept testing the snow during the night. Before daylight I put on my snowshoes and found that the snow would hold us. We got everything packed and the toboggan loaded so that we could leave as soon as we could see. We didn't want to leave until it got light enough to get our bearings for we didn't want to take any chances of getting lost in that country.

It was sure good to be travelling again and we made as good time as we could through some pretty rough going. About 10 o'clock we started breaking through. We swung a little out of our way to see if we could find an old abandoned trap cabin that we heard was on Johanson Creek. We found it just in time for the snow was getting so soft we couldn't travel. It turned out to be a very poor camp. There was no grub, and the old cabin was cold and damp. There was no dry wood handy and we had to wallow through the deep snow to get enough wood to cook our rice and bannock. We were sure hoping it would freeze that night so we wouldn't have to lay over there. Bob and I put in a poor night with a cold cabin and going to bed hungry since we were rationing our grub. Our eyes were very sore from the snow glare.

It froze again that night so we were on the trail before daylight. Bob and I were following up Johanson Creek and wanted to make the summit that day if we possibly could. We blackened our cheeks with charcoal and tied a black scarf over our eyes with a slit in it. About halfway to timberline the going got heavy. The sun became very warm and the glare from the snow nearly blinded us. Our eyes were so painful we could hardly see. We shed our coats early and then took off our shirts and were down to our underwear. Both of us were getting tired but didn't want to stop for we wanted to get over the summit.

Finally we reached the summit where the travelling was a little better.

Leaving the scattered timber we came out onto a sea of white, but with our eyes so painful we weren't able to admire the beautiful scenery. Bob and I had pretty fair going over the top, making 10 miles, and then we went down the Wrede Creek side until we got to the first dry tree top sticking out of the snow. There we got a fire going to melt snow for a hot drink (no tea) and eat a piece of bannock. We were nearly played out. While we were resting beside our little fire we saw a flock of ptarmigan playing on the snow across a steep gully. It would have been nice to have one or two of them, but it would have been nearly impossible to climb down that gully and up the other side in that deep snow, so we had to be content to sit and watch them.

The snow wasn't as deep on this side of the divide. We wanted to go as far as we could so Bob and I wallowed through the soft snow until we got to some dry wood above the canyon, and there we made camp for the night. The afternoon had been quite warm and melted the snow on our moccasins until we had wet feet, so we got a good fire going to dry everything out. It froze again at night and we were on the trail at daylight.

After a mile we had to bypass the canyon, which meant we had to haul the toboggan up the rock ledges with a long rope, work our way along the mountainside, then lower the toboggan down the same way at the lower end of the canyon, crossing and recrossing the creek, which was at times as much as 15 feet below us.

There was a lot less snow as we lost altitude. The weather really warmed up and the snow became wet and sticky, making for heavy going. We stopped for a rest, melted snow for a hot drink and ate some dry bannock. Our grub was down to a little oatmeal and flour. We were hoping we could make it to Shorty's trap cabin that night. We took turns breaking trail and helping the dogs by pushing on the toboggan. The toboggan was getting wet, making it heavy going for the dogs. We wanted to get some meat from Shorty's moose kill, but when we got to the site we saw wolf tracks and found where the snow had settled. The wolves went in under the brush covering and dragged what was left out. All we found were leg bones.

I wanted to camp and cook the bones over the fire to get the marrow out but Bob wanted to go on to the cabin. He said, "There will be tea there anyway." Then I wanted to put the bones on the toboggan. "Oh God, no," Bob said. "We can't pull another pound." "Well," I said, "I'll help the dogs," (the hardest job) "and you can break trail."

I tied any bone that had any marrow in it on the toboggan. It took us a long time to make those few miles to the cabin. Bob would rest on any log or windfall along the way, while I would sit on the toboggan. The afternoon was very warm and the snow was almost slush in places. We were just about played out when we finally made the cabin. We found that Shorty had it nailed up for the summer. Bob pried off a board and only got a little tea.

We got a fire going on a bare spot on the bank of the creek. While Bob mixed up the last of our flour to make two small bannocks, one for to-night and one for the next day, I took the moose bones down and washed them in the creek, then put them in the fire to cook the marrow in them. When they were well done we broke them open and got the marrow out of them. Marrow, bannock and tea made a meal fit for a king. Tea tasted good after being without it for several days. Our bannocks had been burnt some lately for we had run out of grease. This time we used some marrow for grease so they didn't burn too badly. We gathered a bunch of spruce boughs and spread them on a patch of bare ground for our bed. With a good fire going we dried out our socks and sweaty underwear as well as we could.

Bob was quite sick during the night. When we got ready to leave in the morning he had a headache and wasn't in very good travelling shape. We had about 12 miles to go to Shorty's home cabin on the Ingenika. I said I'd handle the toboggan, so we started out. We were going north and the south slopes were bare with shale rock ledges in places. It was some job getting the toboggan up. We had several ups and downs and bare side hills, so I was getting pretty tired. We got to a level stretch through some second-growth pine. Bob said he'd spell me off so I went ahead, coming to a sharp pitch down to a lower level. I ran down so the dogs wouldn't step on my snowshoes and trip me up.

I looked back just as the dogs broke over and started down the hill. A rabbit ran across the trail. Peggy, the lead dog, dove after it anticipating a rabbit dinner. Bob intended to drag his snowshoes to hold the toboggan back, but the toboggan was jerked away from him and upset. Bob ended up going head-first down into four feet of snow. There was no way I could keep from laughing to see those snowshoes sticking up in the air. I had to go back and help Bob get straightened out. Then he saw the funny side.

The further down the creek we went the less snow there was. In the more open places we had to pull across some patches of bare ground, but through the patches of big timber, where the sun couldn't get at it, we had pretty fair going. We stopped for a rest about halfway down and had our piece of bannock and tea. Then Bob and I staggered along, getting into Shorty Webber's cabin that night. Shorty wasn't in and Albright and his family had pulled out for down river with their boat, for the ice had gone out of the river.

We were plumb beat that night and were glad for a warm cabin to spend the night. The unwritten law of the north was to never touch another man's grub unless you were starving. We thought we were in that category so we took enough flour to a make a couple of bannocks and some rice. Shorty had a jar of pickles on his homemade table. We had one that was quite a treat. We had a comfortable night, pleasant to be warm and dry for a change.

We decided to leave our toboggan and backpack ourselves and the dogs the next 70 miles to the mouth of the Ingenika. First, we had to cross the Ingenika, for the trail went down the north side. It was a little early to go wading, but it had to be done. We took the dog packs, put them on our own and climbed down off the shore ice into that nice cold water. The dogs had to swim and we had to watch they didn't get swept under the shore ice. The water was nearly up to our hip pockets and we were happy to climb out on the north side. We didn't take time to make a fire to dry out, but we put on dry socks. We had good travelling on the open hillsides where there was only a little snow here and there, but through the timber and along the river we had to put on our snowshoes. Bob and I waded through enough snow to get wet through to our knees. We stopped for tea on a sunny hillside. While resting by the fire we gazed east down the timbered valley to the Finlay River 50 miles away, and we had snowy white mountains both north and south of us.

We made the 20 miles to the Pelly where we wanted to look around for some horses. When Bob Beattie made his last trip over the mountains he got down to the Pelly when it was freezing over. Not wanting to cross with the four horses, he turned them loose to fend for themselves, hung the rigging up in trees, and walked downriver. We hadn't seen any sign on our way up, but on scouting around we found some fresh sign. Finally we located one horse, a chestnut with a blaze face. A small tough cayuse, Paul had been an Indian Department horse at Jasper and was trailed into the Peace River country. He went up the trail with the Bedaux Expedition and had just survived the second winter in this area. He didn't have much to spare for he was skin and bones. We knew Shorty had a trap cabin near here, but rather than looking for it we made camp on the bank of the Pelly River. While we were breaking camp the next morning Shorty showed up from his cabin.

We had scouted around quite a bit and failed to find any more horses. Shorty said he was sure they had died. Paul, the only survivor, was so thin he could only carry the empty riding saddle. Just like yesterday, we had to start out by getting wet, having to wade the Pelly. The water wasn't as deep but we had to carry the dog packs. I had my camera with me and

Fording the Pelly River. White carries the dog packs while Beattie leads Paul, the only surviving horse. Bob White family collection.

wanted to get a picture of us wading the stream, so I left the camera with Shorty to take the picture. Then I had to wade back and get the camera, for Shorty was going back upriver to his main cabin. We put on dry socks, then started down the trail, driving Paul ahead. We saw lots of caribou signs but were not lucky enough to see any. They were just starting their migration back up to their high country, having come down to the lower levels last fall. The dogs and us would sure enjoy a good feed of caribou meat, for our diet of bannock and a little rice wasn't the best for travelling. After a rough day of ups and downs and wading through patches of snow we made camp at the foot of an open side hill where Paul could get some grass. Glad we were to get a good fire and get our clothes dried out.

The next day, about noon, we came to Indian Tomma's temporary camp. They were the only Indians on the Ingenika. We made a pot of tea and were eating a piece of bannock when Indian Tomma came over. He said, "You no meat, me get some." He brought over a piece of caribou that we cooked on sticks by the fire. While he drank tea and visited with us a young Indian lad across the little meadow was singing "There's a Love Knot in my Lariat", one of Wilf Carter's songs.

"What a beautiful voice," we remarked to Tomma.

He said, "All time sing, that boy." He had learned that song, among others, from phonograph records. Tomma said that the boy had just turned 16 years old. "He man now! So has to do his own cooking and live in his own tipi."

We wanted to visit Buck Buchanan again at the Ingenika mine site three miles south of the river. The river was fairly deep so we thought we'd build a raft. Indian Tomma said, "Me got boat. You take him. Two or three hours you come back. OK."

We crossed over and walked up to the mine. Buck and the German lad were just having dinner. Bob and I sat in with them and had the first good meal we had in a long while; moose meat and potatoes, bread and butter, along with fruit. It was a meal fit for a king. Buck said he intended going downriver in a few days. We would try and arrange a ride with him from Fort Grahame. We got another piece of that German lad's home-cured moose meat, bought some rice, butter and flour from Buck, and thanked them for their hospitality.

Bob and I crossed back over the Ingenika, thanked Tomma for the use of the boat, packed up our dogs, shouldered our packs, rounded up Paul and headed downriver. We had one bad stretch through some willows where the snow was slushy before we got to the horse range about six miles up from the mouth of the river. We looked around, found the horses and left Paul with them, making 13 head out of the 34 that had survived a year ago. That night we camped in the old cabin again.

Bob Beattie had a cache of saddles and pack equipment here, but on the ground where mice and chipmunks were playing havoc with them. We laid over a day to build a better cache. We cut the top off four pine trees about 12 feet up, putting two crosspieces of them, then a deck of poles. Caching our equipment on them we used a makeshift ladder to get the stuff up there. After lunch I left Bob to finish storing the stuff while I headed upriver to the horse range with a pack of salt for the horses.

Bob and I planned on building a raft and floating 20 miles down the Finlay River to Fort Grahame. There were no dry logs near the river bank and we didn't feel like dragging them through the patches of snow and brush. We knew of some dry timber upriver. I said that I would take some rope and if I could find some logs near the bank I would build a raft and float it down. After leaving the horses I found some logs by the river and made a raft with eight of them. The weather had been pretty good lately, but today had been rather blustery with the odd snow flurry. One of these hit us just as Jip and I stepped onto the raft. It was only six miles by trail but about 12 by river. Halfway down there was a rapid. I pulled ashore to look it over. There was a swift channel through the rocks that looked OK, so I stepped back on the raft and sailed straight through. It was different to the trip that we would make through there in the coming summer when we lost everything but what we stood in.

The snow let up by the time I landed. Bob had everything stored away. The next morning we floated out of the Ingenika into the Finlay. Bob and I had an agreement that the first one to spot game would do the shooting.

Rounding a bend Bob spotted a caribou on the shore but missed his shot. When the caribou took off our dogs spotted it, jumped off the raft, swam to shore and took off after the caribou. We floated down quite a piece before the dogs showed up along the shore. They swam out to the raft. We lifted the dogs aboard and they thanked us by showering us when they shook themselves dry.

About 10 miles down were three treacherous logjams quite close together, two together on one side and one on the other. Last year three prospectors were going upriver. They had got by the lower jam and were struggling by the second one when their motor sheared a pin. The boat shot back in the fast water into the logjam. The prospectors lost everything and one of them drowned. The two survivors were lucky that it wasn't long until a trapper boat came downriver, picked the two men up, and took them down to Fort Grahame. The prospectors' dogs were left on their own and were later picked up by trappers. One of them was picked up by Shorty Kierce who was to pack with me later that summer, and the dog came with us.

When we got to the logjams Bob and I decided to chance getting through. We crowded the first jam as close as we dared, getting by that one. Then we paddled away from the second one as much as we could, and had to paddle like the dickens to avoid the last one. We were glad to get through and go drifting down the river again, getting into Fort Grahame in good time. We had left there early in March and now it was almost the end of April. We enjoyed visiting Larry Kemple again and once more camped in the little log cabin. However, we were out of luck in getting much in the way of grub for the store was pretty well sold out. We settled for flour, rice and butter. We were rationing the moose meat we got at the mine.

Buck arrived the next morning and said he would take us as far as Finlay Forks for he was going up the Parsnip on his way to Prince George. We loaded our packs and dogs into Buck's 36-foot boat and were on our way. Our first stop was at Jensens' where we enjoyed a coffee and lunch with our visit. Mr and Mrs Jensen were glad to see spring and intended heading out to Prince George in a week or two.

On our way again we came to the dead-water section above the Ospika. At King Gething's makeshift cabin we saw his boat that he'd dragged up on the shore. When we saw the boat we knew King would like it brought downriver, so the three of us got busy and dragged the 36-foot boat down into the water. We tied it alongside Buck's boat. There was no engine but it had a few paddles. Continuing down the Finlay we spotted a boat tied up at Pete Toy's Bar. They were just starting a tea fire on the bank, so we pulled in and landed. It turned out to be the game warden and Andrew Jorgenson, on their way upriver to investigate a rumour brought down by an Indian of a man's foot sticking out of a logjam. They thought there was a chance of it being part of the man who drowned at the Big Creek logjam. Buck was glad to see Andrew, who had trapped his line.

The warden had a can of bully beef that he shared with us, so we had bannock, tea and beef for lunch. While standing around the fire talking the warden asked Bob Beattie where the young fellow was that went up with him. He pointed to me. The warden didn't recognize me for I hadn't shaved since seeing him on the way up. Our company rifle was sticking up in the boat. He asked Bob whose rifle it was. Bob and I had an agreement that if he asked it would be mine for I had a trapper's licence, so he pointed to me. The warden asked me if I had a licence to carry it so I had to show my trapper's licence. Then he asked me if it was loaded. He wouldn't take my word that it wasn't and climbed down the bank to check the rifle. Luckily we had no shells in it. We were lucky we hadn't connected with the caribou above Fort Grahame for he would have pinched us for shooting game out of season. The warden would have had a fit if he had seen us a few hours later.

After lunch they continued upriver while we headed down, calling in at Allan McKinnon's trading post a few miles above Finlay Forks. Bob and I didn't like the idea of running the Finlay rapids in our powerless boat. Buck said he would run us down if we would help him straighten up the grub cache he had near his cabin at Wicked River. It was on high posts and had developed a lean, and Buck was afraid it might fall over. The rapids were plenty rough and we were glad to get them behind us. We were glad we hadn't tried it on our own, for that 36-foot boat is cumbersome to handle with paddles as we were to find out later. It didn't take long for Buck to fix his cache. We untied our boat from his, bid him goodbye, and shoved our boat out into the river on our last 100-mile stretch.

It was getting late but we wanted to make a few more miles. I watched for game as we sure needed meat and I was the better shot. About seven miles later, while going down Selwyn rapids, I spotted a moose ahead and signalled Bob to hold the boat straight. I fired one shot and down went our moose at the water's edge. It was not too old a bull moose and in fair shape.

With the moose lying there and the game warden only a few hours away Bob got all excited and said, "Hurry up. Just cut off some meat and let's get on our way." He knew the warden better than I did. He said, "If that damn warden catches up with us he will throw the book at us."

We weren't long cutting off both hindquarters. I dug out the liver, cut out the good pieces along the back, and some off the front quarters, for we knew some trappers downriver that would be glad for some fresh meat. We rolled the rest of the carcass into the river, jumped into our boat, and were on our way again. Our two dogs enjoyed their feed of fresh meat.

We passed the Selwyn trap cabin where we should have stopped, but both of us wanted to make the Barnard River cabin, which was a good cabin with a bunk full of good hay. We were still drifting when it began to get dark. Then the water began to slow up, with chunks of ice floating around us. The further we went the more ice, which meant only one thing: an ice jam below. We were hoping it would be below the cabin. It had clouded over and got quite dark, and it was weird paddling through those floating chunks of ice.

The further we went the more ice. The water had blocked up enough to change the lay of the land. We had difficulty finding the landing leading up to the cabin, which we finally did about 11 o'clock. We were getting pretty cold out there and were glad to get a fire going in the cabin and some moose liver on to cook. It had been a long day, and with that bunk full of hay we sure didn't need rocking to sleep.

When we looked out at daylight the ice jam had broke and left our boat high and dry on the shore. After a good breakfast of more liver and moose meat we dragged our boat down and got it afloat. After getting our stuff loaded we shoved our boat out into the current and had an early start. Although it was the 2nd of May it was cold with a fine drizzle falling. To our disappointment there was a fair little breeze from the east that kept turning our boat sideways and slowing our progress. Lots of chunks of ice were scattered along the river bank. When we got a half mile east of the cabin, where the ice jam had been, the ice was piled up 10 feet high on both sides of the river. The ice above the jam had pushed back into the timber in several places, leaving quite a mess.

There were lots of lumps of ice going by us, making better time than we were for they were lower in the river current. When we saw a big chunk coming by we got the idea of getting a rope on it and giving us a tow. When the ice would lead us into rough water we would turn it loose, paddle out and around, and wait for another chunk to come along. It helped us gain some distance as well as giving us a chance to get out of that chilly wind at times. There was an old grease pail in the boat. We set it up on some rocks in the bottom of the boat and got a little fire going in it.

At mid morning we passed the Teepee rapids caused by big rocks in the bed of the river. Normally they don't present too much trouble for there was lots of room around. But at certain stages of water they could be treacherous to anyone not familiar with the river. Two men were to drown there later that summer.

About noon Bob and I decided to land so we could run around and get warmed up. We picked a place where there was very little shore ice, tied up the boat, got a fire going, made a pot of tea, cooked some moose meat on sticks, and toasted the bannock that we had made that morning. Our dogs were glad to be able to run around. They didn't think too much of that boat ride.

Back on the river again, feeling much better, we came to a place where the river widened out and saw a white patch on the water ahead. We drifted on quietly and ended up in the middle of a large flock of white swans when they decided to take off into the wind, the direction we were going. There were more than 50 in the flock. No doubt they had landed there for a rest on their long flight north. They were on both sides of us and some over our heads. What a noise they made with their wings and honking. What a magnificent sight with their white bodies and long necks.

We were now near the Ne Parle Pas rapids. We talked it over as to what we should do, line the boat down or take a chance and run through. Two years before, when we came down with the Bedaux Expedition, we had to walk down. I asked Bob what he thought. He said that at this stage of water it shouldn't be too bad. There were still blocks of ice along the shore that would make it difficult to line down, which helped us decide to run through.

So we found ourselves getting into the fast water at the head of the rapids, quite a sensation as the river drops and you can't see what is ahead. As we started down, the white water on our right made quite a noise. There was a big eddy on the left. As we shot down, Bob hollered to throw the boat over just a little from the white water. We sailed right through and thought there was nothing to it. Then the boat turned toward shore and upriver. By this time we knew we were in the big eddy. When it started out toward that boiling white water it scared the daylights out of us. We didn't quite know what to do for the eddy would ride and fall in the centre. Bob hollered to paddle, but you couldn't do much with the boat going up and down. One second there would be no water, then the next second you'd be in it to the elbow. We both knew if we hit that white water broadside there would be a slim chance of surviving. Just as we were about to enter the rough water the current in the eddy turned our boat down and we got into the clear again. But we couldn't get clear of the eddy until we made another round. We cooled off some and paddled toward the centre until we passed the danger point. Then we paddled for all we were worth to the outside of the eddy. Our boat rode quite high in the water, so we couldn't get much purchase with our paddles. When it started back up the eddy again we were close enough to shore for me to jump, landing in water over my knees. Pulling the boat in, I lined it down a few yards, jumped in, and we were away again. We both realized we'd had a close call.

Now we were in more familiar waters. We passed Fred Chapman's place and Stanley Wallace's, but didn't take the time to call in for we wanted to make Jim Beattie's for the night. About an hour before dark we rounded a bend and saw where there had been a big ice jam. At Jim Beattie's boat landing the ice was piled up 10 feet high on both sides of the river. It looked as if the jam had broken the day before. We had quite a time climbing up that wall of ice chunks and had to do a lot of work chopping out those blocks of ice to make it safe to leave our boat tied up there.

Then we walked the half mile to the Beattie Ranch. They were quite happy when we said we had some moose meat for them, and weren't long in hooking up a team to a wagon and driving down to pick it up. Jim Beattie and his family were noted for their hospitality. We really enjoyed our overnight stay and visit with them, and also the good food, with the bulk of it produced on their own place. We had all kinds of vegetables, milk, butter and eggs, sure a welcome change from our diet of mostly rice and bannock.

It was getting on into the day by the time we untied our boat and got floating down the Peace. We were 40 miles from Hudson Hope and wanted to get there by night. We shoved off into the water and floated down with a wall of ice on both sides until we got to the site of the ice jam. As we were drifting by we couldn't help but admire the beautiful location of the Beattie Ranch with well over a section of the best river bottom land, and 20 Mile Creek coming in from a gap in the mountains to the north. And to think that all the Beattie buildings, including their beautiful 40-square-foot log house, would be burned and the whole valley would be under several hundred feet of water when they built that W.A.C. Bennett dam.

Bob and I had a nice trip down the Peace and landed at the Portage cabin at the head of the canyon a little after noon. We pulled King's boat well up on shore for this was the end of the boat ride. From here it was about an 18-mile hike to Hudson Hope. After a bit to eat we put a pack on each of our dogs, shouldered our packs, and headed out. The trail leads away from the river through a pass between Bullhead and Portage Mountain. About halfway over we stopped for a rest at the Boiler. This big boiler was part of some mining equipment that was shipped in to mine gold at Gold Bar, 10 miles above the Beattie Ranch, about 15 to 20 years ago. The mining fizzled out, and a lot of equipment was left where it was, including this boiler, which got to be quite a landmark on the trail over the Portage. We arrived in Hudson Hope about dark, pretty well tired out, Bob going to his home, while I went to stay with my old friends, the Peck family.

Summer 1936

Jay Sherwood

While Carl Davidson, Bob Beattie, Bob White and the other men involved in Bedaux's Empire Ranch were out at the site, Charles Bedaux became worried about the progress of the ranch, especially since he, Fern and Josephine were planning a trip to the location that summer. On April 3, 1936 he sent a telegram to Jack MacDougall, a member of both his 1932 and 1934 trips to northern BC. "Can you take four dollar day job plus railway expenses to go Edmonton Prince George Hazelton and ranch to find where my goods are and what progress has been made."

MacDougall accepted, provided all his expenses from Hazelton to the ranch were paid. On April 13 Bedaux sent MacDougall a letter. "You will await the arrival of your brother-in-law, Bob Beattie, who is supposed to return to Hudson's Hope in May and from him you will try to obtain the following information." After detailing the items he wanted MacDougall to locate, Bedaux wrote:

> From Bob Beattie when he comes back in May, you will find out what Carl Davidson has or has not accomplished to date. Has he been on the location this winter? Has all the stuff been finally moved up? Have we lost more horses? In other words, has Carl Davidson done his job?
>
> If Carl Davidson, in your estimation, has failed in every respect, you will locate him and after reading it and sealing it, hand him Letter #1. If he has tried his best but simply is not the man for the job, you will instead tear up Letter #1, read and seal #2 and hand it over to him. If you find that he has done his level best and has done a good job of it, then you will tear up both letters and keep him on the job. As soon as you have done that, you will telegraph me which letter you gave him, if any.
>
> After this has been done you will study the best way to go from Hazelton to the ranch and determine whether it is to be done partly by boat and partly by pack train or if it is to be done all by pack train.

If boats are needed, you will find out whether they are available and what they cost.

You will also find out how many horses we have available and how many are needed to move my wife, Josephine and me from Hazelton to the ranch and again find out how much horses can be rented for at Hazelton if some are needed.

There is no use in you or Bob Beattie suggesting our going to the ranch by way of Hudson Hope or Prince George because I will not do it. I am going in by way of Hazelton or I am not going at all. The two men, Carl Davidson and Bob Beattie, should long ago have moved themselves so as to operate between the ranch and Hazelton and not go always tramping around by way of Hudson Hope and Prince George.

Now get busy. By the next steamer I will send you $200.00 on account sending it to the same bank where I send the money to Bob Beattie.

Letter #1 to Carl Davidson said, "The reports I get show me that you are not the man for the job I want done. Your services for me will stop on the 31st of May. I am sorry we had to lose so many horses. I hope you will have better luck on your next job." Letter #2 stated, "From the reports I get, I realize that you have done your very best in my interests but that another man more accustomed to horses is better indicated. In appreciation of the fact that you have done your best, I want to give you plenty of notice, so your services with me will stop on July 31st. Your regular salary will be paid up to that time at your bank. Maybe I will have occasion to give you other work from time to time."

Jack MacDougall began his investigation for Bedaux. He found that Carl Davidson had incurred $1700 in expenses that needed to be paid because people were threatening to seize Bedaux's equipment and he gave Davidson Letter #1. On June 10 Bedaux sent a telegram to MacDougall. "Davidson never authorized to spend this money. In fact was specifically instructed not to. Have already given him fifteen hundred dollars since last July in addition to salary. If you must now pay seventeen hundred to secure our kit I wish you to start suit against Davidson for abuse of confidence and spending money without authorization. Am cabling you two thousand dollars from Amsterdam."

Carl Davidson wrote to Bedaux on June 3. "I suppose you will be surprised to hear that I am in Prince

Jack MacDougall.
Floyd Crosby photograph; LAC PA 171484.

George so soon, but as circumstances are I had to come in." Davidson told Bedaux that, "So far I have not been able to see anything of the land in the circle you indicated on the map but mountains and snow. There was without exaggeration from 10 to 15 feet of snow there. I could not get any satisfaction from what I saw so my intention is to go up to Fort Grahame and take Bob Beattie with me and make a trip in for a month or a month and a half and see what we can find when the ground begins to show." After explaining what he had been doing Davidson said that, "My wife and children are all prepared to go up to your Empire, if I may call it so, which we have not found yet but which we hope to do in the near future."

On June 14 Bedaux wrote to Jack MacDougall.

> Too much unpleasant news has shaken our desire to go to Cassiar this year. When you said that Beattie was responsible for hiring the people, it just became too much. When I hear from you as to whether Beattie should be retained on the job, I will know better what to do.
>
> Whether he stays on the job or not, I want to know if you will take the job at $90.00 a month and with Beattie or another man, start a settlement for us either at the location picked by Carl Davidson or at some other location that Bert McCorkell might show you. There is one place called Caribou Flats that Bert McCorkell knows, which I liked a lot in 1926. Not far from there is a lake where my wife, Bert and I were surrounded by four grizzlies one time. A ranch just around there would suit us if you could find enough tillable land.
>
> Do you want such a job at $90.00 a month as Carl Davidson had? I do not mind spending a little money for extra help for window sashes or doors, providing something is done, but I do want the two men who will take on the job to be together always and not running around in different directions the way Carl Davidson and Bob Beattie have done.
>
> If everything is smooth and all right we will go and see what you have done in the summer of 1937.

Bedaux concluded his letter by saying, "I am sorry I am not going to see you and the boys this year. Write me."

In June, George Myers wrote Bedaux a letter describing in detail his experiences at the location during the winter of 1935–36. Although Davidson had hired and paid him for four months, Myers had actually worked for eight months since he wound up staying at the location over the winter.

> Davidson had promised to see that I was to get outside by November 1, 1935. He was at Prince George at this time trying to find out whether he should keep the men and go ahead with building camps and so while waiting, freeze-up overtook him and so I never saw him until March 30, 1936 and the meeting took place at the head of Sustut River, the location camp. Why it took him so long to get there I do not know but he told me he was laid up for six weeks with broken ribs and there were also a few other reasons, but as to them he can say

in his own behalf, but at the time Carl Davidson was in Prince George waiting for information from you in respect to the building, Bob Beattie and a helper, E. [Ed] Bird, were doing the packing, while I and another man, L. Gerlock, were making hay, which we did until the 12th of October 1935. When two feet of snow stopped any more hay-making we then started to build a cabin to live in as we were still living in tents at this time.

On November 4, 1935 Bob Beattie packed his last load to the camp. Gerlock and I wanted to get out to Prince George. Bob suggested that we could go and he would stay but Davidson had asked us to build a good cache to put all the things in so that the mice would not destroy everything, but we were afraid that he would not build a cache as he was so careless in many ways and so we said we would build a cache and then we would be ready to go. Bob Beattie said that would be all right, that he would go to Fort Grahame in the meantime and be back in 10 days, then we would go, but that was the last of Bob Beattie. He went to Hudson Hope and never came back until March 24, 1936, just about five months in all. L. Gerlock and I were then forced to stay, as we would not desert the horses, 15 head in all. We tried hard to save those horses, but the hay got musty with the wet weather. Horses cannot live on musty hay so that is the reason the fifteen head all died. We were expecting Davidson all this time, so things went until January 15, 1936. The horses had all died by this time and our grub was running short and was very poor. All this time we had no light, no windows, also no baking oven. I had asked Bob Beattie to bring all these things when he was packing and also asked for clothes.

After describing the trip to Fort Grahame in January and the return trip to the location in March, George Myers concluded his letter by stating:

I am writing mostly that Davidson is not as bad as you may think. There are always people knocking other people. There is only one more thing I want to say, Bob Beattie is blaming Davidson for some things that are missing. I know that he is the one at fault for these things. If you care to clear it up when you come this summer, look me up. I only wish to help Davidson where I know he is not at fault. I have written this letter myself and am a very poor writer, so will not write anymore.

Bedaux wrote to Jack MacDougall on June 27, after receiving Myers' letter.

In all my life's experiences, I never saw such a mess as this one. Here I had taken two men, Davidson and Beattie, who had the reputation of going out into the wilderness and building regular towns all by themselves and calling their sons "Sifton" because they had been born on Sifton Pass, but when I gave them a shack development to undertake, they managed to spend, including salaries, close to $7,000 in two years and I haven't even got an inventory of my own goods to show for it, no shack, no land, no nothing and all but 15 horses dead.

The social revolution in France is going on full swing and is playing havoc with me. I must drop any further attempts to develop a ranch in British Columbia until I have time to go there and with a few of you, cruise the country around Kitchener Lake or other places and find a spot that will be likely to hold our interest.

Bedaux asked MacDougall to move all of his equipment to Edmonton. "After that, you and Bob Beattie can go back to Hudson Hope on your own business for I cannot afford, with this difficulty raging in France, to keep either of you on my payroll." Bedaux concluded his letter by saying, "I am sorry things have turned out this way." Bedaux also enclosed a letter to Bob Beattie telling him that his salary would stop on October 31.

While Charles Bedaux was writing these letters, Bob Beattie and Bob White had returned to the location in early May.

Travelling to the Location, Summer 1936

Bob Beattie and I were both very glad to get back from our trip where we could get cleaned up and get some washing done. I got a haircut, shaved my beard off, and was glad to visit many good friends around Hudson Hope.

Bob had mentioned on our way downriver that if he got word from Bedaux that was favourable he would be going back up to Fort Grahame and pack out to the location. He wanted me to go back with him and take charge of the horses. I said it would depend on what I got in the mail. Dr Leibold, who I guided for last fall, had written me several times during the winter, wanting me to outfit a big game hunt for the fall of 1936. There had been two doctors in the party: Dr Leibold, and Dr Care, who Jack MacDougall guided. Bill Pickell was our horse wrangler. Dr Leibold wasn't the easiest hombre to get along with, so I wasn't too anxious to out-fit his party. While in Fort Grahame I had talked with Ed Bird and others who had worked with Davidson and Beattie and they had trouble getting their money. When Bob Beattie offered me the job I said I wouldn't go back unless he wired Bedaux to OK my wages. He sent a telegram to Bedaux in France and word came back that he would OK Bob White's wages at $4.00 a day. I told Bob I would take the job. I would have liked to take out Dr Leibold's party for there would be good money in it, but I thought there would be too many problems.

Bob Beattie wanted to start back as soon as possible. He was taking his family with him; his wife, Bessy, and their three boys, Donny, Bobby and Jerry. King Gething had built a new 40-foot boat and was taking it up the Peace in a day or so on its maiden voyage. We were going to go up with him. I got busy with Bob and family making up packs. Since I would be gone all summer I had a lot of letter writing to catch up. Mother was always the faithful one. She always wrote, whether she got an answer or not. Bob Beattie rented a team and wagon from Shorty Pennington in Hudson Hope and I took two loads of freight over the portage. Then the day arrived when we all went over the portage and camped in the log cabin at the landing, ready for the start upriver in the morning.

King was one of the best river men up there and never got excited in fast water. His new 40-foot boat was quite wide and powered by a big inboard motor. It was the biggest boat to date to ply the upper Peace. When we pulled out into the river on the morning of May 9 we were fairly heavily loaded with freight and 14 people, counting the kids. There was King Gething and his two helpers, the Beattie family, and myself. Short Kierce, a trapper on the upper Finlay, was also on the boat. There were two prospectors, Old Dutch and his partner from Dawson Creek, who were to drown in the Teepee rapids later that summer. There were also two fur buyers, Frank Taylor, who used to buy for the Hudson's Bay Company at Finlay Forks, and Lyle Mason, who was a newcomer at the fur-buying game.

We made fair time except where the current was swift in some of that fast water. We called in at the Jim Beattie Ranch, unloading mail and supplies, and taking on some vegetables, our last chance of getting any for the summer. Then we stopped at Brennan Flats (or Gold Bar) where Billy Mahaffey was operating a very primitive gold digging operation. There were several Hudson Hope boys down in the pit losing sweat for $1.00 a day. We left mail at Stanley Wallace's, Dick Hamilton's and Fred Chapman's place before reaching the Ne Parle Pas rapids where Beattie and I had nearly met our Waterloo on our way down when we got caught

Bob Beattie's family with King Gething's new boat. Bob Beattie family collection.

in the big eddy at the foot of the rapids. King unloaded all the passengers and had us walk up. He and his bow man followed a lead up the south side and made it without any trouble. It was a nice warm day to travel, but toward evening, when we got into the higher mountains, it got quite chilly. We camped for the night below Wicked River in some spruce trees along the river bank. The Beattie family put up a tent while the rest of us rolled out our bedrolls under the trees, and we cooked over an open fire. King was quite satisfied the way his new boat had performed.

After a little shower during the night the sun came out bright but was late getting down to us on account of the high mountains surrounding us. We loaded up and got away in fair time. About 10 miles up we came to the Finlay rapids. King got part way up and hit fast water. We would make a little headway, then slip back again. Finally King dropped back, and swinging over to the south side, let six of us off on a rock ledge. We got out on a point of rock. When King tried again we pulled on the rope and he finally made it up. Just above the rapids we entered the Rocky Mountain Trench, having passed through the main range of the Rockies.

We called at the Finlay Forks trading post where there were a few trappers with fur for sale. The fur buyers put bids on some of the furs and some were sold. Lyle was so low on his bids he never got a skin. Then we started up the Finlay River to Fort Grahame.

We came to Indian Joe's camp where Lyle tried to pick up some cheap fur, but the other buyer stepped in and gave the Indians a fair price. King unloaded some supplies here. The Finlay had a few shallow places where the river widened out, so King had to pick his way up. After a few more stops at trappers' cabins along the way, we arrived in Fort Grahame that evening where Larry Kemple, the Hudson's Bay factor, welcomed us. We

King Gething's boat at Ne Parle Pas rapids. Glenbow NA 1095-20.

landed in front of the store. The first to be unloaded was the mail. Then we all got busy unloading the freight, which had to be carried up the bank. We set up a tent for the Beattie family and a canvas lean-to for the men.

On our way upriver Beattie had made a deal with Shorty Kierce to be my helper on the pack trail for the summer. I was somewhat disappointed for I wanted him to hire one of the Peck boys in Hudson Hope for they were good boys on the trail. Beattie said he and I were to pack together. But he had decided to hire Shorty. Shorty was a nice chap. He only weighed 130 to 135 pounds and was not much over five feet tall. Shorty had trapped up the Finlay with Del Miller this past winter. He had never handled horses and had no pack trail experience, so I didn't know how we were going to make out. We spent the next day making up packs and filling our pack panniers with our grubstake for the summer.

King Gething headed back downriver in the afternoon taking some bales of fur for Larry. Lyle hadn't been able to buy any fur on the trip. Shorty Webber was at the post, so Bob Beattie made arrangements with him to take our packs 20 miles upriver to the mouth of the Ingenika.

Making camp at the mouth of the Ingenika we saw horse tracks and found where two horses had gone up the Finlay. Early the next morning Shorty and I struck out with a lunch to find horses and maybe get some meat. Bob and I had last seen the horses about seven miles up on the hillside back from the river. We looked around most of the day and located 11 head. There should have been 13, so we knew the two we had tracked hadn't got back to the rest. About noon I jumped a black bear and was lucky to get him down with two shots. We dressed him out and found him in fair shape. After locating our horses and leaving them some salt we packed the bear back to camp. The Beattie boys weren't fussy about eating bear meat, but any meat was better than none.

Early the next morning Shorty and I again tried to track the two horses that went up the Finlay. After a tough time tracking them through a lot of windfall and brush we came out on the river bank, followed their tracks up a gravel bar, and saw where they had swam the Finlay. When we got back into camp late that night we were a pair of tired hombres. We decided to let the two horses go for the time being.

The next day was spent sorting out pack saddles and packs for 10 horses. We would have one saddle horse to cross the streams. The following morning Shorty and I struck out at daylight to wrangle the horses, getting them into camp for a late breakfast. We had rigged up a sort of corral out of windfall. When we got the 10 horses packed we turned them loose in the corral to see how they liked their packs. The only one that bucked was the old veteran, Paul. We had packed him with a small trunk, a roll table top, brooms and shovel, thinking he would be the old reliable, but he sure fooled us. We had to laugh at him trying to buck off his pack. But no damage was done and he was good from then on.

Bob and his family were to wait and go up with Shorty Webber, 70 miles by boat to where we were to swim the river. Shorty Kierce and I started out, the horses working pretty good. We camped in a small meadow where the ponies had good grass. The horses weren't in too good shape, some barely making it through the winter, so we had to make easy days and had two more camps before reaching Pelly River.

Shorty and I got along well. He was a willing worker but admitted not being too good with horses. He suggested he do the cooking while I handled the horses, which suited me fine. I also found out that he was no wizard on the cooking. I ate more burnt bannock that summer than all the years I was in the north. But Shorty did the best he could.

On the whole the weather was quite good with some hot days that melted the snow on the mountains, causing the rivers to rise. When we got to the Pelly it was too high to cross without raising the packs. We had to repack and put them up as high as we could. I head and tailed three at a time and led them across so they wouldn't stray off the ford into swimming water. The ford was quite wide and the water cold, straight from the snow banks. I couldn't keep my feet out of the water and after several trips they were darn near paralyzed. My faithful saddle horse, Dusty, got so he didn't want to go in, and I didn't blame him. We finally got all the packs and Shorty across without any mishap and set up camp about 300 yards up the Pelly from where it entered the Ingenika. This is where our pack horse Paul had survived the winter.

When we woke up we saw that the river had risen quite a bit. Going up along the Ingenika we hit a few bad spots and had to cut some trail, making camp late that night about five miles below where we were to cross the river to Shorty's cabin. We made camp on the trail and put the horses upriver. The horse feed was very poor. I should have hobbled them but didn't have the heart to do so. The horses were in poor shape and would need all the help we could give them. Sometime after midnight I heard the horses go past camp, heading downriver. I gave them about an hour, thinking they would graze on the odd patch of grass. Then I rolled out, picked up a bridle and took after them. They had never stopped. When it got daylight I knew I had a long walk ahead. I trailed them back 13 miles to our last camp on the Pelly. They had just got there. After catching one to ride bareback I had quite a time getting them started back up the trail.

About halfway back I met Shorty coming to meet me. I said, "Did you bring anything to eat, Shorty?"

"Hell no, I never thought of it."

We caught a horse for him to ride. When we got into camp we were ready for something to eat. He got busy cooking some hotcakes while I started saddling up.

The day turned out to be a scorcher, bringing more water down from the mountains. When we were opposite Shorty's cabin we signalled Bob. The Beattie family was camped in Shorty's old cabin. Shorty was down-river, so Bob came across in an old boat Shorty had there. The Ingenika was really booming right up into the bush on both sides with quite a bit of driftwood coming down. The plan was to swim the horses here and start up Wrede Creek. I was against putting the horses into that fast water in their condition for there would be a good chance of losing some. We agreed Shorty and I would bring up another pack load providing we could swim the Pelly.

We relayed the packs across the river, lining the boat quite a piece up-stream before we started across. We had to watch out for driftwood. Some were pretty well submerged and hard to see. Eventually we got everything across. After one of Bessie Beattie's good meals Bob put us across the river. The horses were having it rough with practically no feed the night before and all this day. I knew if we camped anywhere short of the Pelly we would have another long walk unless I hobbled them. I asked Shorty if he was game to ride through.

"Hell, yes," he said. "We'll have to walk after the buggers anyway."

It got dark not too long after we started, which made it slow going. Shorty and I were both riding but had to walk at times to get warmed up. We got into camp a little after two o'clock. Riding down off the side hill heading for the camp on the bank of the Pelly, we rode through water up to the horses' knees, so we knew the rivers were over their banks. We camped on a slight rise so we figured we'd be OK for the night, but the Pelly was a mad-looking stream not too many feet away.

We were a pair of tired hombres after we unsaddled and turned the horses loose. I had travelled over 50 miles that day, 14 of it on foot, and Shorty nearly as much. The horses were glad to get into their good range again, the last grass on this 70 miles of river. When the mosquitoes woke us up the sun was shining. A few feet from us, and just an inch or two from coming over the bank was the wildest-looking piece of water you ever saw. The Pelly was bouncing down in a mad rush of foaming water with all kinds of driftwood, and trees 60 feet long. Some of them had very little bark on them, no doubt skinned up coming through the canyon a few miles up. We realized we were completely surrounded by water and were on the highest spot around. We moved back under a jack pine and figured we could stick it out. After getting a bite to eat we waded out to the hill, the water nearly to our belts, and realized how high the water was. The whole Ingenika valley was under water, with the Ingenika River over its banks and running through the timber. There was no chance of getting across the Pelly. We decided we would have to sit it out.

Our first problem was to get some meat. Shorty and I took turns going out with the rifle but had no luck. I decided to go further back on top to look for a lake I had heard about. After climbing over lots of windfall I located the lake and was sitting on a rock along the shore swatting mosquitoes. I had rolled a smoke, but delayed lighting it up on the chance of seeing some game. While looking to the right up the lake I heard a splash. Looking to the left I saw a big moose wading out into the lake not 50 yards away. With a quick shot I got him through the side. He kept going and swam out into the lake. I was about to take a shot at his head when the moose started to turn and I thought he might make it back nearer to shore. But he died before he made the turn. So there was my moose out in the lake. I tried tying poles together and shoving them out, but the moose was too far away. In desperation I peeled off my clothes, swam out, and pushed him into shore. I got the moose out far enough to get the insides out of him. The water wasn't that cold so I enjoyed the swim.

I beat it back to camp. We were both happy to have meat. Time was getting on, but this was the beginning of June and the days were long, so we got busy and wrangled the horses. With two pack horses we rode out to pack our moose in. We had quite a time getting through the windfall, but late that night returned to camp with our moose meat. We turned our horses loose and ended up working most of the night getting light poles ready to start drying meat in the morning. We knew that once the sun came up the blow flies would be out in droves. Shorty had spent some time with the Indians and had helped them dry meat, so he was a great help. Surrounded by water, our camp space was limited. We had to wade out to the hill to get light poles to hang the meat on. That water from the snow banks sure was cold. It took me just below the belt, but above on Shorty. He was a tough little guy and didn't seem to mind too much. We got the meat all hung up, and early the next morning we got busy cutting up meat and getting our smudge going. We got a lot of meat hanging on poles and had to watch the smudges continually for the flies were bad. We had to keep the smoke coming steady and yet not let the fire blaze up. The sun came out and it was hot, a good day for drying meat.

We were happy to get meat for our dogs for we had been short of grub and they were getting pretty hungry. My dog, Jip, wouldn't touch a thing around camp, but Shorty's dog, Rum, would steal anything he could. Jip would watch Rum and get after him when he got near the kitchen packs. At that camp we had a big cake of two-coloured toilet soap. We put it at the foot of the tree where we hung the towel. Rum got hold of it before Jip could stop him and ate most of it. I don't know if it did him any good, but it didn't seem to do Rum any harm.

We heard a motor boat on the river, and a short time later Shorty Webber walked into camp. He had come down the Ingenika but he couldn't come up the still-wild, roaring Pelly to our camp. He tied up at the point and waded up through the timber to our camp. Shorty brought some badly needed baking powder that Bessie had neglected to put in our grub box.

Shorty also told us about Bob Beattie's near-tragic adventure at Shorty's cabin. While we were riding back downriver, the Ingenika rose so fast that when the Beatties were sleeping in the old cabin that night Bob woke up and thought he heard water running. On stepping out of the bunk the old hewn planks on the floor were floating. He sounded the alarm, went out into the darkness, and saw river water running all through the yard and well back into the timber. The only building clear of the water was Shorty's log grub cache up about 10 feet on posts. Bob got a ladder and finally got Bessie and the three boys up into the cache. While wading through the water to the cache young Bobby fell into a hole and nearly got washed away in the dark. Bob spent the rest of the night wading around building a raft out of Shorty Webber's new house logs that he had piled up there. He made a good-sized raft and piled all the stuff he could on it. When daylight came the family set up camp on the raft, stove and all. They were to spend the next five days there.

Shorty arrived back there later that day and helped them get things straightened out. They knew we would be held up at the Pelly and also knew we would need the baking powder. Shorty said he would go down in the boat, then on down to Fort Grahame and see what damage the flood had done. We were glad to see Shorty and doubly glad to get the baking powder, for we sure didn't look forward to bannocks made without baking powder. We gave Shorty what meat he wanted and sure didn't envy his trip downriver with all that driftwood.

We spent five days in our camp, a lot of the time drying and taking care of the meat. The mosquitoes were bad night and morning, but the hot days were good for the meat drying. We cut some logs and dragged them out for our raft when it would be safe to swim the horses. The water finally settled within its banks, so we decided to try the crossing in the morning. That afternoon we roped the raft together, tied it up, and cut all the sweepers that hung out over the water for quite a piece down the river. It would be difficult to get our loaded raft away from the bank in that fast water. We dug the bank down where we were to enter the horses, sacked up all our dried meat, and made up the packs.

Early the next morning we wrangled the horses. The few days rest and good grass had done them a lot of good. After loading all the packs and rigging on the raft it was ready to go, so we put the horses over the bank into that fast water. They shot downstream and out into the Ingenika, then came out on a point of land. We turned our raft loose and worked like the dickens. We got fairly well across when the raft got hung up on a rock and the water started boiling up on one side.

Then Shorty panicked. He kept saying we might drown. To make matters worse the dogs peeled off to swim ashore. They shot down with the current, out into the Ingenika and out of sight around the bend. Shorty kept saying, "They are gone, they are drowned."

I finally told Shorty to get hold of himself. We couldn't pole the raft loose so I had to step off, and with quite a bit of prying got it free. I had to be careful I didn't get left behind when it came loose. We went out into the Ingenika and got the raft to shore around the bend, and tied it up.

Our first concern was to get the horses before they got too far down the trail. After that cold swim they would feel like travelling. We caught up to the horses within a mile and got them back to the raft. We unloaded the raft, saddled up, got the packs tied on, and started down the trail. We ran into a lot of wet trail where the river bottom had been flooded. One section of the trail, at the foot of a high clay bank, was completely washed away. We had to make a long detour up the mountainside to get around a deep gully. We also had to pick our way around some bad windfalls. But we made it down to the horse range camp in two days.

We had been living high on the hog on that good fresh moose meat, but thought we would welcome a change in our diet. There was a good fishing hole at this camp. About sundown Shorty and I rustled a pole and went down to the river where we managed to catch six nice grayling, which were sure good eating. We wrangled our horses early next morning, went down to our cache at the mouth of the river where we made up packs for the 10 horses, and returned to our same camp. That evening we got a few more grayling. The mosquitoes had been very bad since the flood, and we had the added chore of putting up our mosquito bar over our beds. Sometimes it was necessary to get in under the net, before it was time to go to bed, to get away from the hungry hordes.

We made it back to the Pelly in two days. The first camp wasn't the best, and the horse feed was skimpy. I didn't hobble the horses but turned them upriver. We set up camp on the trail on a bit of a side hill. The light breeze we got now and again helped the mosquito situation some, but it didn't help Shorty's temper. Shorty got working on a bannock. When he started cooking it, the smoke kept following Shorty around the fire. Shorty was cussing and finally got so mad he jumped up and kicked the fire, bannock and all, down the hillside. I was busy covering up packs and putting up a lean-to for it looked like we might get a shower. I gave Shorty a little time to cool off, then hollered out, "What are you having for supper tonight, Shorty?" He laughed then and we both got busy gathering up the pieces and started another bannock on its way. Camp cooking has its problems.

During the second day we decided against putting the loaded pack string through all that windfall on the detour we made on the mountainside. We swamped a new trail down the steep side of the deep gully and angled back up the other side. We led our saddle horse up and down a time or two to make a few tracks in the moss, then were lucky enough to get all the pack horses across without any trouble. If any of them had slipped off the trail we would have had quite a time getting them back up.

When we got to the Pelly the water had gone down some so the river was fordable. We had to repack, get the packs up as high as we could, and relay the packs across. It meant several trips back and forth with the saddle horses. It was a cold job and we were glad when we got all the packs across.

We rolled out early the next morning knowing we had a big day ahead of us. We wanted to get all the way up to Shorty Webber's. With no horse feed on the north side of the river we would have to swim the horses across that day. There were a lot more wet spots on the trail due to the flooding of the river flats. Where the trail sneaked along the river's edge the cutbanks underneath were washed out and we had to pick our way around over the top. Our moose meat wasn't fresh anymore so we were living on the dried meat. If the sacks where we had the dried meat got wet or damp the blow flies would blow the meat right through the sacks.

When we arrived at Shorty Webber's we thought Bob Beattie would have a raft ready. Shorty W.'s two boats were also gone, so Shorty K. and I built a light raft, for our first job was to swim the horses across. Bob had cut some of the brush on the other side to give the horses a better chance to get out.

The horses were thirsty, so when we turned them loose quite a piece up the river they went down to get a drink. We got behind them and shoved them in. There was very little driftwood but the Ingenika was quite fast.

Gold mine on the Peace River. Glenbow NA 1095-19.

The current took them down quite a way but they made a good landing on the other side. Shorty and I followed on our little raft. The horse feed was a half mile up Wrede Creek. I took the horses up and found they had lots of good grass to work on.

Then we all enjoyed a good meal that Bessie had cooked up. They still had their camp set up on the raft. We added a couple logs to our little raft, then brought all our packs and rigging across the river without getting anything wet. Then we got busy making up packs for a start up Wrede Creek in the morning. We were to have more awkward packs from here on, for this stuff had been brought up in the boat.

When I brought the horses into camp the next morning we had to sort them out. Bessie and three-year-old Jerry were to ride a horse called Pinto. The other two boys, Donny and Bobby, were to ride the old reliable Dusty. Shorty, Bob and I were to spell off on a bay horse we called Shorty (Clark). We had another horse in the string called Shorty (Hudson), named after their respective owners. So with Shorty Webber and Shorty Kierce it got to be a little confusing. An old sway-backed horse we called Bigenough was to be our stove horse. The stove was a fair-sized kitchen stove with an oven that weighed 80 to 90 pounds stripped. It had to ride right up on top, making an awkward pack. A stocky horse called Blue was to carry a small trunk on one side and a cabinet type Philco radio on the other, a very wide pack that caused us a lot of trail cutting.

After a lot of sorting out, cleaning up the yard and piling up Shorty's building logs, storing and covering up the stuff we were leaving for our next trip, we got started up the trail. In the afternoon the trail came out along the creek bank. I was cutting some trail and walking, leading

Shorty, the saddle horse. I came to a big poplar that had blown down over the trail with the top landing in the stream. We had to go out near the creek bank to get over the log. My saddle horse got over OK, but Blue broke through the overhand of the creek bank with his hind foot and would have landed on his back in the creek if his halter shank hadn't been hooked to the saddle horn. I called for help. When Bob came up Blue was sitting in the creek. I was hoping the halter shank would hold. We had quite a time getting him back up the bank and were hoping the radio hadn't suffered any ill effects. We crossed a fast-running stream coming in from the north and made camp at a slough that had enough grass for the night.

While unpacking, Bobby came to me and said, "You know, Bob, I'm mad at you."

I said, "What did I do now?"

He said, "You didn't cinch our saddle and we fell off on a rock." The trail had led over a big flat rock. When the boys were riding over it they leaned over to look at the rock. The saddle turned and the boys landed on the rock. Luckily they didn't get hurt too badly, mostly their feelings. I told Bobby to get after his dad for that, for Bob was to look after his family's horses while I did all the saddling of the pack horses. They were three great boys and were having the time of their lives.

The next morning we expected we might have a tough time getting up through the canyon. At the foot of it we came to a sheer rock wall on our side of the creek, so it meant crossing over. It was a wild-looking stream, tumbling down over a lot of big rocks. After talking it over we decided I would try crossing on old Dusty. If I could make it we would raise the packs and relay them across. The water went over the seat of the saddle on the upper side at times, yet it would only be stirrup deep on the lower side. The falls above and below made so much noise we couldn't hear each other. I made it across OK and cleared a place for the packs on an upper level. I put Dusty at the water's edge to coach the other horses across. Bob and Shorty raised the packs and sent the horses across. I would catch and unpack them, then send them back for more packs. About halfway through they put Ginger through without raising his pack for he had a case of milk as one side pack, and a case of tomatoes on the other side, which the water wouldn't hurt. As I caught Ginger when he came out, he sort of panicked from the roar of the water. When I let him climb up to the upper ledge his pack hit a tree that knocked him off balance. His hind feet went through the overhang of the bank. He went over backwards and fell 10 feet into the boiling water below the falls, landing on his back. The water rolled him over and over until he got down to where we crossed. He tried to get up but couldn't stand. Bob couldn't get to him from his side. I went out on Dusty, got hold of his halter shank, and held his head up so he didn't drown. I couldn't drag him out with all those rocks. He struggled again and moved down nearer the falls. I waded in on foot to try and get the pack off. As soon as I cut the rope he struggled and I had to reach for some alders to save myself from going over the falls. When I looked around the pack had disappeared over the falls, but Ginger for some reason missed going over and was getting out on the other side.

I felt bad about losing the pack. Bob hollered over to not let it bother me and get the rest of the packs across. Bessie and the kids didn't want to ride across. I cut a big tree almost a foot through and dropped it across. When it hit the water the force took the top of it downstream. I cut another one, a little bigger, which held and made a bridge we could walk on. We stretched a rope across above the log, which was a poor hand rail for the span was too long. We helped Bessie across on the log. It was pretty scary 10 feet above that boiling water. We told Bessie not to look down. Donny walked across on his own. Bob wouldn't carry his two younger boys so Shorty and I packed them over. Bob crossed on the horse. We dragged the stove and radio across on the log. We all felt bad about losing the one pack horse load with the case of canned milk, case of tomatoes, the B and A batteries for the radio, and most of Bessie's supply of shoes. We had a wash tub tied on top of Ginger's pack, but after his fall into the creek it was pretty well flattened out. On a later trip, when the water had gone down, we walked that creek for several miles but all we found was a piece of board from one of the cases.

While we were getting our packs together Bessie handed out some lunch. It was getting late and there wasn't a speck of feed here. We had to climb the mountain to bypass the canyon. We had quite a time getting the pack horses up those wet moss-covered rock ledges. We had to help Bigenough in a few places with his stove pack. After getting up we crossed over the shoulder of the mountain. Getting down on the other side was just as bad or worse. Shorty (Hudson), a chunky bay horse with a blaze face, slipped over a ledge and rolled over but got up on his own, none the worse. A little further down, Potlatch, a big raw-boned bay horse, slipped off the trail and landed with his back downhill. We had to unpack him to get him up. We got down to the creek and soon came to a rock wall on our side. We found a pretty good ford, so we crossed over the stream. A short piece up we came to some good grass and weren't long in deciding to camp.

It had been a long, hard day for all of us and we were glad to set up camp. Bessie Beattie was a wonderful person who never complained and just took everything as it came. We were within a short day of the summit and right in the mountains. The next day we reached the summit in a cold rain and decided to camp for there was good grass. Bob and I couldn't get over the transformation that had taken place since late April. At that time there must have been 20 feet of snow in places, and now, around the middle of June, there was grass high enough to wave with the wind.

The rain eased up as we unpacked. Bob said they would set up camp if I would take the rifle and try for some meat. I liked to hunt. I climbed the mountain to the south. Across two basins to the east I spotted what could be two goats. I worked my way across the first basin and could see two goats quite plainly, but there was a deep canyon between us. I looked around and spotted a caribou lying down quite a distance below me. I worked my way down to get a shot. Our rifle had got its sight out of line and was shooting a little to the left. I missed with my first shot. The caribou jumped up and started to the left, which was lucky, for it got in the way of my next shot and down it went. It was a cow caribou that had lost its calf, no doubt to the wolves. It wasn't in too good shape but would make meat. I let the insides out, made up a pack of one hind-quarter and got back to camp when it started to rain again quite heavily.

After a cold wet night the sun came out when we were eating breakfast. Shorty and Bob were to wrangle the horses and start packing while I was to take the dogs out and pack in the caribou meat. I found the caribou hadn't been touched and got busy cutting it up. I made up the dog packs and a heavy pack for myself. While angling down the mountainside I looked up and saw a big black wolf not more than 50 yards in front of us. He didn't seem scared. We just looked at each other. He must have been quite a scrapper for he had plenty of white scars on him. He still looked at us. Then I reached down, picked up a rock, and tossed it in his direction. He just trotted off. The wolf had smelled the meat. He was pretty hollow looking and it seemed as if he could have used a good feed. After travelling over many snow banks we arrived in camp and got the meat packed on the horses, fighting hordes of mosquitoes.

We headed south across the summit and followed down Johanson Creek. There were still plenty of snow banks everywhere and all the hollows among the rocks were filled with water. Bob started out on foot, with the two boys following on their horse Dusty, then Bessie and Jerry on Pinto. Shorty and I were to follow with the pack string and our saddle horse, Shorty. There were some wet places on the lower levels, so we followed along the mountainside. It was pretty rough going climbing up and down those moss-covered rock ledges. Every gully that came down the mountain had a torrent of water that presented some problems. I was leading the pack string across a stretch of water. I hollered back to Shorty that I would come back and take him across. He was leading Bigenough and shouted that he would climb on behind the stove. He led him up to a big rock and climbed on. Shorty couldn't see over the stove pack, and all I could see of him was his short legs sticking out. Hot-headed Shorty got into trouble halfway across and started jerking on the halter shank. I thought he was going to upset Bigenough among the rocks. He finally said to hell with it, jumped off, and waded ashore. We angled down the mountainside and made camp in some pines on a high bank along Johanson Creek. It was another cold rainy night but we had good shelter and lots of dry wood. The next day we followed down Johanson Creek a few miles to where it met the Sustut River, which we followed up to the location.

Summer at the Location

After we got unpacked, the boys gave me a hand to take the horses down to a nice bunchgrass meadow. We took along some fishing lines to try our luck in the river. We found a nice pool in a bend of the river and cut some willow poles. I had just tossed the line out and handed Donny the pole, intending to get yet another line ready for Bobby, when Donny hollered, "Bob, I got something really big." I gave him a hand. We played the fish around for a while in the pool, then eased him down to a bar, got behind him, and got it up on higher ground. It was a beautiful lake trout and must have weighed 12 pounds. The boys were really excited when they took the fish into camp. We were to get a few more later on and they sure were good eating.

The first priority was to hunt some meat. Shorty would take the rifle early in the morning and try for a moose while Bob and I scouted around and started cutting some building logs. We found some nice pine logs but they were across the Sustut River. We cut some and figured we could find some way of skidding them across the river. Shorty arrived back in camp before noon, driven frantic by the mosquitoes. He hadn't seen anything.

Bessie gave me a bit of lunch and I took the rifle. The mosquitoes were so bad in the bush that I decided to climb the mountainside to timber line and try for mountain goat or caribou. The mosquitoes followed me above the timber. I finally took several runs into the wind and got rid of most of them. I climbed up and over the shoulder of a mountain where I could look down into a saddle between two mountains. To the west was a big basin with a nice blue lake almost 2000 feet below. To the east the mountains sloped off, with numerous snow banks around. I sat down to look over the country and see if I could spot some caribou. All I saw was a black wolf heading for the pass below. I guess the hot sun got the better of him and he stretched out on one of the snow banks to cool off. I climbed down into the saddle, then climbed up the narrow ridge of the mountain to the north. Part way up I spotted two goats, which soon disappeared over the side to the west. When I got to where I had last seen them I couldn't see how they could even get a toe hold on what looked to me like a sheer mountainside. I looked over as far as I dared but could see no sign of them. They must have steady nerves for a misstep there would plunge them 2000 feet to that blue lake below.

I climbed further up the mountain and finally spotted two more goats coming down from the top of the mountain. I dropped down and lay flat with Jip beside me. They worked their way down toward us. The closer they got the more that Jip would look at me, as much as to say, why don't you shoot. They got quite close and one turned partly sideways so I let go a shot. The other goat then ran by on my right. I took a shot at it as it went by. Jip wanted to jump up, but I kept him down for it was a sheer drop on either side of the ridge and I didn't want to scare the goats over the side. They were both hit hard. The first one we got to landed on his back with his hind feet hanging over the cliff. I managed to pull him back onto safe ground and got him dressed out. We worked down the ridge and found the other goat stretched out in the middle of the ridge. They were two nice big billy goats with two nice sets of horns. I dressed out this second goat and cut off a hindquarter for my pack. By the time I climbed down, crossed the saddle, went up over the next mountain and started down on the south side it was dark. They had built up the fire in camp to act as a beacon. I was pretty well beat by the time I picked my way down through the bush and into camp. Goat meat is considered the poorest of all the wild meats, but nevertheless we were all glad to have fresh meat in camp.

The next morning Bob, Shorty and I, along with three dogs, headed up the mountain to pack in the goat meat. We made up a pack for each dog. Bob and I wanted to favour Shorty with a lighter pack since he was so much smaller, but he insisted on carrying as much as we did. They were two big goats and we all had heavy packs. We worked our way back to camp. When we got to timberline we ditched our packs for a rest. We wandered around looking the country over for it was a perfect day to be up on the mountain. We spooked a blue grouse with a family of about a dozen small chicks. Their colour blended with the mossy surroundings so well that after a few seconds we couldn't find any. We shouldered our packs again and struggled the rest of the way down through the bush into camp. Those pack straps really cut into our shoulders. Shorty wasn't long in getting out his hunting knife and cutting both straps to let his pack drop. Bob was a little provoked at him for they were both good saddle latigo straps.

We built a smudge for our horses whenever we could for the mosquitoes really bothered them at times. Smudging them also made for good camp horses. I gave them a ration of salt now and again, which made them easier to catch. I never put a hobble on any of the horses all that summer, and didn't have too many long walks.

The next morning we salted some of the meat and Bessie canned some. We had to get a team lined up to skid in some logs. I knew Dusty was broke to harness and we picked on a big brown horse called Jumbo. After driving them together for a while they worked out pretty good. We spent the rest of the day skidding in logs from across the river. The river was fast and cold and came up a little over our knees. We got in enough logs to keep Bob busy until we got back. Shorty and I were going to take the pack string over the mountains to Shorty Webber's for another load of freight, which would take about a week.

Shorty and I struck out the next morning, making good time as we were travelling light. We ran into a wicked snowstorm going over the summit and darn near froze until the sun finally came out and thawed us.

Shorty and I got into quite an argument on the trip. Bob wasn't the best of providers and we weren't living too high on the hog. Riding along a mountainside I spotted some puff balls, picked the best ones and put them in our kitchen pack.

Shorty said, "What are you doing that for?"

I said, "We'll fry them up when we make camp."

He said, "You can't eat them. They are poisonous. They will kill you."

"No", I said. I had eaten lots of them while living with the Hudson brothers on the Halfway River. In camp, when I was slicing them for the pan Shorty still insisted they were poisonous and begged me not to eat them.

When I got them all fried up and started eating them Shorty said, "Hell, if you are going to die I might as well die too."

I enjoyed the feed, and I think Shorty finally did. They are not as tasty as the mushroom, but much alike.

Then it became my turn to doubt Shorty. He said, "When we get down into the pine country I will get us some pine mushrooms."

I knew the ones he referred to. They had a slight yellow colouring. "No, Shorty," I said, "you can't eat them. They're poisonous."

He said he had eaten lots of them while living with the Millers on the Finlay. Sure enough, the next day we camped in the pines and Shorty brought in and fried up some of those pine mushrooms.

When Shorty started eating them I was like him. I said, "Shorty, if you are going to die, I may as well die too." One thing in their favour, they smelled like mushrooms. Anyway, we suffered no ill effects from either feed.

We had a pretty fair trip. The crossing at the mouth of the canyon wasn't as bad for the water had gone down quite a bit. When we arrived back at our home camp Bob had begun to realize they were getting short of supplies and want us to head right back out to Fort Grahame to get what mail there was along with the goods we needed. We were to take the horses about 120 miles to the mouth of the Ingenika, then raft down the Finlay to Fort Grahame and get a trapper there with a boat to run our supplies up. We spent one day skidding in more logs, so Bob would have more for his building since we would be gone two to three weeks.

We started out with six of our horses carrying light packs. The rigging of the loose horses was packed by the others. We didn't have much time to scout for game. The only fresh meat we got going over the top was one blue grouse and a whistler. The latter are good eating when fat, but the one we got was tough when we cooked it in front of the fire. Bessie had apologized for the bread she sent with us. It turned out to be one of her very few failures. The bread had neglected to rise and was a little soggy. Coupled with Shorty's soapy prunes, both of us were on the sick list by the time we got to Shorty Webber's cabin on the Ingenika. Most trail cooks would pack their kitchen packs with grass or even spruce boughs to keep the packs from rattling, but Shorty had neglected to do that. The prunes had got wet and fell apart, then bounced around on the pack box with a cake or two of Lux toilet soap.

We rafted the rigging across early in the afternoon intending to travel late and make camp at the Pelly River. I climbed on Dusty without a saddle and led the horses down to the river. Shorty chased the rest in after me and we had an easy swim across. Shorty followed on the raft. We left it roped together, for we would need it on the way back. After getting packed up we decided to try for a fish or two, for we thought that might get us feeling better. Both of us got a nice rainbow. We arrived in camp at the Pelly late that night, both of us feeling pretty rough.

The next day was a tough one for we were no better. We camped about halfway to our horse range camp. The following morning I was feeling better but Shorty was still sick. We decided to travel straight to the horse range camp without stopping and try for some fish at a good fishing hole near there. During the day I got ahead of Shorty, and when I turned into camp only five horses followed me. I unpacked those that had packs and got busy setting up camp. No more horses showed up and after a while I got worried that something may have happened to Shorty. Just as I started to saddle my horse a pack horse came out of the bush up the trail followed by more horses, then Shorty. I said, "What happened? You sure had me worried."

He said, "I darn near died a couple of times today. I had to get off and lay down a couple of times along the way."

By this time we had decided the cause of our sickness was Shorty's stew made of macaroni, rice and the whistler meat. The meat had been OK but had been unwrapped in the hot packs too long. I had eaten sparingly of it, but Shorty had taken on a big feed and was really sick. I think the sour bread and soapy prunes contributed to it as well.

We got out our fishing lines but had no luck. Since Shorty was sick it gave me a chance to cook and make a bannock that wasn't burnt. You start your bannock cooking over the fire, then drag out enough coals to put behind your fry pan to keep the bannock from getting a chill. Tilt the pan up to get the heat from the fire. The more it cooks the more you tilt it. By rotating the bannock in the pan you can get it all a nice golden brown if you are lucky.

We tried our fishing hole again before sunset and got five nice grayling. We gave our dogs one apiece and cleaned and boiled the other three for ourselves. They were sure good eating. Shorty and I cut some dry trees down along the river bank and roped together a good-sized raft. Since there was no horse feed from here to the mouth of the river we intended leaving them here. However, we were going to put the saddles and packs on the raft, float down to the mouth of the Ingenika and unload the rigging before taking the raft down the Finlay to Fort Graham.

Early the next morning we had the raft loaded and ready to start. It was only six miles by trail, but about twelve by the river. There was only one bad rapid about halfway down. Bob and I had rafted down that section of the river late in April. We looked the rapid over and I asked Shorty what he thought of it.

He said, "I'm game if you are."

I was a little worried after he had panicked on the Pelly crossing. I had rigged up a sweep on each end of the raft and all we had to do was keep it straight and sail down through.

When we hit the fast water Shorty got excited and kept saying, "Can we make it? We'll never make it." Then he gave a big jerk on the sweeper, which turned the raft nearly crosswise.

I couldn't get it back for we were near the rocks. I knew then that it was all up and that we would never make it. I hollered to Shorty to get ready to jump for a rock. It was all over in a few seconds. The raft slid up on a rock. The force of the water sucked it down and everything went.

Shorty piled off into a rock. I just had enough time to grab two things, a riding saddle and a pack box that had a few extra pack manties and my two goat heads. The rest of the stuff went sailing down the river.

That was an awful feeling and one of the worst disappointments I ever had in my life. There we were standing on the rock in our ragged overalls with the water boiling around us. I had a new pair of overalls in our pack for we intended to change into better clothing when we unpacked at the forks. They went down the river along with our bedrolls, rifle, axes, our canvas fly that we used instead of a tent, all of what little grub we had, our kitchen utensils, and all of our pack rigging. It all added up to quite a loss.

My worst loss, and what I felt so bad about, was losing my camera and six exposed films. I had gone to a lot of trouble getting pictures since we left Hudson Hope and I had what could have been some good ones: the high water on the Pelly and Ingenika Rivers, our horses swimming the rivers, as well as the pack horses climbing over snow banks and the rocky mountainsides. I had carried that camera and got some good pictures on the Bedaux Expedition. To lose the whole works sure made me feel bad.

Shorty felt bad, for he thought he was more-or-less responsible.

"Well, Shorty," I said, "at least we still have our skins, and it's no use crying over spilt milk. The thing is, what are we going to do now?"

We talked it over and thought if we jogged three miles down the trail we might be able to salvage some of it if it came near the north bank where the current normally went. There were a few ups and downs on the trail and we had worked up quite a sweat as we were coming out through the timber toward the river. When we got to the bank we could see it was no use. The water in the Finlay was fairly high and had backed up into the Ingenika so that the current was out from the bank.

We sat down on a log to cool off just as our stuff came floating around the bend, all of it way too far out to get any of it. We checked the things off as they floated out into the Finlay. There were riding and pack saddles, some pack boxes, my bedroll, the pair of angora chaps that I had been wearing and figured on laying claim to at the end of the season. Buckled in the belt were my spurs that I thought a lot of.

As Shorty and I sat there we realized that all the stuff hadn't come down, and we thought it might have got caught in some eddy. We walked back up the trail, got some poles from a logjam, and went out to try and pry our raft loose. My riding slicker was trapped between the logs and I couldn't reach it in the fast water. While we were working on the raft it let loose and shot downstream, not to be seen again. Shorty and I had quite a time prying the raft loose from the point of the rock where the force of the water had it pinned.

Eventually we got it free, loaded the box and saddle, and floated downstream to see what we could find. In the first eddy we found some pack saddles, some empty boxes, and our canvas fly. Further down we found some bales of blankets. We had made our extra saddle blankets into side packs. Those packs were really soaked and when we picked them up they nearly submerged the raft. We rounded a bend and saw a bundle hung on a rock where the water broke into a back channel. We landed and Shorty went over to pick up his bed roll. It was so soaked he couldn't lift it. Shorty dragged it to shore and walked on it to get some of the water out. We got it on the raft and floated down to the forks.

It was dark by the time we got our raft unloaded and a fire going. We had no axe and had to gather up scraps. We dragged in some windfall, got a fair-sized fire going, and hung up some of the wet blankets to dry out. We hadn't had anything to eat since early morning. Shorty and I scouted around an old log cabin that was often used by trappers going up- and downriver. We found a handful of rice in a baking powder can and a beat-up aluminum pot that we straightened out and scoured with sand. When the little dab of rice was cooked we ate it out of the pot with chips we had whittled. There wasn't much rice. We ate about half, saving the rest for morning, for it would take most of the day to float down to Fort Grahame. We were a pretty dejected pair of hombres when we rolled ourselves up in our damp saddle blankets that night.

After getting pretty well rested, the first thing we did was to check our saddle cache to see if we had enough saddle equipment with what we salvaged to outfit our pack string. There was another cache of Bedaux stuff in Fort Grahame. We were hoping we could get the rest of the stuff there along with the axes and kitchenware. Shorty and I shared the bit of rice, then got on the raft with our two dogs.

I had made up my mind to handle the raft myself and was glad when Shorty agreed to it. I had rigged up some crude oars so I could row backwards to slow the raft down, giving us more time to look things over in the bad places. While I was trimming off some knots from the paddles with my jackknife it slipped out of my hands and disappeared down through a crack in the raft. There went our only remaining tool. Talk about luck.

We were a little anxious as to what had happened at the Big Creek logjams. When we rounded the bend above the jams Shorty stood up to see what he could see. He said the three logjams were still there. I was rowing backwards to slow us as much as possible. As we were nearing the first jam Shorty noticed a new back channel that had been cut through between the logjam and the west bank. I asked about sweepers. Shorty said that he couldn't see any but it was narrow and crooked. We decided to try it and I turned the raft into the channel. I told Shorty that if we tangled with a sweeper and had to jump for it to go for the main bank for it could be days before any trapper would come along. We kept our eyes skinned for sweepers. There were a few trees leaning out over the channel but we ducked under them and sailed right through. We sure were relieved.

Looking back up to the three logjams, they hadn't changed much, except to get a little bigger. Shorty and I thought back to the time over a year ago when three men had lost everything they had and one drowned in this jam. Shorty's dog, Rum, was one of the survivors of their dogs. As we were relaxing on the raft I saw a sight I had never seen before. At the bend of the river below us, where Big Creek entered from the east, there was a big, high cutbank with a lot of good-sized timber. We were looking in that direction when the whole hillside let loose for several hundred feet and slid quickly into the river. There was such a volume of dirt and trees that it just seemed to push the whole river in our direction. We were over on the west side of the river and only felt a few of the waves. It was quite a sight, and to think it took place as we were there. We soon ran into dirty water, which continued on downriver.

We were wondering what we were going to do about a rifle. Shorty said he had an old 38 Colt revolver that Frank the Indian wanted to trade him last spring. He said that if he was around he would see what he could do in a trade for a gun. We floated around the bend and landed at Fort Grahame late in the afternoon, quite a sight as our overalls were in rags.

We met several trappers we knew: Bob Fry, Del Miller, Shorty Webber and others. When they found out what had happened they said, "Don't worry about it, boys. You saved your lives. That's the main thing."

All we had on the raft was my two goat heads wrapped up in a tarp. They asked when we had last eaten and I said we hadn't much the last two days. Shorty Webber said to come up to his tent and he would cook up something. He put potatoes on to boil. He said that we should have been here the last couple of days for they had a real wing-ding of a party. Several of the trappers had pulled out to go downriver this morning.

"You know," he said, "we didn't drink it all." He took us back in the bush and from a cache behind a tree pulled out a bottle of Hudson Bay rum, pulled the cork and said, "Here. Take a shot. It'll make you feel better." On our empty stomachs that rum sure made us feel good. We enjoyed our visit with Shorty and other trappers and the good meal he cooked for us of potatoes, bacon and eggs, bannock and tea – the first eggs and potatoes we'd had in a long while.

Then we went over to the Hudson's Bay store to see Larry Kemple.

Larry was a good head and let us have our overalls, shirts, socks and underwear at cost. We got Mrs Kemple to sew up some small mosquito nets to put over the head of our bed rolls. We looked in the Bedaux cache and got some bed blankets. With a sponge-off that evening, clean clothes and dry blankets we felt like the King of England.

The next morning I said, "Shorty, we'll take it easy today, and pull out in the morning." We spent the day making up our list of supplies and getting stuff we needed from the Bedaux cache. Shorty Webber agreed to take the supplies and us up to the mouth of the Ingenika in his boat. Shorty Kierce met Frank the Indian. The only trade he could make for his 38 Colt revolver was a 30-30 Winchester rifle without a stock. He wanted me to have a look at it. It was a long-barrelled 30-30 Winchester and a good-looking rifle. We knew of a rifle stock hanging in a tree in an old Indian camp 50 miles up the Ingenika, so I asked Indian Frank about it.

He said, "That Winchester stock, you take him."

I said to Shorty, "It's up to you, but I'm sure we could fix it up and no doubt make you a good gun." Shorty didn't want the 38, so he made the trade.

That afternoon King Gething arrived with the mail boat, and my good friend, Don Peck, was with him.

The Indians had a big pow-wow going in a log cabin that evening. Don and I were feeling pretty good on a drink or two of rum and went down to see what was going on. Somehow I got hold of a button accordion (I had one once but never really learned to play it). The Indians we knew would slap me on the back saying, "You make good music." All of us had a good time. Don called a few square dances.

The next morning I sent my goat heads down with Don Peck. We loaded our supplies into Shorty's boat and he took us up to the mouth of the Ingenika. After unloading the boat we got Shorty to run us up to where we wrecked on the chance we could find the rifle and axes, but the water was too fast. We worked a can of honey to shore and managed to get it. We sure appreciated Shorty Webber's help.

Shorty Kierce and I were in a lot better shape when we set up camp than the last time we had been here. I told Shorty we'd each ride a horse, so we got busy and made up packs for nine horses. The next morning we walked up, wrangled the horses, brought them back and had to fit new saddles on most of them. We packed up and headed back to camp at the horse range. In two days we made the Pelly, picking up the rifle stock at the old Indian camp on the way. The Pelly was down enough so we could ford it without raising the packs.

We were anxious to see if our rifle stock would fit but soon found out that it was for a Savage rifle, not a Winchester. But with a little whittling we got it to fit after a fashion. We had to drill another hole through the wood, which we did by burning it through with red-hot nails, used a four-inch spike as a bolt that we riveted on a rock, then wrapped it up with tape. It was a pretty crude but solid job.

"Well," I said, "Shorty, there's your rifle. Better try it out."

He wasn't much of a rifle man and was a little afraid of it. We picked out a small rock down in the river. Shorty's shot hit in the water halfway to the rock. "Well," he said, "I know where it shoots anyway."

Then I took a shot and hit dead on, and I knew that Shorty had a good gun. The rifling in the barrel was in real good shape.

After crossing the Ingenika at Shorty Webber's cabin we headed up Wrede Creek again. On the second day we passed Indian Tomma and his family who were on their way to visit some relatives in the Kitchener Lake area, about three days' travel northwest of our home camp. They were taking their time travelling on foot, everyone carrying big packs except the bucks who only carried their axe and rifle. They had about 12 dogs, each carrying big packs. Some of the squaws had a child on top of their big packs.

That afternoon Shorty spotted a moose in a draw. I said, "You take the rifle and go after him. I'll take care of the horses." After a while I heard a shot, then later Shorty rode up. I said, "Did you get some meat?"

"That damn rifle," he said, "is no good." I asked him if he wanted to sell it. He said that he would sell it to me for 10 dollars. I gave him the money and became the new owner of the rifle. It turned out to be a very good gun and I still have it 46 years later.

We also had some mishaps. The cinches became a little loose and Jumbo's pack started to turn, so he bucked it off, scattering his things along the mountainside. A little later Shorty (Hudson) tried to buck his pack of, but his halter shank being tied up short, he couldn't get his head down. When I called him he came running to me and we got him straightened out.

I wanted to try for a caribou so we made camp at timberline. It was always risky camping anywhere near or above timberline, for wicked storms can come up in a hurry. Shorty said he'd set up camp, so I took off up a narrow basin to the north. There were lots of whistlers around and they announced my coming all the way up the basin. I spotted some caribou high up on the right side but couldn't get very close. I took a long shot and hit one, who headed down the mountain then went out of sight. I worked my way up the mountain, then saw it quite close and still coming in my direction. Before I could get my rifle up to shoot it piled up dead not far in front of me. It was a nice fat caribou. I made up a pack and took it into camp.

In the morning we didn't light a fire but headed up the mountain with our two dogs and packed the caribou down into camp. By this time it was raining pretty good. We decided we had better move camp right away. While Shorty made up the packs I wrangled the horses. As we were packing up it settled into a driving rain with a high wind blowing. When we got through packing we were soaked right through.

We travelled for two and a half hours and camped when we came to some good wood and shelter. We got our lean-to set up in a sheltered place and soon had a good fire going. We got some grub on to cook, then peeled off and dried out our clothes. The fire felt good after our cold ride. We lined our shelter with lots of balsam boughs so had a comfortable camp. The caribou meat cooked on sticks by the fire had enough fat on it to make it tasty. It had settled in to a steady cold rain with the odd flurry of snow and it looked like it would be with us for the rest of the day. We decided to hang up a whole hindquarter of the caribou by the fire and start it cooking. We kept turning it during the day. As it cooked we would cut pieces off to eat. With a good bannock fire we had bannock that wasn't burnt, boiled rice with lots of butter, and with some dried fruit boiled up and tea, who could ask for more. It was a miserable wet day, but we enjoyed it.

The next morning Shorty and I were packing Slim, one of our best pack horses, a tall bay with high withers and a good saddle back. We always put a heavy pack on him. It was job enough for me to hold the pack up with my chest until I got the basket hitch on it. It was doubly hard for Shorty, so I nearly always went around to give him a hand. This time he held the pack up with his head and was reaching over his head to tie the basket hitch when the ropes got all tangled up. Before I got there to help, hot-headed Shorty just stepped back and let the pack drop. It hung in the ropes and swung under the horse. I grabbed Slim's halter shank in time to prevent any damage but I was put out and told Shorty that it was a good way to spoil a good pack horse. Shorty wasn't cut out to be a packer. We got on the trail and made the home camp that night. The Beatties were glad to get the supplies and mail, and also the meat, for Bob hadn't had any luck.

We had had quite a time with one of our pack horses, Potlatch, the last several days. He had developed cracked hoofs on both hind feet. One got so sore he had a bad time getting along the rocky mountainsides. We had a horseshoeing outfit with us but no horseshoes. One night we dug up a tent rod, got a good fire going, flattened the rod out on a rock and made a pair of shoes. We made the holes for the nails with a coal chisel. We had to throw Potlatch to get the shoes on, for his feet were so tender. The horseshoes proved successful and he wore them until the end of the season.

The next morning we got busy and skidded in some poles for the roof of the building that Bob had pretty well up. Halfway through the morning I developed a sharp pain in my right side and got so sick I had to lie down. When it was still bad in the afternoon we came to the conclusion that it was appendicitis. There wasn't much we could do about it but hope that it would pass. Bessie suggested that cold packs might help, so late in the afternoon I went down to the river. While the boys fished they kept me supplied with cold rags from the river, which I held on my side. They seemed to do some good. I didn't eat any dinner or supper.

After not too good a night I ate some breakfast but didn't feel much like working. Bob said, "If you feel up to it you can go out and maybe get us some more meat."

My side was sore, but I thought walking might help it. I always wanted to hunt the mountain southeast of camp, so I crossed the river and started up the very steep north side. After getting quite a piece above timberline I looked down and boy, did I feel like a fly on a wall. I worked my way on up to the top, and the view was well worth the climb. Our camp looked like fly specks down there in the valley. Off to the left was a big basin with a nice blue lake several thousand feet below. A shallower basin led off to the right. Ahead, across a connecting ridge, were jagged mountain peaks sticking out of snow banks. Around these peaks on the snow were some caribou. The only way to get to where they were was across that ridge. I looked at it quite a while before I decided to tackle it. I had to straddle the ridge and inch my way across for it fell away sharply on both sides. Any rock I couldn't get over I pushed off and it went clattering down the mountain. It was a bit scary and took me quite a while, but I finally made it.

The view from that mountain was wonderful. It was good to walk around on the cool snow banks, but the caribou had gone, following south along the mountain ridge. I came to another basin on the left that connected with a valley on the right through a gap. While sitting on the ridge, taking in the sights and trying to spot some game, I saw a grizzly bear that seemed to be looking for whistlers and was working toward the gap below me. It gave me quite a thrill. I didn't know whether I dare tackle him with my rifle. The grizzly fooled around down there among the rocks in the basin on the left and finally went out of sight. I didn't feel like going down there after him, so I went down and followed up the valley on the right, thinking the caribou had gone that way.

On nearing the foot of a big glacier two caribou started up the mountainside. I took a quick shot, and to my surprise, they both dropped and rolled down. The rifle shot echoed in that basin so it was hard to tell where the noise really came from. Another caribou was standing there so I shot it. When I stood up another caribou was running right toward me, so I dropped it. It was all over in a few seconds. I was sure tickled with my newly-acquired rifle. It was a cow and a yearling that I got with the first shot. They were running side by side. The other two were in good shape. I got busy, dressed them out, and started back to camp. I had enjoyed the day but was plenty tired when I got into camp that night for I had walked a long way. My side was still sore but there was not much actual pain. It was to be 10 years before it got that bad again and I had the appendix taken out.

The boys got quite excited when we talked about going back for the meat, so we all decided to go and take all the horses. Those that wouldn't be carrying packs could run loose. Luckily we had a nice day. We crossed the river, went around the foot of a mountain, then up into the basin. Nearing the kill site we spotted a caribou. I wanted Shorty to take a shot but he said that he was scared of that gun. I got off a shot and hit the caribou but it didn't go down and went running down the valley. When we got to the kill we strung a rope around a big rock and tied up all the horses. While skinning out our meat Donny spotted an animal up in the rocks quite a piece off. It looked like a wolverine. Bob said, "Try a shot and see if you can hit him."

I took a fairly coarse sight, and darned if I didn't hit him through the small of the back. Right away it set up the darnedest squealing and growling that wolverines are noted for. He was part way up a rock ridge that was formed by the glacier. This rock ridge was 200 to 300 feet high and extended across the mouth of the basin at the foot of the glacier. These rocks had come down and piled up with the movement of the glacier over the years.

The dogs went up after him, but I was afraid to let Jip tackle him, for one swipe of their paw with those claws could open a dog right up. Shorty and I scrambled up and stunned him with a rock and got him down. The fur was no good, but I skinned him out for a trophy.

We packed in enough wood to make our tea and after making up our packs we had lunch. Then we all climbed over the rock ridge and went for a mile or two up the glacier, which continued up and through a pass. I took Bessie's camera to get some pictures from the summit. On the way up I noticed a line that continued around the top of the basin. When I

Indian Tomma Finds Some Gold

On one of our trips back to the home camp we found Indian Tomma and his family camped nearby. They were on their way back from visiting their relatives over Kitchener Lake way. Tomma was quite excited over some gold they had found over there. He had two lighter-flint vials full of coarse gold. He said they had got that out of two or three shovels full of gravel, which if true would be a tremendous strike. Since we had the only horses in the country he wanted us to go back with him and stake out some claims. The sight of that coarse gold gave us a touch of gold fever, but much as we would have liked to go and have a look, it was too late in the season. We could be snowed in on the wrong side of the mountains and we had our work cut out for us as it was.

Although Shorty Webber and Tomma trapped in the same general area they didn't get along too well. Tomma said, "That man, not much good man." But when we couldn't go back with him, he told Shorty about it. Shorty went back there the following spring with two pack dogs. He was gone over three months. The Kitchener Lake Indians were a rather hostile bunch. When Shorty didn't show up people thought they might have done away with him. Shorty finally came out but he had no gold with him.

got up to it I got the scare of my life. That line was a crack in the ice several hundred feet deep. The crack was four feet wide and covered with a crust of snow in many places. Luckily for me I came on it where it wasn't covered. The glacier was covered with rocks of all sizes that had tumbled down from the high mountains around. Several streams of water ran down the glacier to disappear under the rock ridge, appear below, and run down the valley.

It had been a nice day and the family enjoyed the outing. We started back with the horses and the dogs led us to where they had pulled down the wounded caribou. It was in the creek and the three dogs had eaten a big chunk out of both hindquarters. It started to rain and we got quite wet before getting into camp. As we neared camp we smelled smoke and knew we had company. Indian Tomma and his troop had arrived late that afternoon and set up camp near ours.

We gave the Indians one of the caribou. They weren't long in getting some of the meat to cook on sticks by the fire. Indian Tomma brought word that a white man had been brought up the Ingenika by boat and set out to walk over the mountains to our camp. He said all he could remember of his name was Jack. He had walked through his camp and continued on our trail. When they continued on the next day they failed to see his tracks on the trail. When they started down the mountain Tomma thought the man was lost, so he set fire to an isolated pine tree near the trail, figuring that Jack would come to see the smoke and find the trail.

After a wet night I wrangled the horses and started down the trail with a light bedroll and some grub on an extra horse. I had a feeling that this was my good friend Jack MacDougall from Hudson Hope. Bob said that he had word in the mail that wasn't too favourable and that Bedaux might shut things down.

I kept going until I got to an open mountainside and was glassing the countryside for any sign of smoke. I heard a yo-ho, which seemed to come from my back trail. We answered back and forth until we got together. It turned out to be Shorty, who went out to catch me. He said that Jack MacDougall had walked into camp shortly after I left.

When Shorty and I arrived back in camp I was glad to see my old buddy, Jack MacDougall. He confirmed what I had been thinking, that Bedaux was folding things up. Charles Bedaux had got in touch with Jack in Hudson Hope and hired him as his investigator to go out into that wilderness country and fire Davidson and Beattie, and to try and salvage what he could of his equipment. Jack had to go out to Edmonton, then on to Prince George where he caught up to and laid off Carl Davidson. In Prince George, Jack was lucky to meet a Finlay River trapper, Del Miller, who he knew quite well. "Sure," Del said, "You can be my bow man" when Jack asked him about a ride up the Finlay.

They started down the Crooked River north of Prince George. Del's boat was loaded, making it difficult to take some of the bends. Jack was a better trail man than he was a boat man. At a sharp bend Del told Jack to get ready to throw the bow over. Jack had a good grip on his long pole. At the right moment he struck his pole in the bank to throw the boat over. Instead of the boat going over, Jack went over the side into the water and the boat buried its nose in the bank. After Del fished Jack out of the water he had a good laugh out of it. They travelled down the Crooked and Parsnip rivers, then up the Finlay to Fort Grahame. After Del unloaded a lot of his freight he ran Jack 70 miles up the Ingenika to Shorty Webber's cabin where Jack started out on our trail on foot, carrying a light bed roll and some grub.

The second day out he went through Indian Tomma's camp. Continuing on he got off our trail and on the tracks of two prospectors and three pack horses that were travelling from Takla Lake north to McConnell Creek. Jack spent the night with some prospectors who were camped there digging for gold. He then had to cross over a mountain range to the south to get into our valley. Going east down the valley he made camp several miles short of ours, arriving into our camp not long after I had left.

Indian Tomma and Yellowjackets

Yellowjackets were quite troublesome on the pack trail this summer. I generally rode in the lead and didn't get stung too often. About half the pack string generally got by before the yellowjackets got stirred up too much. The rest would take off through the bush. Shorty got stung several times. When Jack came and insisted on doing quite a bit of the walking he got stung quite often. One night he came into camp with one eye swollen shut.

We asked Indian Tomma what they did when they got stung. He said, "Fill mouth with fireweed leaves, chew them up, and hold it on the sting." We only had a few chances to try it out but it seemed to help.

Jack MacDougall was Bessie's brother and brother-in-law to Bob, and we soon found out why he was there. He had orders from Bedaux to take everybody off his payroll and try and salvage what he could of the equipment. He rehired me to help him pack out what Shorty and I had spent most of the summer packing in. We were now into August (the best time of the year to be in this part of the country) so we knew we had to get over the summit before we got too far into September. We decided to relay the packs over the mountains to the Ingenika. Jack was a good packer and we had packed together a lot. We decided to pack pretty heavy and unpack at noon to be easier on the horses. We had no saddle or cinch sores on our horses and we wanted to keep it that way.

Jack wanted to make a trip right away and take Shorty to the Ingenika, so he could go on out. Bob and family were to wait for a later trip. We got busy sorting out and making up packs and left in good time one morning with 10 horses heavily packed and one saddle horse for the three of us. We camped that night a little short of the summit. The next day we went over the top, down through the canyon on Wrede Creek, and camped at our paradise camp, so named by us because it had everything. At the foot of a slide on the mountainside there was a heavy growth of red top and blue joint grass. There were a lot of raspberry canes, currants, gooseberries, and the best concentration of huckleberries I ever saw in the north. When we started out I asked Jack what he wanted to do.

He said, "You keep looking after the horses. I'll do the cooking."

That suited me fine for Jack was a first-class trail cook who had spent quite a bit of his life on the trail. It was just like being born again to eat Jack's hotcakes and his nicely browned, well-cooked bannocks. Poor Shorty used to do the best he could, but I sure ate a lot of burnt hotcakes and bannocks that summer. Shorty and I were telling Jack about the berries ahead and said we would pick them if he would make the pies.

When we got into our paradise camp, a dry place in the pines along the creek, the horses went back through the timber to lots of grass at the foot of the slide. Jack got busy and scrubbed off the side of one of the pack boxes, smeared it with grease and flour, and got working on some pastry. Shorty and I went out and came back with a mixture of raspberries and huckleberries. It wasn't long until Jack had two pies cooking in the reflector alongside a good fire. They turned out as nicely browned as any that would come out of an oven. We had got some ptarmigan and one blue grouse coming over the mountain, fried them up, and with a fresh bannock and the pies, made a meal fit for a king. The mosquito season was pretty well over, so life was beginning to be well worth living.

We packed down to Shorty Webber's cabin the next day where we made a cache of our stuff. Jack and I rode down on our side of the river to the ford Shorty and I had picked out coming up. We hit a few boggy places but got a passable route blazed for future use.

The next morning we put Shorty and his dog, Rum, across the river on a raft. Shorty and I had had our differences during the summer but had become very good friends. When Shorty put a pack on his dog and a light pack for himself, I felt a little sorry for him starting on his 70-mile hike by himself. That was the last I ever saw of Shorty Kierce. We heard afterwards that he rafted the Pelly OK and reached Fort Grahame safely.

Jack had sold a number of horses to the Bedaux Expedition in 1934, and three of them were in our string: the chunky pack horse we called Blue; Dusty, the old reliable all-round saddle and pack horse; and Ginger, a skittish but real good pack horse who fell over the bank in the Wrede Creek canyon and recovered with no ill effects.

When Jack and I got ready to hit the trail back up Wrede Creek we had a brain wave and decided to ride back without a saddle for we had quite a number of riding saddles to pack out, and they make an awkward pack. When we got up in the mountains we regretted the idea and missed our saddles.

On one of my earlier trips with Shorty we had met Bear Lake Bob and a few other Indians who were hunting on the mountain by Johanson Creek. They were from Bear Lake, more than 60 miles to the south and a little east. He said, "By and by lots of fish stop this place," pointing to the creek. We asked what kind. "Lots of salmon, he come, maybe August time." It was hard for us to realize we were actually over on the Pacific watershed.

So this trip we stretched our morning drive to get down to Johanson Creek. While I was tying up our horses, Jack ran down to the creek and

A Pair of Boots for a Grizzly Skin

Indian Tomma's son, Alex, came to our camp on the Pelly one time during the summer and complained about his feet. He said, "Don't know what's the matter, my feet all time sick, maybe you got 'em boots, we trade."

I had traded for a fairly expensive, heavy-soled hob-nailed logger pair of boots with one of the Bedaux crew. I thought I could use them in my mountain climbing but found they were too heavy for me, so I had them hanging in a tree. Alex tried them on and wanted them. He said, "Maybe trade."

I wanted that grizzly bear skin he had hanging up near his camp and a pair of moose-hide moccasins. "Sure," he said. "Me trade." The Indians had got the grizzly on the mountain to the north. They had shot two sheep up there. Going back for them the next day, they found the grizzly had dragged them both off and buried them so they got the grizzly.

Quite a while after that I saw the same boots hanging in a tree. I said, "What's the matter, Alex? No wear 'em boots."

He said, "Feet not sick anymore. Boots too heavy."

came back as excited as any school kid could be, saying they are there. I had to have a look, and sure enough there were 15 or 20 red salmon with green heads working their way upstream. We had a quick lunch, then whittled out some makeshift spears, but had no luck in getting any.

When we got into our home camp that night Bob and the boys had got one and Bessie had it cooking in the oven. Boy, was it ever good, about the nicest fish I ever ate. It was still in good shape and real tasty. After we ate we all went down to the river to watch for fish going up. This was pretty well the end of their run, but there were still bunches of six to eight moving up. We got in the water and would drive the salmon up the shallow riffles, and with sticks try to kick them out onto the bars. We had all kinds of fun and got well soaked, but did get two nice salmon for our efforts.

A few days later the salmon started dying off after they had spawned, and in a week or two it was a gruesome sight to see the bars along the river lined with dead salmon. They didn't smell too good and the flies got to them and they became full of maggots. It made me feel as if we didn't want to use the water out of the river. On one of our trips out, Jack and I had unpacked for dinner and spotted two geese down on a bar of the creek. It was a long shot, but my bullet glanced off a rock and killed one of the geese. We plucked and dressed it, and hung the goose by the fire that night to cook. It was nicely cooked by morning and we saved it for our noon meal. What a disappointment when we went to eat it. It tasted real fishy and we thought of those maggoty fish, so my dog Jip got a lot of the goose.

Bedaux had some big tarps made of sail silk, which he designed as a lean-to for his tractor trucks. In the sag where water would accumulate he had cemented on some long flexible rubber tubes to drain the water away. That was the stretchiest rubber you ever saw, so Jack and I made ourselves some slingshots. With a little practice we kept ourselves pretty well supplied with ptarmigan and blue grouse. The rock ptarmigan weren't very big, but good eating, and very hard to see for their summer plumage blends in so well with the colour of the moss and rock of the mountain-side. One day we got a few ptarmigan and scared up a blue grouse. Jack threw a shot at it on the wing with his slingshot, injuring one wing. Jip knew it was hit and went after it, and how he found it down the mountainside, among the rocks and brush is more than I know. He brought it back and dropped it at our feet.

When we left the home camp on one of our trips we followed a new route we had picked out. It meant going over two summits but would avoid a lot of bad trail. We arrived at the first summit about camping time. The weather was perfect, no wind, no mosquitoes so we decided to take a chance and camp above timberline. We stretched a rope between two gnarled and stunted balsam trees, and stretched our canvas fly over the rope. We were carrying a number of Bedaux's folding cots with us, so Jack decided to play Dude and set up one of those cots to sleep on. I scrounged enough balsam boughs around to cover up the rocks and rolled my bed out on them. Jack rolled his bed out on the cot. It was a perfect camp with beautiful scenery all around. We sat around the fire until it got dark. We weren't in our beds very long until we realized that we weren't so smart. A clap of thunder woke us up, then lightning, more lightning and thunder, until it developed into one of the wildest nights we ever saw. The wind got up to a regular gale, then the rain came down in sheets. Our canvas fly went up and down like a yo-yo until one end broke loose. I just covered my head and hung onto a corner of my bed tarp so it wouldn't take off. It wasn't long until Jack started grumbling, for when he had set up his cot it sloped down to his head end, and when the deluge came the water ran down the cot canvas until Jack's head and shoulders were in a puddle of water. There wasn't much he could do about it. Those mountain storms come and go with very little warning, but sure can be wicked. When the storm passed in an hour and a half I just stayed put but Jack had to get a dry blanket to wrap around his shoulders. He didn't have too much to say when I asked him how he liked his Dude bed.

It was cloudy and cool the next day with a shower in the afternoon.

When we got to our paradise camp that night we piled and covered the packs for we had decided to go back and bring the Beattie family over the mountains in case the weather turned bad. From the home camp Bessie and the children rode two horses while Bob, Jack and I walked, for we wanted to take out as many packs as we could. We made it to our paradise camp in two days. As soon as we got into camp I got a bite to eat, then took the rifle and climbed the mountain to the west. I knew there was goat there. The day was running out and all I saw was a nanny goat and her kid on a ledge. The kid was so cute rolling around on the ledge at his mother's side. I didn't know what to do. The kid was so cute and wasn't meat enough. If I shot the nanny the little one would be left alone, so I got them both. I put them over a steep cliff and made a detour down to where they were, field dressed them, and got into camp a little after dark. Jack and I were going back on our last trip in the morning. The Beattie family would camp here until we got back. Bob would have plenty of time to bring in and dress out the meat.

We made it back to our home camp in two days. Riding through several rain and sleet storms going over the top, we made up 10 pack horse loads, leaving a few things of very little value, as well as the mower and rake. At our first camp on our way back we had to pick a place with plenty of dry wood, for it had showered during the afternoon and settled into a cold rainy night. As we went over our last summit, we ran into rain that ended in enough snow to whiten the ground, making it miserable for us since one of us was walking. We were glad the rain petered out before we got down to the canyon on Wrede Creek, for the rock ledges can get pretty slippery when it's wet. When we got into camp that night Bessie had a good meal waiting for us. The goat meat was nice and tender. Looking back up the gap through the trees, when we were saddling up the next morning, that whole summit country was absolutely white, so it looked like we had got over the height of land just in time.

By Horse to Hudson Hope

We got packed up and trailed down to Shorty Webber's, taking the family. They were to set up camp there until we were able to get a boat to take them out. The next several days were spent relaying our packs down from the paradise camp. We started down the Ingenika with 10 horses packed. Jack still wanted to walk. Jack tried our new ford and found it quite deep and narrow. We figured by head and tailing the horses in groups of three we could get across without raising the packs. When Jack came back to get me and the last horse, the wind had developed into a regular gale. A big old poplar that had been cut partway through by a beaver landed in the water right beside us. The wind was so strong that while we were working our way across, riding double, the spray from the river blew up on us. We were pretty well soaked by the time we got across. There was a stretch of fire-killed timber between us and the trail above. The wind had blown more of the dead trees down. With our small trail axes we had some tough cutting to get up to the trail. When we got onto the trail we followed it down to the campsite at the Pelly. We made it down to our horse range camp in two days. There we tried our luck at our favourite fishing hole and got some grayling and a few rainbow trout. The way Jack cooked them they sure hit the spot.

While riding down the trail that first morning through thick second-growth pine, Jip was on ahead. Normally a very friendly dog, he started the darnedest racket of barking and growling. Two Indians hollered out, "You call 'em, your dog." The Indians had got a black bear and with their dogs were packing it back to camp.

The next morning we packed up and went the six miles to the mouth of the Ingenika, where we intended swimming our horses across the

Finlay. We were hoping a boat would come along to save us rafting our packs across. We had about half of the logs cut for the raft when we heard a boat coming up the river and were glad to see Shorty Webber. We got busy stripping the rigging off the horses and took them down to the Finlay. There was no trouble getting them into the water, for they were pretty well used to swimming. They drifted downstream quite a piece before getting out on a gravel bar on the other side. We hoped they wouldn't stray too far before we got across.

We loaded our packs and rigging into Shorty's boat. It was really too much for one load but Shorty figured he could handle it. We floated down the short distance of the Ingenika OK, but when we got into the fast current of the Finlay, the water started coming in over the side, scaring the hell out of all of us. Shorty, a very experienced river man, couldn't do much but drift with the current. He got pretty excited as the water kept slopping over the side. Finally, around the bend, he got into some slow water and made a landing. We unloaded all our stuff onto the gravel bar and bailed out Shorty's boat. He said we were lucky we didn't swamp the boat.

Jack made a deal with Shorty to go up and bring down the Beattie family and what freight he could handle. We tracked our horses out several miles to where they had found some grass. We brought them in, got packed up, and started for Fort Grahame. We camped about halfway at the Police Meadows. It was raining off and on when we rode into Fort Grahame the next day. We set up camp and turned our horses on grass a mile or two downriver. I kept one horse on a picket.

Jack was hoping to hear from Bedaux as to what to do with the horses but he got no word. King Gething was due in with the mail so we decided to wait. When King did arrive, after three days, there was still no word from Bedaux. Jack and I both thought a lot of our horses, so we decided to trail them out over the main range of the Rockies. The most direct way was through Laurier Pass onto the head of Cypress Creek, down that creek to the Halfway River, and on to the Peace. The Indians said that we'd never get through for the trail had been blown in with big windfall for a year or more.

We decided we would go up the Finlay and try to get through Akie Pass. The Indians said we might make it through. There had been traplines through the pass but no pack trails. The trip would be further, about 325 miles out to Hudson Hope. We knew we were taking a chance, this late in the season, of getting snowed in, in the high mountains, but with all the snow and rain we'd had, we thought we should be in line for a spell of good weather.

Akie Pass. Bob White family collection.

While riding down from camp one morning to check our horses, Jip and I jumped a dandy black bear. We chased him and he climbed about 40 feet up a big tall poplar. I sure wanted that bear but didn't have the rifle with me. I tied my coat around the tree as high up as I could and tied Jip to a tree a little piece away, hoping they would hold the bear until I got back with my rifle, but when I got back he was gone.

Larry Kemple had a fair-sized boat so Jack made a deal with him to bring the freight down from the upper Ingenika and take it to Hudson Hope. Larry was quite short of supplies at the Hudson's Bay Company store for many of the trappers had outfitted for the winter and the winter freight boats hadn't arrived yet from Prince George. We stocked up with some provisions, rounded up our horses, and got ready to hit the trail for upriver.

Ed Bird, a friend at Fort Grahame, wanted us to pick up some potatoes and carrots at their garden patch beyond Police Meadows and take them up to Alex Pierre's place at the mouth of the Akie. Ed had married Alex's daughter, Maggie. We camped that night at a beautiful spot near where they had their garden. There were some nice big trees and a good hay meadow close by. We loaded three pack horses with Ed's vegetables and headed upriver past Ben Cork's cabin at the lower end of Deserter's Canyon. The valley is quite narrow here so the trail passes by his cabin. We delivered the potatoes and carrots to Alex and made camp nearby. The Pierres remembered us camping there two years ago coming down with the Bedaux pack horses. Alex was still whipsawing lumber and had just about enough to build the new house they were planning. Alex had six horses, the only ones in the country apart from ours. I asked him about the two of ours that had strayed from the Ingenika last spring. He said they had drifted in with his halfway through the summer and were running with them about six miles up the Akie. His horses had a bell on, so he thought we'd have no trouble finding them. We enjoyed our visit with the Pierres.

The next morning we started up the Akie. The river was running a good flow of water with the added snow from the headwaters. We had no trouble finding the horses and sure enough, our two were there. They looked like typical wild horses and were in great shape. One was a black gelding with a blaze face, originally a Westergaard horse from the Halfway River country, called Major. The other was a jet black gelding called Nigger, from the North Pine country. They wouldn't let us catch them, so we worked them down onto a gravel bar by a logjam. Finally we snared Major, and leading him around, we got Nigger to follow and snared him. I knew Major wasn't broke to ride but thought Nigger may have been ridden. They were both a picture to look at. I told Jack that I would try Nigger out, and we could ride him and the other would follow. I put the saddle on and took him down on the river bar. When I got on I found I had a well-broke horse. We put a light pack on Major and started up the river. Our first consideration was to get some meat for we could only get a small piece of bacon from Larry.

Our first attempt was for a beaver. We came onto a big beaver dam across a stream coming from the mountains. I suggested that we pull a big hole in that beaver dam, and when they show up we might get a shot at one. Jack didn't think too much of the idea but he said that it would be better than no meat. We walked out through some mulch and opened quite a hole in the dam, then knelt down in the water waiting for our meat to show. Jack finally said, "To hell with this, I don't want meat that bad," and walked out. In a short while a beaver showed, but he saw me first and made a big splash before I got a shot, so I gave up too.

A little further up the valley we spotted some hoodoos halfway up a high clay bank. We figured this was a good place for goat. Although Jack had spent a lot of time on the trail he had killed very little game. When he saw goat there I wanted him to have the best chance, but he just missed them. I went further up around and was lucky to get a half-grown goat. We dressed it out, wrapped it up in tarps and put it in the packs.

Continuing on I was following snowshoe blazes that led me into a muskeg. Several horses bogged down and we had quite a time getting one out. Then we backtracked and followed up the river, which meant crossing and recrossing it. If we picked our crossing we could get across without getting the packs wet. Some of the horses got careless and wandered into deep water, wetting some packs. Dusty, who had the kitchen pack, was the worst culprit. He just took to the water and swam across. We had to unpack him right away to salvage what we could of our sugar and salt. The valley was quite narrow with very poor grass. We camped that night on a bar where we only had goose grass for the horses.

The next morning, while I was saddling up, Jack hollered out, "Look out, I've thrown some rifle shells into the fire." He was cleaning out some of the pack boxes that had got wet. Our rifle shell boxes had come apart. He thought about eight shells went into the fire but only five had gone off. I was saddling Pinto at the time and had him between me and the fire. I just stood there. Jack had dropped down behind some packs. We were lucky and had no damage done.

Alex Pierre had said that the head of the Akie was good grizzly bear country. Jack and I had visions of getting ourselves a good bear skin. Our goat meat didn't pan out too good, what with wrapping it up warm and getting it wet in the river crossings.

About noon one day I came onto a cow and two big bull moose on a gravel bar ahead. I piled off and took a shot at the cow with no result. I kept shooting until I emptied the rifle, then got more shells from my horse. After several more shots I saw where two shots had landed on the bar halfway to the moose. The moose were milling around there on the bar. The bulls, being in their rutting season, would as soon run toward as away from you. Jack had come up and got off a few shots before they finally took off. It finally dawned on us that we had stocked up on dead ammunition in Fort Grahame. The Indians had complained during the summer. "That rifle shells, no good," they said. "Bullet hit moose, stop, fall down, no kill moose." We were sure we had some of that dead ammunition. It sure changed our plans about going after our grizzly bears.

During the next few days we saw lots of grizzly sign, but we had opened up the bells on our horses to keep the grizzlies out of our way. We crossed that river 14 times in one day. When we got to the forks we took the left branch, which led up to a glacier with a saw-tooth range beyond, and no possible chance of getting horses through. We backtracked to the forks where we camped for the night. We were surrounded by high mountains here, and horse feed not too plentiful.

Scouting around on the mountain ahead, we saw some axe marks leading east, we thought maybe to the pass. We had to find a way to get our horses up there. The next day we rode up through a canyon of the right fork. We were lucky not to run into a waterfall. Finally getting up the side, we worked our way up the mountainside to the blazes, which we were able to follow to the pass. There were just a few snow banks around.

As we entered the pass with high mountains on both sides we came to a small meadow with pretty good grass and decided to make camp. There was very little tree growth looking east through the pass, but we could see what turned out to be a long narrow lake up ahead.

Jack said, "I'll make camp if you want to take your rifle and walk up along the lake and see if you can get us a moose. It looks like good moose country. I won't turn the bells loose on the horses until you get your moose!"

That suited me, so away I went. When I got closer I could see it was a long narrow lake, beautiful scenery here in this nice open pass. We were lucky to have good weather, and I hoped it held until we got out of those high mountains. Walking along the north side of the lake I spotted a cow and bull moose across the lake on the south side. It wasn't that far across and I figured I could reach them with my 30-30 Winchester. I wasn't sure how my rifle shells would work. I thought I had my good shells, but they got mixed up when the packs got wet. The big bull had a nice rack of horns but the bulls aren't the best of eating during rutting season. I took a shot at the cow and, to my surprise, she dropped.

There she was on the other side of the lake and no wood handy to make a raft. To go around the east end was quite a bit shorter, so I started that way. The lake drained east, with a swampy bog at the end, which I had to wade through. It took me above the knees in places. Going back up the south side I had to take to the water, for the sheer rock wall of the mountain extended down into the lake. It meant quite a climb up over the shoulder of the mountain. I decided to try and wade around. It wasn't too bad until it got up to my waist. Boy, that water was cold. It was getting deeper, but I only had a short piece to go and didn't want to turn back. I kept on, the water came up to my armpit before I got through. I was sure glad to get out of that icy water. When I got to the place where the moose had dropped, she was gone. There wasn't much blood around. I must have just creased her. Our thoughts for a nice juicy steak would have to wait for a later date.

I had to walk fast back to camp to keep warm after getting soaked. On getting into camp, Jack asked if I had any luck. I said we would have to go on eating the goat meat. The goat meat had been too long in the warm packs and was getting a little tainted, so we were going pretty easy on it. I got busy and dug out some dry clothes. They weren't too dry either for our dunnage bags had got wet in the Akie River crossings. Jack had cooked a good meal of rice. The first half we would eat with pepper and salt with our meat, the other half we would eat with butter and sugar, along with stewed prunes, a nicely browned bannock and tea.

We awoke to a nice bright morning, but everything was covered with white frost and plenty of ice around. Our horses were right near camp. We continued east through the pass and followed down the stream that drained the lake. The first 10 miles were nice open travelling and beautiful scenery. While riding around the rim of a hollow I heard splashing in the creek and a two-year-old moose came trotting out. I had the rifle across the saddle in case we saw some game. I took a shot from the saddle as he disappeared in the brush. We went down and found a nice moose waiting for us. We dressed it out and camped for a few hours to give the meat a chance to cool.

Travelling down the valley we went through several old burns. When we got into poplar and willow country we realized the havoc that the September snowfall had done. The snow took the smaller trees across the trails until you couldn't follow them unless you cut your way through in many places. The different hunting parties that were out had done considerable cutting, but it was too big a job to cut it all out. We had to do some trail cutting, but not having very wide packs we could jungle through pretty good. When all that snow melted it caused high water in all the rivers and creeks, washing out banks and changing some of the fords.

There were three hunting parties in this general area during the heavy snow: the Jim Ross party; the one that I was originally to guide; and the Knox McCusker party. Mac and I weren't married at that time, but we both married sisters later on.

We crossed the Sikanni River, went south over a height of land, and camped that night on the Sikanni Chief River. The next day we went over another height of land and down into the Halfway River valley. We camped at Billy's fish hole, named after old Indian Billy, who used to camp there a lot and fish.

We awoke to a cold, frosty morning. While wrangling our horses I climbed up a little knoll to look over the meadow. I noticed a pile of rocks that could have been a grave. On a stone that had rolled partway down I saw some engraving that was really well done. It said, Angus McDonald, 1898, no doubt one of the Klondikers who didn't make it. This was part of the Westergaard brothers' trapping area. Travelling down the Halfway River we camped at Two Bit Creek. The Westergaard brothers and I shared a trap cabin at this point, the western boundary of my registered trapping area. We were still 140 miles out of Hudson Hope.

The next day, as we were riding east through the gap with Pink Mountain on the north, we admired those open flats with scattered poplar, a fair growth of willow and rich black soil. Getting through the gap, the river makes a sharp bend south, at the Elbow. I had another trap cabin here I called my Elbow Cabin. Below the Elbow we had to cross the river. It would be swimming. We decided we wouldn't go to the trouble of making a raft. What few perishable we had, including our bedrolls, we'd wrap up and put high on the packs. It was a short swim, but we got wet. It wasn't too far to our camp on Mosquito Flat. When we got too cold we got off and walked. Larry Kemple was good enough to loan me his camera for the trip out from Fort Grahame. I would hang it and the rifle on my neck to keep them dry.

We made camp and got a good fire going to get warmed up and dry out our clothes. This flat was where a plane cracked up in the fall of 1933. They had put up a cabin and rebuilt the ship that winter. I had spent many a night with the crew while trapping my line that winter. Next morning we visited B.C. Brady on Cypress Creek. Bob and I shared a trap cabin with Brady on the Cameron River. Crossing Cypress Creek we rode down to the MacFarland crossing on the Halfway, a fairly deep ford and another swim. The weather had been turning colder, so we built a fire as soon as we got across to dry out some. Ten miles further down we had to cross back again to the west side at the Stony Crossing. After another nice short swim we kept going down to camp on Horseshoe Creek. This creek is noted for its good fishing. After getting a fire going and warming up, Jack went fishing while I took care of the horses. Jack came back with some nice rainbow trout, which really hit the spot.

Now we were within three days of the end of the trail. We could go down the Halfway to the forks or up the south fork (Graham River), then south along the Butler Range to Hudson Hope. I wanted to see Bill Beckman and maybe the Westergaards, who lived a few miles below the forks. But it meant crossing the Halfway two more times. I asked Jack if he'd mind.

He said, "Hell, no! I'm getting to like these nice cold swims."

As we were riding down to the Forks the next morning it looked like old man winter was around the corner. It was quite cold and snowing. That swim across the river sure didn't look very enticing but we piled into it anyway and swam across to the north side. We went in and had coffee with old trapper Frank Wagner in his little log cabin and got dried off some. Frank was glad to have someone to visit with for he led quite a lonesome life there alone.

We continued downriver and camped with our good friend, Bill Beckman. Last night, at the Horseshoe Camp, I had to hobble all the horses for the first time all summer. They were getting nearer their home range. You could see they were anxious to get downriver. I had to do the same at Bill's. When I wrangled them the next morning it had snowed several inches and was quite cold. I got on the horses' tracks. They had got several miles down the trail and were still going when I caught up to them. Old Bigenough was in the lead. His home range, along with several others, was 20 miles further downriver. When I took the hobbles off I had quite a time getting them started back up the trail. It's odd how strong their homing instinct can be. It was two and a half years since they had left their range. We enjoyed our visit with Bill.

We had to cross the Halfway River here and head south. About a mile upriver was a long angling ford. Bill thought we might make it without swimming but we hit swimming water on the far side. As soon as we hit dry wood we got a fire going and dried ourselves out. There was good moose country between here and Hudson Hope, and we wanted to get one to take in with us. While Jack poked along on the horses I ran ahead on foot with the rifle. I wanted a cow moose, but had a chance at a fair-sized bull and took it. We dressed and cut up the moose, made a pot of tea to give the moose a chance to cool, then moved down to Red River, where we camped and hung up our meat.

It had settled into a winter's night, snowing and cold, making us glad we only had one more day. We got a good fire going to dry out a lot of saddle blankets as they were starting to freeze. Later we had to pack the meat in the packs before it froze too hard. We were lucky to have so much fat on the meat. It was still snowing and darn cold when we packed up the next morning and started on the last lap of our trip. We were heading for Jack's home place on Lynx Creek, four miles below Hudson Hope. We rode right through without stopping for lunch, arriving before dark.

So ended our long trip where we saw some beautiful country, and quite a bit that wasn't so beautiful. I was thankful to have had a fellow like Jack MacDougall to trail with for the last two and a half months. We figured we had travelled approximately 325 miles since leaving Fort Grahame. With the cold weather it was going to be nice to sleep in a building after camping out all summer.

Afterword

Jay Sherwood

In August, Jack MacDougall wrote to Bedaux describing the situation regarding his Empire ranch. "Davidson and Beattie seem to have antagonized both the white men and the Indians in the country to such an extent that they seem to have a grudge against the outfit and will rob or do anything in their power to make it as hard as they can for any one trying to do anything." MacDougall told Bedaux that he had intended to let Bob White go, but "after making a trip over the trail I saw that it was impossible for one man to pack on such a trail, so it was necessary for me to keep Bob White with me." He said, "It is necessary at present to have someone with the outfit all the time now, so I must keep Bob White with me, although I hate to put you to so much more expense."

He explained that Bob Beattie had to remain at the location, because it was "that time of the year the Indians are travelling up and down the valley and they seem to think that everything belongs to them." He believed that once they got Bedaux's equipment to the Ingenika River the cheapest way to get it out was by boat.

MacDougall also told Bedaux about the care of the horses. "The authorities in Prince George told me that if there was nothing done for the horses this winter they were going to arrest whoever was in charge, and as I can not get any one in here to winter them I shall take them out to my own place and feed them. I don't know what you intended me to do with them but that is the best I can do and if it doesn't meet with your wishes I will winter them myself at no expense to you except taking them out."

Of the location site, he said: "The snow in the Sustut valley is so deep that it makes it impossible to do anything with it at all. Besides, there is not a place to put up sufficient hay to feed any amount of stock." He closed his letter by stating, "I hope I have done right so far as I sure have tried and have had an unpleasant job to do."

MacDougall had hoped to receive a quick response, but Bedaux did not reply until early November, after MacDougall had brought the horses out and was back at his ranch near Hudson Hope. Bedaux wrote:

Many thanks for your letter of August 10th. I know you are taking care of my interests to the best of your ability.

However, I must refrain from spending any money in Cassiar at this time. As you have moved the horses to your place, the best thing for you to do is to sell them and use the money to pay whatever bills remain unpaid...

I wish I could afford to hire you and another man to cruise during the winter to find a new location for a ranch but before I do that I must wait until the European situation clears up.

So all I want now is to:

(1) dispose of the horses;
(2) bring all the goods together, except the agricultural machinery;
(3) make a list of them;
(4) wait for better times.

In a year or two the European situation should be settled and we should be able to resume our plans for a ranch. I have not given up the idea, far from it, but I simply must not spend any unnecessary money at the present time.

In another letter on January 15, 1937, Bedaux emphasized that he wanted to keep the saddles and bedrolls belonging to him, Fern and Josephine.

From 1937 to 1939 Bedaux's BC correspondence dealt mainly with expenses that still needed to be paid. In April 1937 Jack MacDougall wrote to Bedaux's secretary.

Last summer I went to work for Mr Bedaux and he knew at the time that it was going to cost him some money. Now all the expense of moving that outfit was financed by me as I could not do business in Mr Bedaux's name at all, so you see I am responsible. So my creditors give me one month from date to dig up eight hundred dollars or they are going to tie up my outfit... I am appealing to you once more to please try and send me $800.00 so I may get these bills straight and have a little peace for a while. This does not include my wages at all. If they will do Mr Bedaux any good he can keep them but please send me enough to pay up the rest or I am busted flat, which I think under the circumstances is hardly fair.

In the spring of 1937 Shorty Kierce wrote to Bedaux requesting payment for his wages, and in early 1938 Lou Gerlach also wrote to Bedaux. "I am sick for over a year now and as I went to work for you in good faith, you would oblige me greatly if you would make the inquiries and forward me that money at an early date, as I am in need of it badly."

In early January 1938 MacDougall wrote to Bedaux's secretary asking for payment of Bob White's wages. "Regards Bob White's wages I sent you a bill for his wages from August 4 to October 20, $312.00, and if he did not earn them, a man never did. He was working with me and when I say working, I mean he was working. Please try and pay him. The money he had coming to him before August 4th, I don't know anything about, except that Bob Beattie hired him and he did his work. Mr Bedaux knows as well as I do that Bob White does his work."

In late January 1938 a frustrated Jack MacDougall wrote again to Bedaux's secretary. "I worked for my money once and it seems I have to work a lot to try and collect it. I have made two trips to Fort St John and one to Dawson Creek to try and sell this outfit of Mr Bedaux's, and although my time is not worth much, most likely from your way of looking at it, I have a living to make." He concluded his letter by saying: "I simply cannot carry him [Bedaux] any longer and it is not fair for you to expect me to. Mr Bedaux must have known it was going to cost a lot of money to get that stuff out – look how much it took to get it in, but why slip it all onto me. I'm beginning to think I was a sucker." In February Gladys Pride, Bedaux's secretary in New York, wrote to Bedaux's secretary in Europe. "I do believe MacDougall is entitled to some consideration and if we don't try to satisfy him some way it is going to be very difficult if Mr Bedaux should ever wish to go to British Columbia again."

In November 1938 Larry Kemple placed a claim for collection against Bedaux because his cost for bringing Bedaux's equipment down from the Ingenika had not been paid. Alexander Young, an attorney in Prince George, wrote to Daniel Cook, a lawyer in New York. "Bedaux had an agent, a man by the name of Jack MacDougall of Hudson Hope BC, who hired my client to freight certain of Bedaux's personal belongings from the Pelly River to Hudson Hope. The contract price made between MacDougall and Kemple for his work was the above mentioned sum and the contract was made during the latter part of September 1936. I understand that MacDougall wrote Bedaux several times about the matter and I have also written him but no replies have ever been received."

MacDougall finally sold most of Bedaux's equipment and used the money toward his expenses. In March 1939 Bedaux paid MacDougall $500 as a final settlement. He also inquired, "Who is Kemple? Do you owe him anything."

Despite the acrimonious correspondence between Bedaux and his former employees in British Columbia, Fern Bedaux made a small donation to a church in Hudson Hope in the spring of 1939. Maude Ferguson wrote her a thank-you letter. "I do hope you will get back to see us again some day. We often speak of you, and I have the picture frame Mr Bedaux kindly made for me still hanging in the living room."

In May 1939 Alexander Young also made a claim against Bedaux on behalf of Carl Davidson. "My instructions are to demand a settlement of the above mentioned amount [$751.40] on or before the 30th inst., and if not paid by that date to take immediate action.

The final reply in Bedaux's BC correspondence, dated August 24, 1939 (just before the start of the Second World War), went to Alexander Young in Prince George. "In Mr Charles E. Bedaux's absence, we have received your letter of May 5, 1939, addressed to New York, the contents of which is quite a surprise to us. Mr Davidson has been liberally and adequately recompensed for everything connected with Mr Bedaux's Canadian expedition. No further payments will be made."

After 1936 Bedaux's attention turned away from British Columbia. In 1937 he hosted the wedding of the Duke of Windsor, formerly Edward VIII of England, to Wallis Simpson, at his chateau in France. The wedding was arranged by Herman Rogers, brother of Rae, who had accompanied Bedaux on his 1926 trip to BC. After the wedding, Bedaux arranged for the Duke of Windsor to make a tour of German factories. A similar tour of American factories was planned, but negative publicity forced this event to be cancelled and the newspapers labelled Bedaux a Fascist sympathizer. Bedaux and his efficiency methods came under increasing criticism by organized labour in the United States and officials of the American Bedaux Company demanded he sever his connections with them.

Bedaux went back to France and despite labour and social unrest, spent most of his time there. After Germany invaded France during the Second World War, Bedaux offered his services to the Vichy regime, and he was put to work reorganizing the coal mining industry. With the encouragement of the Nazis, Bedaux began planning to build a railroad and a pipeline in North Africa. In December 1942 Bedaux was arrested in North Africa and taken to the United States on a charge of treason. In February 1944, while still awaiting trial, he committed suicide. After the death of her husband, Fern became a recluse, spending almost all of her time at Candé, the Bedaux chateau in France.

Bob White remained in the Hudson Hope area until the fall of 1938, marrying just before he left. Bob's brother, John, had died of a ruptured appendix in the early 1930s. Bob would now inherit the ranch at Maple Creek, and his family needed help in operating it. Bob lived on the ranch for most of his life, moving into Maple Creek during his last few years. But he maintained connections with the Peace River country. Family members recall that most summers Bob would take his family up to the Hudson Hope area for a few weeks and visit his friends. He also corresponded with many of these people. Bob attended the 1959 and 1964 Bedaux reunions, and wrote Fern Bedaux a letter on the occasion of the first reunion.

When Bob died in 1985, his niece, Edie Dean, wrote "A Tribute to Trapper Bob".

> In loving memory of the late Robert Graham White – husband, father, grandfather, brother, uncle and friend.

Fern Lake. LAC PA127448.

He was a true outdoorsman. His love and understanding of the great natural world around him gave him an insight into nature's "scheme of things" that few people in the world today possess. A rancher, hunter, guide and trapper at different times throughout his long life, he learned to deal with nature in all her moods and loved the challenge. He was most at home under the open sky, whether astride a horse, rounding up a herd of cattle, stalking big game along a rocky hillside, or piloting a raft down a swift northern river.

He was a gentle man. His love of the wild and the creatures in it extended to his love of people – people of all ages, creeds and races. He had perfected the art of storytelling, in the hours he spent around the campfires, during his guiding and trapping years in the north and he could hold a captive audience for hours. Many of his happier moments in later years were those he shared with family and friends, over a cup of tea or a card game, while he recounted incidents from his long and adventurous life....

He's found his God – not in some pretentious man-made structure of worship, but he found him in the gentle hills and valleys of his native Cypress Hills and in the mountain trails and rivers of his beloved Peace River country in northern BC.

He's gone now. Like the creatures of the wild, who were as much a part of his life, his days on earth, too, have been fulfilled. We who have known and loved him, must count it a privilege that such a man has passed our way.

The 1934 Bedaux Expedition produced few tangible results:

- Bedaux's five Citroëns were no match for the rugged landscape of northern BC.

Bedaux Pass. BC Archives B-07384.

- Frank Swannell made a map of northern BC for the provincial government. Though it was not produced to regular surveying standards it did provide some new information about the geography of the northern BC Rockies.
- The expedition generated more discussion about a road to Alaska. However, the present-day Alaska Highway does not follow Bedaux's route. Bedaux's expedition planned to travel mainly east to west across northern BC. Even today there is no continuous road along the route he followed and sections of the northern BC Rockies still remain largely wilderness. Redfern-Keily Provincial Park and Kwadacha Wilderness Park retain a landscape that would be familiar to Bob White and Charles Bedaux. The site of Bedaux's proposed Empire ranch is within Sustut Provincial Park.

The main influence of the Bedaux Expedition was at the personal level. A large portion of the $250,000 Bedaux spent on the expedition went directly into the BC Peace River economy. In the middle of the Depression the money that Charles Bedaux paid was a financial boon to many people, providing needed cash. The cowboys worked hard, but made good wages. Many businesses in Fort St John supplied goods and services to Bedaux. Bedaux purchased horses and equipment from many ranchers and purchased a large amount of local food. He bought 50 pounds of butter at $2 a pound from a family in the Halfway River valley. He paid Del Miller $150 for six days work in delivering a message. At the end of the expedition Bedaux hosted a banquet in Hudson Hope for its participants.

Bedaux also had a direct influence on the lives of some of the expedition members. Jack Bocock and Al Phipps went to South Africa to work at a gold mine Bedaux owned. Bocock remained in South Africa the rest of his life. Although Al Phipps returned to Canada after two years, he married a woman he met in South Africa. For some of the young cowboys Charles Bedaux represented a way of life that they had not previously known about, and he inspired a few to venture into the world beyond the Peace River country. Cecil Pickell's daughter states that Bedaux was the inspiration that led her father to a successful executive career in the oil-and-gas industry in Calgary.

Charles Bedaux visited British Columbia three times and had a connection with the region for 13 years. It appears that he had a genuine fondness for the northern BC landscape and its people, yet at the same time he failed to understand how to relate to it. In the Rocky Mountains, around the headwaters of the Muskwa River, surveyor and geographer Frank Swannell named several geographical features for members of the Bedaux Expedition, including Fern and Charles Bedaux: Fern Lake, Fern Peak, Lombard Peak (Fern's maiden name), Bedaux Peak and Bedaux Pass. These names are a reminder of this unusual adventure that brought provincial, national and international attention to the wilderness of northern British Columbia during the summer and fall of 1934.

Acknowledgements

There are many people who provided assistance in this production of Bob White's manuscript. Rosaleen Ward of the Hudson's Hope Museum first showed me a copy of the handwritten *Bannock and Beans* and assisted in establishing contact with White's descendants. Ross Peck shared his wealth of knowledge about the early settlers of the Hudson's Hope area and was my host for a week during the summer of 2008. He took me to meet and interview several descendants of Bedaux Expedition members. We also spent a day in the Halfway River valley visiting some of the landmarks of the 1934 adventure, including the place where the Citroëns plunged over the cliff into the river. I appreciated the many hours Ross spent providing his insights and knowledge about *Bannock and Beans*. My thanks also goes to the many descendants of the Bedaux Expedition members who took the time to share their family information with me. Anita McWilliams allowed me to use the typewritten transcription of *Bannock and Beans* that she made several years ago. It was of great assistance with the sections of White's manuscript that were difficult to read.

During the Victoria Day weekend of 2008 I spent three days at Maple Creek, Saskatchewan. My thanks to Edie Dean, Bob White's niece, for being my host, sharing her material, and for taking me out to the family ranch in the Cypress Hills where I spent a wonderful afternoon visiting more of White's nieces and nephews. White's grandson, Bob McAtamney, provided invaluable assistance in locating his grandfather's photographs and making them available. I appreciate the support and enthusiasm that Bob White's descendants have provided for this publication.

Carl Davidson's son, Eric, allowed me to copy his father's material related to Bedaux's Empire Ranch. Carl's papers provided many valuable insights into Bedaux's planned ranch. My thanks goes to Jack Boudreau for providing the contact with Eric. Bev Field shared her memories of the Bedauxs' visit to the Cassiar Ranch in 1926 and provided a copy of her father's account of the 1926 hunting trip. Robin Philips shared her material about her father, Jack Bocock, including his 1934 diary. Arlene Myers provided material from the Bob Beattie family.

My thanks again to my wife, Linda, for the many things she did to help with the book, and the rest of my family for their moral support. I also thank Gerry Truscott of the Royal BC Museum for his willingness to undertake the publication of *Bannock and Beans*, especially on a tight deadline. I hope that this book justifies your support for publishing material about our province's history.

Credits and Copyright Information for *Bannock and Beans*

Bob White material edited by Jay Sherwood.
Copy edited by Robert Moyes.
Page design, layout and typesetting by Gerry Truscott, RBCM; typeset in Franklin Gothic Book 10/12 and Abobe Garamond 11/13.
Cover design by Chris Tyrrell, RBCM.

All images reproduced with permission from the source credited in the caption:
    LAC = Library and Archives Canada
    Glenbow = the Glenbow Archives, Glenbow Museum

Maps on pages 8 and 9 by Rick Pawlas, © Royal BC Museum.

Front-cover photograph from the Bob White family collection: Bob White on his horse, Sliver, in 1935; White rode Sliver from Cypress Hills, Saskatchewan, to Peace River country.
Back-cover from Library and Archives Canada: Charles Bedaux easing a Citroën down a slope to the Cameron River. LAC PA171637.

Sources Consulted

In preparing the background and contextual information for this book, I consulted a variety of sources, including books, newspapers and archival material. I found several articles about Charles Bedaux in the *New York Times* and other article about the expedition and Bedaux's activities in the region in the *Peace River Block News* (1930 to 1934) and the *Prince George Citizen* (1926).

In July 2008, I interviewed relatives of several of the people mentioned in this book: Arlene Myers (granddaughter of Bob Beattie) at Charlie Lake, Bev Field (daughter of Bob McCorkell) at Fort St James, Lyle Westergaard (son of Nels Westergaard and nephew of Einar Westergaard) at Fort St John, Mary (Girlie) Powell (daughter of Jim Beattie) at Hudson's Hope, Robin Phillips (daughter of Jack Bocock) at Calgary, Robbin Spencer-Pickell (daughter of Cecil Pickell) at Fort St John and Ross MacLean (brother of Art MacLean) at Fort St John.

Other published and archival sources:

Beattie, Bob, family collection. Fort St John, BC.

Bedaux, Charles. Fonds: R7591-0-7-E. Library and Archives Canada, Ottawa.

Bocock, Jack, family collection, Calgary, Alberta.

British Columbia Provincial Secretary: GR1668. BC Archives, Victoria.

Christy, Jim. *The Price of Power*. Toronto: Doubleday Canada, c1984.

Davidson, Carl, family collection, Cluculz Lake, BC.

Dean, Edie. "Bob White" (tribute), Bob White family collection, 1985.

Freer, Willard. 1934 Diary. Copies at Hudson's Hope Museum and North Peace Museum, Fort St John, 1934.

Lamarque, Ernest C.W., fonds. Whyte Museum of the Canadian Rockies, Banff.

Matheson, Shirlee. *Keeper of the Mountains*. Saskatoon: Thistledown Press, 2000.

Pickell, Cecil, family collection, Fort St John, BC.

Swannell. Frank Cyril. MS392 (journals and correspondence), 98002-17 (photographic prints and negatives). BC Archives, Victoria.

Swannell. Frank Cyril. Fonds: R2076-0-1-E. Library and Archives Canada, Ottawa.

Ventress, Cora, Marguerite Davies and Edith Kyllo (editors). *The Peace-makers of North Peace*. Privately printed (?), 1973.

Ungar, George (director). *Champagne Safari* (documentary film). National Film Board, 1995.

White, Bob, family collection, Maple Creek and Shaunavon, Saskatchewan.

White, Bob. Photographs: HP41310-41383. BC Archives, Victoria.

White. Bob, collection. Hudson's Hope Museum.

White. Bob. Photograph files: NA1095, PA750. Glenbow Museum, Calgary.

Royal BC Museum

British Columbia is a big land with a unique history. The Royal BC Museum, as the province's museum and archives, captures British Columbia's story and shares it with the world. It does so by collecting, preserving and interpreting millions of artifacts, specimens and documents of provincial significance, and by producing exhibitions, publications and public programs that bring the past to life in exciting, innovative and personal ways. The Royal BC Museum helps to explain what it means to be British Columbian and to define the role this province will play in the world tomorrow.

The Royal BC Museum administers a unique cultural precinct in the heart of British Columbia's capital city. This site incorporates the Royal BC Museum (est. 1886), the BC Archives (est. 1894), the Netherlands Centennial Carillon, Helmcken House, St Ann's Schoolhouse and Thunderbird Park, which is home to Wawaditła (Mungo Martin House).

Although its buildings are located in Victoria, the Royal BC Museum has a mandate to serve all citizens of the province, wherever they live. It meets this mandate by: conducting and supporting field research; lending artifacts, specimens and documents to other institutions; publishing books (like this one) about BC's history and environment; producing travelling exhibitions; delivering a variety of services by phone, fax, mail and e-mail; and providing a vast array of information on its website about all of its collections and holdings.

From its inception more than 120 years ago, the Royal BC Museum has been led by people who care passionately about this province and work to fulfil its mission to preserve and share the story of British Columbia.

Find out more about the Royal BC Museum at

www.royalbcmuseum.bc.ca